The teaching of English in schools   1900-1970

The teaching of English in schools 1900-1970

David Shayer

Department of English, Caerleon College of Education

Routledge & Kegan Paul   London and Boston

First published 1972
by Routledge & Kegan Paul Ltd
Broadway House, 68-74 Carter Lane,
London EC4V 5EL and
9 Park Street,
Boston, Mass. 02108, U.S.A.
Printed in Great Britain by
C. Tinling and Co., Ltd., London and Prescot

ISBN 0 7100 7321 6

Contents

one   **Introduction** Concepts and confusion -
the English scene in 1900   1
*The state of English in 1900 – The fallacies: the
classical fallacy – The Old English fallacy –
Composition and the imitative fallacy – The moral
fallacy – Correlation and subject status – Grammar
and the content fallacy*

two   **1900-20** Progress or paralysis? Some voices in
the wilderness   26
*Social implications: the Revised Code mentality –
New Board initiative 1902–10 – The fallacies
persist: grammar – Liberal advocates: Edmond
Holmes, Montessori and 'activity' – English and the
Recapitulation theory – Progress in attitudes to
writing: O'Grady, Greening Lamborn and Finch –
Caldwell Cook – Dorothy Tudor Owen and the
psychology of expression – School poetry 1900–20 –
Secondary English 1910–20 – The 1914* Suggestions:
progress 1900–20

three   **1920-30** The Board reports - creative consolidation
and advance   66
*The 1921 Report – New moves in speech work –
George Sampson – Textbooks: progress in composition
– Creative advances: Nunn, Lamborn and
Tomkinson – Reaction: the progressives attacked –
The social context and the silent revolution – The
Scholarship problem – The Dalton Plan and 'content'
attitudes – Other Board publications 1920–30*

four   **1930-40** Reaction - old themes for new citizens   103
*The Primary School Report – Further reaction:
conservative misgivings – Pritchard and the senior
schools – Textbooks: little change – English and the
School Certificate – The problem of essay marking –
Creative pressures: pupils' verse writing –
Achievements in the elementary schools – The New
Criticism: Richards and Leavis – English and the mass
media – A. J. Jenkinson's survey – Citizenship concerns*

Contents

five **1940-70** The New English - priorities and purpose
in a democratic society   135
*Creative criteria – Marjorie Hourd and the Romantic
view – A. F. Watts and the contribution of linguistic
theory – The grammar debate continued – The
challenge of the secondary moderns – The answer for
the moderns (1) A. E. Smith – The answer for the
moderns (2) David Holbrook – Creativity and
democracy: culture or anarchy? – English or social
studies? – Creative English and the grammar schools
– Some official views: SSEC, Newsom and Plowden
Reports – Children's poetry writing – Creative writing:
a definition – A new grammar? Further linguistic
considerations – The new look in textbooks – Current
attitudes to literature: the relevance of 'the relevant'
– Texts and examinations: wider horizons? –
Conclusion*

Bibliography   188

Index   201

Each fresh improvement seems such an advance on what has gone before that by and by the young teacher gets a little frightened at his progress because of the shade into which his present brightness casts his previous work. The disturbing question forces itself upon him: If my past methods are so inferior to my present, may it not be that my present will look contemptible when I have reached a still higher level? Then comes the doubt: Am I really making progress after all, or am I merely changing without necessarily going forward?

Professor John Adams, *The New Teaching*, 1918

Until some general change occurs, the teaching of English will not flourish as it should. There will be – as there have been – small advances on particular sectors, partly offset by small retreats on others. 'Appreciation' (officially recommended in 1921) replaced pure grammar (officially recommended in 1911), but by now both these prescriptions have fallen into relative disrepute . . . Dictation has disappeared, and exercises in comprehension, with 'objective' answers, have swept the board . . . Probably a slow general improvement is taking place the whole time; but this is scarcely perceptible in any one teacher's life-time and the improvement would be difficult to demonstrate to a sceptic.

No substantial and permanent progress is likely to take place until 'English', literature as well as language, is regarded by all in authority as the central subject in the education of every English child of every age and every grade of intelligence.

Language, Ministry of Education Pamphlet No. 26, 1954

Chapter one   Introduction
Concepts and confusion — the English scene in 1900

English 'method' writers have for long been strangely reluctant to
look very far over their shoulders; for them the need to establish or
strengthen what they believe to be good present practice has over-
ridden the desire to dwell on the practices of the past, and perhaps
this deliberate concentration of vision is not surprising when some of
those past methods are recalled. At the same time there is always the
danger that following one's nose will lead one in circles rather than
forwards, with consequent impressions of considerable advance
when no such advance has been accomplished, and the justification
for this present study rests quite simply on the conviction that until
some kind of detailed long-term perspective is brought into the study
of English method, bad teaching habits will be perpetuated, good
practices will be shelved erroneously, and successful but old-
fashioned theory will continue to be periodically rediscovered to the
amazed cheers of the 'progressives'.

How can such a long-term view be acquired? The answer is that
we must take a close look at the considerable body of historical
evidence that is still available, although it must be said at the outset
that this evidence will not necessarily provide us with the whole
story. It would be almost impossible to determine in exact detail (by
visiting several hundred schools over whole terms) the kind of
English teaching which is going on in this country now, in 1971;
still less is it possible to say exactly what kind of English work was
going on in the nation's classrooms in 1910, or in 1925, or throughout the decade 1900–10. In the absence of such direct observation
we must fall back on other forms of evidence, almost wholly of a
written kind, which can provide information at second-hand. This
is not the most satisfactory procedure but it is the best we have, and,
as I hope to show, these secondary sources provide information
which is both consistent and reliable. I refer to such items connected with English teaching as method books, textbooks, examination papers and syllabuses, Board and Ministry Reports, the
memoranda of other official and professional bodies, and the comments and statements of informed contemporary opinion. Over a
period of time these sort themselves, as regards method attitudes,
into quite distinct patterns, which, if not always completely in touch
with the actual (to us hypothetical) classroom situation generally,
are near enough to be acceptable as a defining framework if not as
the actual working details at the centre.

The approach is basically descriptive, and although it is impossible
to remain on the fence when discussing such items as the positive
values of creativity, the influence of the examination system, or the

benefits (or not) of teaching formal grammar, the intention is to clarify the issues as far as possible, both with regard to their present form and also to their past nature and development, and in so doing present today's teacher with the *raison d'être* for much of his method, be it good, bad or indifferent. Once isolate the specific components of 'English' as they have developed over the last seventy years in this country, and lines of perspective can be drawn which can serve to put our present vantage point into a clearer light. Why, in fact, within the bounds that constitute 'English' do we teach what we do teach, and why have certain practices become traditionally accepted as sacred (sacred cows in some cases) where others have either never been seriously tried or have been abandoned in the distant past? To what extent do teachers merely continue an established pattern (experienced in their own and their teachers' education) without considering that the spiral could and should be broken? What must disturb anyone who looks into the history of the subject in this country is the extent to which (teaching) practices have been established for reasons often only tenuously connected with well thought out English theory, and have then assumed a permanence generation after generation which is seemingly unshakeable.

Let it also be said at the outset that the notion of 'progress' becomes an extremely tendentious one when English teaching comes to be discussed, and it is not the intention of this study to try and prove a graph-like upward curve of increasing enlightenment from 1900 to the present day. This would be extremely difficult to prove in any case, and I am not sure that the 'progress' key is the right one to apply. It is true that much 'English' before 1920 was of a very dubious nature; but this certainly does not mean – as some present writers seem to think – that *all* pre-1920 English was so much antiquated lumber; nor indeed does it mean that all post-1945 theory has been marvellous.

The state of English in 1900

The year 1900 – although quite arbitrary – is as good a starting point as any, and English teaching at all levels in 1900 was in a somewhat sorry plight. As a university discipline in its own right the subject was making determined but slow progress. Outside Scotland, where it was approached very much as a study of rhetoric and style, development had been late. London University's first official English paper (for the Matriculation examination) was something of a landmark in 1839, and the strong linguistic-grammatical bias of that paper is an indication of the tendency at this time to equate 'English' with 'language'. ('Define a verb. Explain the origin of the form of the preterite tense in English, and point out accurately its signification, distinguishing it from the Aorist. Give the preterites and perfect participles of the following verbs: Ride, write, wash, sit . . . etc.')[1] Not until 1859 was English literature accepted as part of the London B.A. course, and despite the efforts of men such as F. D. Maurice and Henry Morley to encourage genuine literary studies, English at London remained of the linguistic (and subsequently 'historical') kind well into the twentieth century.

The newly-founded provincial university colleges such as Owens, Manchester (founded in 1850), Leeds (1874), Birmingham (1880), Liverpool (1881) and Nottingham (1881) were also teaching English literature but as D. J. Palmer points out[2] it lay very uneasily between history on the one side and grammar and rhetoric on the other, with classics hovering balefully in the background. Oxford resisted the subject until almost the end of the century, and then admitted it only grudgingly in the compromise form of philology and Old English studies, while Cambridge, although emphasising the purely literary side much more from the very beginning, was equally cautious.[3]

In the teacher training colleges the situation in 1900 was very unsatisfactory. A narrow range of literary texts was certainly studied, but the 'payment by results' examination attitude had reduced both teaching and study to a utilitarian minimum. Things were not so bad in 1900 as they had been twenty years earlier, and a small proportion of students was now reading for university degrees, but Certificate study still often meant no more than memorising the set texts for examination purposes. Indeed, it was not unknown for the students to memorise the textbooks as well (invariably of a potted, factual type), whole groups sometimes reproducing an identical rote answer in the same examination.[4] At the same time the kinds of questions set in Certificate papers at this time were often not really literature questions at all, being historical-biographical ('Write a short account of the life of Milton or Macaulay'), merely reproductive ('What does Johnson say of Milton's juvenile productions?'), or of the 'Write short notes on four of the following – Bedivere, Merlin, Excalibur' variety (Certificate papers for 1901). Parsing and clause analysis of passages of poetry – especially Shakespeare's –was also common if somewhat misguided practice, though the general standard of written work among students was deemed to be exceedingly weak.

At secondary school level English was still in a dubious position, so much so that in 1904 the Board of Education felt obliged to include in its Regulations a directive requiring *all* State secondary schools to offer courses in English language and literature. With a few 'modern side' exceptions the boys' public and grammar schools had generally ignored English to plough their traditional classical furrows, although in the girls' schools literature had for some time been accepted as a subject in its own right. The 1921 Report, *The Teach-*

ing of English in England, was not over-generous in its praise for some of the teaching methods in the girls' schools,[5] but literature was encouraged for all that, helped also, for good or ill, by the Oxford and Cambridge Local Examinations, begun in 1858, which many of the pupils sat.

The following comments sum up the lie of the land in the secondary schools generally around 1900: 'is it not time to make it [the study of English literature] a central subject in our schools, as it is in France and Germany, and not a mere accessory to the time-table, to be struck out before examinations or at other times of pressure?' (Alice Zimmern, 'Literature as a central subject', the *Journal of Education,* 1900); 'it is a notable fact that . . . literature, as such, has comparatively little recognition in English schemes of study. From the syllabuses of a large class of important schools it is expressly excluded.' (P. A. Barnett, 'English literature and English schools', the *Journal of Education,* 1902).

As for English teaching at the elementary school level in the usual standards, excluding the 'secondary' higher tops, we need only look at the Board of Education's 1900 English Schedules to see the nature of the instruction given.

Standard 1 (7 years)

Reading	To read a short passage from a book not confined to words of one syllable.
Writing	Copy in manuscript characters a line of print, commencing with a capital letter. Copy books to be shown.
'English'	Pointing out nouns.

Standard 2 (8 years)

Reading	To read a short passage from an elementary reading book.
Writing	A passage of not more than six lines, from the same book, slowly read once and then dictated.
'English'	Pointing out nouns and verbs.

Standard 3 (9 years)

Reading	To read a passage from a reading book.
Writing	Six lines from one of the Reading Books of the Standard, read once and then dictated.
'English'	Pointing out nouns, verbs, adjectives, adverbs, personal pronouns and forming simple sentences containing them.

Standard 4 (10 years)

Reading	To read a passage from a reading book or history of England.

| *Writing* | Eight lines of poetry or prose, slowly read once, then dictated. |
| *'English'* | Parsing easy sentences, and showing by examples the use of each of the parts of speech. |

Standard 5 (11 years)

Reading	To read a passage from some standard author, or reading book, or history of England.
Writing	Writing from memory the substance of a short story read out twice; spelling, handwriting and correct expression to be considered.
'English'	Parsing and analysis of simple sentences. The method of forming English nouns, adjectives, and verbs from each other.

Standard 6 (12 years)

Reading	To read a passage from one of Shakespeare's historical plays, or from some other standard author, or from a history of England.
Writing	A short theme or letter on an easy subject; spelling, handwriting and composition to be considered.
'English'	Parsing and analysis of a short complex sentence. The meaning and use of the most common Latin prefixes in the formation of English words.

Standard 7 (13 years)

Reading	To read a passage from Shakespeare or Milton, or from some other standard author, or from a history of England.
Writing	A theme or letter. Composition, spelling and handwriting to be considered.
'English'	Analysis of sentences. The most common prefixes and terminations generally.

What is interesting about these Schedules, and the deadening hand of Lowe's Revised Code is still very apparent, is the careful division of English into quite separate components – almost into separate subjects – and the fact that the overall term 'English' is applied to the grammar work. At the same time the term 'composition', as used in standards 6 and 7, has a seemingly unusual and significant meaning, being applied not so much as we would apply it today ('a' composition being something the pupil writes or makes) but in the sense of 'expression' or manner of presentation – an important distinction as we shall see when we come to consider composition work in schools during the first two decades of the century. The reference to Milton should not be taken to represent a last-ditch attempt at some kind of literary humanisation, since the chosen passage would be worked on for the entire year until it was known by heart, grammar included.

Such a programme as that given above more often than not represented the sum total of English work done by children in the elementary schools at the beginning of the century, though we must remember the nature and purpose of elementary schooling (not 'education') as it was conceived at the time and also the fact that the overriding consideration was still to combat sheer illiteracy. The diet remains incredibly unimaginative for all that.

The fallacies: the classical fallacy

When an overall view of English teaching at the beginning of this century is taken, a number of interesting misconceptions appear (they might well be called 'the great fallacies') and an attempt to delineate them accurately is desirable if only because a number of them are still active in subtle ways today and have shown over the last seventy years the regenerative powers of a Medusa's head. Broadly speaking they are characterised by the tendency to study English in ways quite unsuited to that subject, or to study it for entirely the wrong reasons, with consequent distortion of the study material. Each fallacy operates through a tendency to excess, or the unrealistic promotion of fringe concerns (not harmful in themselves and when kept in perspective) to positions of central, perhaps exclusive, importance. Thus to include within the fallacy framework such things as grammar study, or Old English study, or figures of speech study is not to dismiss these items out of hand but to insist that we get our priorities right and strive not to lose sight of what really matters.

The first misconception – and it was to dog English teaching until the thirties – we may call the 'classical fallacy'. Its origin lies in the uneasy transition from the almost exclusive study of the classics as the one true literary discipline to the acceptance of English at the turn of the century, with the belief that despite its pale substitute nature it (English) could be respectable – providing (and only providing) it was treated 'classically'. While it was regarded by many as an upstart, its advocates were too anxious to prove its integrity by distorting its real nature, a somewhat ironic capitulation when one considers that classical studies themselves were excessively biased on the grammatical-linguistic side at this time. The situation was not helped by the fact that the early teacher of English (certainly in the secondary school) was more likely than not a converted classicist and was prone 'to fall back upon the methods of the Classical curriculum in which he had been trained'.[6] As a result literary study became 'allusion hunting', grammar (including clause analysis of texts, particularly poetry), figures of speech spotting and paraphrasing

(Chaucer was eminently satisfactory since he involved 'construing'); editions of English texts were closely modelled on the format of classical texts, with copious if often pedantic and irrelevant notes; composition became the imitation of models and the mastering of complicated sets of rules; and the verse composition of senior pupils an arduous course in prosody (particularly scansion), poetic diction, marking the caesurae (see Virgil), and stylistic ploys.

If, for example, a textbook such as L. C. Cornford's *English Composition*, 1900, is examined, we find the business of writing English expanded into an incredibly complicated and tortuous process. Before even pen can be set to paper a score of difficult rules must be mastered and sundry models carefully studied. Here, in short, is English composition presented in the worst Latin manner, with all the spontaneity crushed and an air of deadly aridity hanging over the process. What is so false in such an approach is the assumption that writing in one's own language is purely a matter of externals, the confronting of a mental obstacle course that the writer will best get through if he keeps his personal feelings in abeyance.

When approaching the need for pupils to write verse A. E. Roberts and A. Barter (*The Teaching of English*, 1908) are perfectly frank on the matter; if students of the classics are required to write Greek and Latin verses, students of English ought to do the same – and along identical lines. 'Before any exercises in verse are attempted by the pupil, some definite lessons in versification should be given ...'[7] (they include scansion and metres, phonic elements, caesurae, enjambement, 'poetic' vocabulary – the whole box of prosodic tricks).

As early as 1891 H. Courthope Bowen had pointed out in his *English Literature Teaching in Schools* that the emerging study of literature was suffering 'from the endeavour to transfer the method used for Latin and Greek to the teaching of English',[8] and in the same year John Churton Collins in his *The Study of English Literature* (a plea for genuine literary – as opposed to merely philological – studies at Oxford and Cambridge) had written:[9]

> Since its recognition as a subject of teaching it [English literature] has been taught wherever it has been seriously taught on the same principle as the Classics. It has been regarded not as the expression of art and genius, but as mere material for the study of words, as mere pabulum for philology. All that constitutes its value as a liberal study has been ignored. Its masterpieces have been resolved into exercises in grammar, syntax, and etymology. Its history has been resolved into a barren catalogue of names, works, and dates. No faculty but the faculty of memory has been called into play in studying it.

Really the transfer of method is not so surprising. If the classics had represented the road to a liberal 'literary' education, so called, then such treatment of any new equivalent subject was to be expected – though the effect was merely to highlight the inadequacy of the traditional classical methods rather than help the new studies. After 1915, in fact, there was a strong (but not universal) movement away from the use of classical-format editions of English texts and the 'plain text' editions became more popular. A number of letters to the *Journal of Education* at this time show the growing impatience of some teachers for the pedantries of editors. In an article in the *Journal* for May 1907 the writer describes a school edition of *Samson Agonistes*; total pages 258; text 53; Milton's biography 22; the background of Greek tragedy 68; 'allusions', philology and grammar 115. Another typical school edition (of *Marmion*, edited by F. Marshall, 1904, for Junior Local candidates) supplements the 188 pages of text (and these include copious footnotes anyway) with a further 100 pages of material, including two maps of the Flodden campaign with suitable logistic comments. A typical note reads:

> Plight (1) (M.E. 'pliht', danger; also engagement, pledge) = pledge
>   (2) The feminine form of 'plait' (M.E. 'plait', a fold; L. 'plicare' to fold) = a fold, to fold.
> In the line 'Whose fate with Clare's was plight' 11, xxviii, 3, some editors substitute 'faith' for 'fate' as making better sense.
> 'But we plight our faith to another, not with another's faith.'
> If we take 'plight' in the passage as the passive participle of 'plight' = to fold, we get an intelligible rendering. The meaning then is that Wilton's fate was interwoven with that of Clare because of their mutual love.

Candidates in the 'Locals' were questioned on this kind of thing, for example 'Explain the following, *giving derivations where necessary*: The barrier guard, pikes, brigantines, kirtle . . . etc.' (Cambridge).

Above all the 'classical fallacy' dominated the attitude to grammar teaching. Not only had the English language been tortured in numerous nineteenth-century grammars into Latin form (conveniently fixed once and for all) but it was also assumed (as in traditional Latin study) that the rules, tables, and diagrams of grammar must be mastered first before actual reading or writing was possible. The Board of Education emphasised the illogicality of these attitudes as early as 1910 in Circular 753, *The Teaching of English in Secondary Schools*, but they persisted well into the forties and have not completely disappeared even now. Had the approach to Latin at the time been exclusively of a 'direct' kind with pupils reading simple texts from the very beginning and learning the grammar afterwards, there is no doubt that the approach to English generally and to grammar study in particular would have been different, with a consequent reshaping of much English teaching method. It is no exaggeration to say that the attitude of British schools to grammar has been firmly determined by outside other-subject influences (the United States, for example, lacking the classical heritage, took a slightly different line) which at base have nothing to do with English at all. It may be that for a very long time now (over 100 years) the schools have been barking up a wrong and unimportant tree – promoting a form of grammar study which was never relevant to English at any time.

Closely linked with this was the obsession with rhetoric – another harking back to ancient practices – and the excessive emphasis upon the rhetorical possibilities of the English language. Once again the literary text was approached not as an end in itself but solely as a repository of rhetorical bits and pieces. Perhaps the most obvious result of this was what came to be the inevitable inclusion in the standard school composition textbook of extensive lists of figures of speech (Anacoluthon, Epistrophe, Prosopopoeia, Epanorthosis, etc.) – a feature which remains in modified form today – with the assumption that pupils must be able to spot these in their reading, and indeed undertake reading merely for the purpose of spotting, an exercise which is splendidly examinable. As with so many things, what begins as a necessary (if at school level, minor) adjunct to the assessment of an author's skill and his ability to say what he wants to say, becomes the monster cuckoo that drives everything else out of the nest.

The Old English fallacy

The second fallacy, which was more evident in university and sixth-form English, we may call the 'Old English fallacy'. The earliest university English courses placed considerable emphasis on the importance of the study of Old and Middle English and philology generally, frequently at the expense of literature. The nineteenth century had seen considerable advances in philological study (particularly from Germany) with the formulation of the basic Indo-European system, and British scholarship was anxious to maintain the standard and scope of linguistic studies not only at research, but also at undergraduate level with the consequent desirability of a preparatory Old English section in the school Higher Certificate course – totally unsuitable though such a course might be.

At the same time the linguistic emphasis came to represent a further attempt to make English a respectable discipline (and not the soft option of the aesthetic undesirables – the 'novel reading tripos') and it was not surprising that at Oxford, for example, where Old

B

English and philological studies had already been functioning for some time, English proper should be introduced only through a forced and somewhat unhappy marriage with the existing subjects. Despite the efforts of Walter Raleigh to reduce the Old English load and/or make it optional before 1920, Old English remained (and remains) strong in the Oxford English School. It is not that Old English studies have no place in an English degree course, but that a false emphasis (English 'really' being such studies) is patently wrong. In fact Quiller-Couch was nearer the mark when (in Lecture 6 of his *On the Art of Reading*, 1920) he made the point that English will be prevented from becoming respectable academically at any level just as long as there is an excessive emphasis on Old English. The second decade of the century saw an increasing number of attacks on the Old English monopoly. Stanley Leathes in the English Association's Pamphlet No. 26 ('The Teaching of English at the Universities', 1913) demanded that Old and Middle English studies be made entirely optional in all English degree courses. Leathes was answered in 1922 by R. W. Chambers in Pamphlet No. 53, where Chambers insists that all English students should be thoroughly versed not only in O.E. and M.E. but also in Latin and Gothic for good measure, the necessary study beginning at school level.

Old English was of course included in the Higher Certificate up to the 1920s and a number of school Old English grammars were published. The 1921 Report, considering both schools and universities, tends to face both ways on the matter to the point of downright inconsistency, both criticising the subject adversely yet in effect recommending its continuation. A rather strong attack becomes 'retain if used in moderation' becomes 'great importance of' becomes 'but be careful' in the course of the Report's argument.[10] In fact the inclusion of Old English in the Higher Certificate school courses had ceased by the mid-twenties, though the situation in the universities with regard not so much to inclusion but as to emphasis has been another matter.

Composition and the imitative fallacy

The pseudo-classical study of models was also a symptom of another prevailing attitude of this time, and this attitude is revealed most clearly when the general approach to written English in schools is considered. 'Imitation' was not simply an isolated classroom exercise, but a whole way of thinking that was taken for granted by a great many teachers, if not by the vast majority, certainly until 1920 and even beyond. Briefly, the pupil (elementary or secondary) is always expected to imitate, copy, or reproduce. Not only are all composition subjects imposed upon him from above, but also detailed outlines for each which must be filled out according to a carefully prearranged pattern; in fact, composition becomes the expansion of pre-determined notes, the teacher's or textbook writer's, not the child's, and the final mark awarded will depend as much on the pupil's ability to keep to the straight and narrow of the imposed framework as on his spelling, punctuation and handwriting.

'Write on "The Cat": 1. Where found. 2. Why kept. 3. Fitted to be a beast of prey – (a) teeth, (b) claws, (c) pads. 4. Fitted for night prowling – (a) fur, (b) eyes. 5. Fitted to be a pet. 6. Habits.'

(Longman's *Junior School Composition*, 1901)

'Describe a cow; general appearance. Horns . . . teeth . . . hoofs . . . tail. Food. Breeds. Uses.'

'Write on "Our Town" as follows: 1. *Introduction* – Name; Meaning; Situation; Population. 2. *Appearance* – General appearance, chief streets, buildings, parks, etc. 3. *General Remarks*. Principal trades and industries. Any historical facts, etc.'

(Nelson's *Picture Essays*, 1907)

'Write the story of a bluebell saying (i) where it was (ii) what it thought (iii) what the wind said to it . . . etc.'

(E. Covernton, *The Teaching of English Composition*, 1909)

Expanding Aesop's Fables was also a common composition exercise.

Expand the following outline . . . into narrative:
1   Ass carrying salt – passing through stream – falls – salt melts – ass relieved of burden.
2   Again fetches salt – this time lies down in stream.
3   Master determined to punish it – loads it with sponges – ass lies down – burden made much heavier.

(D. Salmon, *Exercises in English Grammar and*

Composition, 1900 edition)

Sometimes the outlines were embellished with further suggestions or warnings from the omniscient writer:

The Story of a Shilling

Hints
  Where and when was it born?
  What did it look like?
  Who was its first owner?
  What did he do with it?
  Invent some adventures for it, and tell what became of it in the end.

Cautions

1   In writing an autobiography, take care not to begin every
    sentence with 'I'.
2   It is still worse to use 'myself' or 'self' in order to avoid
    saying 'I'.
3   Never use 'and which' where 'which' is sufficient. 'And
    which' is only permissible when 'which' has preceded.
    'The shilling which he gave me *and which* I lost' is right
    but 'The old shilling *and which* was nearly worn out' is
    wrong.
                        (J. H. Fowler, *A First Course in Essay-Writing*, 1902)

Along with this went a close study of model passages for the pupil
to imitate in stylistic as well as content terms, with such directions as
'Write a composition based on the events in the passage above; keep
as close to the original as possible'; 'Write out a conversation between the willow-tree and the wheat using the text as a model' (E. J.
Kenny, *Composition from English Models*, 1913). The wholesale
adoption of phrases or even sentences from the original was not only
permitted but encouraged by the teacher.

This imitative approach (did the majority of teachers know any
other?) was wholeheartedly recommended in the Board's first (1905)
Handbook of Suggestions for Teachers. We even find E. Covernton
advocating a method of 'double translation' – the pupil expanding
the given outline, then comparing his version with the original full-
length passage from which the outline was extracted.[11]

The system also included the frequent use of dictation exercises
(another hangover from the Revised Code days). There was no
shortage of textbooks containing collections of 'suitable' passages for
dictation purposes, and it is interesting to see the kind of standard
which was expected of elementary pupils. In W. Williamson's *A
Class Book of Easy Dictation and Spelling*, 1902 (ominous title),
intended for seven- to eleven-year-olds, we find this:

> Now as on a memorable evening when I had crossed the street
> in a drizzling rain, and looked that way with foreboding, there
> were two or three guards, in the Cardinal's livery, loitering in
> front of the great gates. Coming nearer, I found the opposite
> pavement under the Louvre thronged with people, not moving
> about their business, but standing all silent, all looking across
> furtively, all with the air of persons who wished to be thought
> passing by.

Now granted that this is aimed at the eleven-year-old rather than at
the seven-year-old, it certainly represents a spelling level which, if
not difficult for some, is most decidedly not 'easy' for most. Williamson appends a table of 'suitable' words for this age range, including:

accede, aerated, anemone, apparel, asthma, boudoir, burlesque, catarrh, chamois, diphthong, eyrie, heinous, heliotrope, lieutenant, lymph, meerschaum, mien, plebeian, privilege, succour, syringe and wrought – all useful stuff for the budding elementary essayist.

When the children were not taking dictation, learning lists of useful words by heart or expanding outlines, they might be replacing the punctuation in passages such as the following from E. E. Kitchener's *English Composition for Junior Forms* (1912):

> o blithe new comer i have heard
> i hear thee and rejoice
> o cuckoo shall i call thee bird
> or but a wandering voice

Equally popular at all levels was 'reproduction', where the children had a short story or prose passage read to them, then wrote down immediately afterwards as much as they could remember, this memory exercise remaining standard 'English' procedure until the 1930s. (A collection of suitable reproduction extracts can be seen in H. A. Treble's *English Prose Passages for Repetition*, 1913.) Reproduction was also enthusiastically recommended by the Board of Education both in the *Suggestions* and in the 1910 *Circular 753*.

To complete the picture we find James Welton in a then much-used training college textbook, *Principles and Methods of Teaching*, 1906, actually maintaining that it is extremely useful for pupils to *copy out* passages from suitable books since this provides 'a direct training in composition'.

Of course, the assumption that the child was merely a miniature if unrealised adult, although no longer respectable psychology, was still very strong in the classroom. Teachers assumed that pupils should write like adults from the beginning, and every effort was made, through the use of examples and suitable models, to impose adult language structures upon them. The idea that a child must master each separate stage of language development himself, working out each stage to his own satisfaction and thus 'internalising' it before progressing to the next rung of the ladder, was hardly considered. Thus the teacher, with the aid of a well-chosen Belles Lettres style, did everything, the child – passively imitative – practically nothing.

Edmond Holmes, a former Chief HMI, directed a bitter attack on this mentality in 1911 (*What Is and What Might Be*), pointing out that children are not even permitted to make mistakes in their writing, being controlled and supervised at every phrase. 'The golden rule of education', he writes, 'is that the child is to do nothing for himself which his teacher can do . . . for him.'[12] If the pupil were to start doing things for himself he would make mistakes, and this could not be tolerated because 'successful' learning is seen as the complete avoidance of errors, and the falsity of this notion (says Holmes) is nowhere more false and inappropriate than when applied to the necessary trial and error process of acquiring a reasonable competence in written English.

Here again we see the 'externals' and the mechanical drills being catered for, but without any genuine understanding, insight, growth or personal application at the centre. 'Writing' becomes a series of artificial gestures, the donning of adult clothes by the child, which is going to appear forced even where it does not appear ridiculous.

If such attitudes strike us today as being very strange (or worse) some excuse can be given from the point of view of the numbers of children which teachers had to cope with at the beginning of the century. Classes were very large indeed by present standards, frequently in excess of 60 pupils, and classes of 70 or 80 were not unknown before 1910. The LCC tried to initiate a '40 and 48' scheme (to restrict infant classes to 48, 'junior' classes to 40 children) in 1912, but the War and subsequent economic troubles ensured that classes of 50 and 60 were still to be found throughout the country as late as 1930,[13] so that some degree of regimentation was necessary for purposes of sheer control, and 'writing by numbers', though hardly satisfactory, is understandable in such circumstances. It is no coincidence that increasing experiment in the subject has been closely linked with a decline in class numbers – though one still gets the impression that many teachers preferred a situation of rigid control and kept to it long after physical classroom circumstances allowed a freer, more relaxed approach.

When we look at the kind of children's writing that was considered to be above-average by educationists before 1910, we find a synthetic artificiality which speaks eloquently of the mechanical nature of the writing. E. Covernton reproduces three pieces by seven- and eight-year-olds in *The Teaching of English Composition* which are practically identical and evidently merit praise as much for their accurate copying of the original notes and given outline as for their very 'literary' style. One of them begins as follows:

> Once upon a time there grew in a cool green wood the
> prettiest blue-bell you ever saw. A pretty fairy dwelt in its bell.
> When the blue-bell awoke it felt very happy; for had not
> Spring, all clothed in green, come at last? The Spring was
> rather late that year, so the blue-bell arose later than usual . . .

W. J. Batchelder also reproduces pieces in a similar style in his *Notes on the Teaching of English*, 1913, and even P. B. Ballard (who took such a sensible view over grammar) gives us the following essay by a fourteen-year-old girl, full of clichés and coy artificiality, and calls it 'remarkable'.[14]

The present is a time calculated to arouse the warmest feelings
of loyalty and patriotism in the coldest heart that ever beat in a
land governed by our beloved Queen. Sixty years of happiness,
peace and safety have rolled by under the sovereignty of the
greatest monarch England has ever known; and now we call
aloud to Britain's every son and daughter to celebrate the grand
jubilee of love and loyalty. From far-off Australia to mighty
India, from rocky Gibralter to icebound Canada, the glad
voices of a million happy subjects come in one great hurrah . . .
Never has the throne of Britain been filled by one so loving, so
lovely, so truly queenly and withal so womanly . . . Sorrow has
not spared her, Queen Empress as she is; Death has come and
asked her best-beloved at her hands . . .

Another good example can be seen in William Boyd's *Measuring
Devices in Composition, Spelling and Arithmetic*, 1924, where the
following (by an eleven-year-old) is offered as a criterion of excellence with which to judge pupils' compositions generally (Boyd's
concern being to produce a reliable marking scale).

'A Day at the Seaside' – what pleasure is in those words – for
with them comes the echo of the waves lapping up on the
golden sands and the memories of those thrilling donkey rides.
To children who live in the smoky towns the experience of a
visit to the blue sea is delightful and one may well notice the
eager looks on the faces, pinched and pale, of the slum
children, as they are packed into the railway carriage, bound for
the seaside. Poor little mites, is it not sad to think that they
have come into this beautiful world to see the lovely country
and seaside once in so long a while? However, after their
teacher (for doubtless they are some little flock belonging to a
Sabbath school) has seen that no one is lost, she points out the
shimmering sea in the distance and, laughing with glee, they all
march joyfully down the path, perhaps singing some glad
refrain . . .

Boyd's comment on this piece is extremely interesting (and revealing): 'This is a highly exceptional production . . . The elevated
style and the detached point of view . . . suggest an *adult* rather than
a juvenile mind' (my italic). Pupil X, who is unquestionably very
intelligent, has had 'detachment' instilled into him as a matter of
course since he first began to move from exercises with words to
exercises with clauses and phrases.

In case it should be doubted that this kind of thing was what
teachers wanted, the sceptic should take a look at the 'model' essays
which were offered to pupils in the composition textbooks as being
the required *ne plus ultra* of written work. Take for example the

specimen compositions given in John Eades's *New English Course*, 1914, presumably written by the author himself for Standard Four children (ten to eleven years).

'Christmas Eve.' For weeks I have looked forward to this happy night; and, now it is here, I do not think I shall be able to sleep at all. Last year I tried to keep awake, to watch the entrance of Santa Claus; but my eyes would not stay open, and at last I dropped off to sleep. This year I intend to go to sleep as soon as I can, so that the time will pass more quickly; and when I wake up in the morning it will be Christmas . . . etc.

Spring is the first season of the year. It begins in March and ends in June. It is the season of new life, when everything in Nature looks sweet and lovely. It is very welcome, especially after a long, cold winter.

This is the time of the year when the trees begin to bud, the flowers begin to show themselves, and the grass once more takes on a beautiful green.

During the springtime the snowdrops, crocus, primrose, tulip, wallflower, pansy, iris, lupin and certain other flowers may be seen. The snowdrop comes first and is followed by the crocus, daffodil and hyacinth. The first wild flower is the dandelion and that is soon followed by the daisy, buttercup and bluebell . . . etc.

Of course, an intelligent pupil, by dint of careful copying and imitating, can assume the style of a third-rate middle-aged female novelist, though the process becomes entirely artificial and completely disconnected from his actual personality. The writing comes from the top of the head, while the living child goes its own way underneath, and as long as composition is only this, no pupil, however intelligent, is ever going to see that writing can be a direct and frank expression of something one really *wants* or needs to say from the centre of one's interests, hopes, fears, beliefs, memories or temporary absorptions. It is very doubtful whether any pupil trained in this way would ever regard the writing process as being anything more than an artificial classroom exercise, put on for teacher's benefit, and would not relate the business with the 'real' world, 'real' feelings or personally 'real' situations at all. What happened to the less intelligent child who couldn't master the system we can only guess at; presumably he trailed after his brighter peers occasionally getting two or three consecutive sentences together in the right style but for the most part producing work of an inadequate and unacceptable standard.

Now it may very well be that pupils pre-1920 (or even pre-1930) were better age for age on the 'technical' side (in their spelling, punctuation, sentence construction and paragraphing) than their descendants today, but if we have lost some ground here we have almost certainly gained in making – or attempting to make – the writing process personal and enjoyable, and therefore more real to children, so that to sit down and write *means* something. There is also the completely immeasurable long-term effect as regards reading. Where writing is artificial the child's – and perhaps, later, adult's – approach to reading is going to be slightly wrong; the child who has learnt that to communicate through writing is as natural as talking or gesticulating, may well approach other people's written expression in a much more pleasurable and sympathetic way.

This is not to say that the technical aspects of written English do not matter; on the contrary, they are as important now as they have ever been, but it would be entirely false (and here, I think, lies the beginning of the answer to those who claim that standards in school English have fallen over the last fifty years) to compare written work now with written work in 1910 or 1920 by merely totting up the 'technical' scores and spelling mistakes in each. The fact that pupils were given and made to follow quite detailed outlines when producing compositions should make us ask whether the written specimen from 1910, say, is as original in terms of content and phraseology as it appears. Our criteria for judging written work, together with our philosophy of written expression, have changed, so that direct comparison with earlier specimens is apt to give a misleading impression. What is of pressing importance is that the present teacher of English should retain the indispensable formal core (without which expression becomes gibberish) and relate that to the freer, more personal approach characteristic of pupil expression since 1940. This ideal compromise has not yet been established in enough schools.

The moral fallacy

If children are to be little adults, they must also be well grounded in morality, and here the fourth fallacy appears – that of using literature primarily as a means of purveying 'moral' lessons. This has a distinctly 'Victorian' sound, but was still sufficiently widespread in 1920 for The 1921 Report to fire a few parting shots at it. Elementary reading primers had traditionally included 'improving' material but the fallacy had now extended into the reading material at upper elementary and secondary school level also. Henley's *Lyra Heroica* (a standard school anthology) is only one example of this tendency with its 'Sound, Sound the Clarion, fill the fife' or 'It is not yours, O Mother, to complain' approach. F. Langbridge's *Ballads of the Brave*, 1890 ('Poems of Chivalry, Enterprise, Courage and Constancy') is another. The poems and stories read to young pupils should embody 'fine actions' writes James Welton[15] and school poetry is valueless unless it produces 'ennobling sentiments'.

One gathers from Arnold Smith's 1915 criticisms (*Aims and Methods in the Teaching of English*) that this use of literature for moral or patriotic purposes was quite common: 'The English curriculum in certain schools has an ethical basis, so that a boy learns patriotism one year and some other civic virtue the next. Shakespeare's *Henry V* is supposed to inspire a love of the fatherland; we have anthologies of verse to inculcate the same feeling, literature being studied not merely for its own sake but for some didactic purpose.'[16] As late as 1931 we find Macmillan producing a junior class reader of blatantly moral passages – 'Helping mother', 'Personal Hygiene', 'Little Deeds of Kindness' – with the claim that the book is designed 'to develop literary appreciation... to appeal to pupils' sense of duty; to stimulate patriotism and a just pride in the achievements of our countrymen...' Poems considered suitable for this include 'Who Taught the Birds' (Jane Taylor), 'Which Loved Mother Best?' (Joy Allison) and 'I Lie Down with God' (Eleanor Hull).

Correlation and subject status

If English was not diluted by didactic concerns it was likely to be diluted in a merger with geography or history. One of the magic words in education for the decade 1900–10 was 'correlation', not the statistical device, but an attempt to link subjects across the timetable divisions. In practice this often meant that English virtually disappeared or became a matter of second-rate texts which happened to fit the study plan of the moment (with the use of such anthologies as Ernest Pertwee's *English History in Verse*) while composition tended to become purely a matter of 'other subject' topics. Literature was particularly vulnerable to the inroads of history and the distinction between the two was not completely established until the nineteen-twenties. We have already seen that the 1900 Elementary Schedules admit readings from Shakespeare *or* from a history of England and another obvious link lay in the use of works by Anson, Macaulay, Carlyle, Gibbon or Southey (*Life of Nelson*) as set secondary texts. There was also a strong bias towards studying any literary text to discover the light it might throw on the historical events of its time (this was a marked feature in the early School Certificate literature papers) and at a more pedestrian level it was common practice in the elementary schools for pupils to learn by heart long lists of authors' dates as part of the 'literature' lesson.

This correlation was strengthened in the secondary schools by the 'grouping' principle advocated in the Board's 1904 Regulations – English being only one in the group of literary subjects which included history and geography. When literary studies began to break free of history after 1910 the principle of correlation was hotly defended – by G. F. Bridge, for example, in the *Journal of Experimental Pedagogy* in 1914 (Vol. 2, No. 6) where he sees the increasing gap between the subjects and the growing tendency to read literature 'purely for aesthetic and emotional enjoyment' as being very undesirable and dangerous; no longer will pupils be trained to read 'for information' (clearly the only kind of reading worth anything).

We can thus see that English, hopefully spreading its wings to meet the new century, was likely – if it survived the initial neglect and rejection – to be either confused with somebody else or strangled with good but misguided intentions. Few people stopped to consider the real nature of the subject, or came near to discovering that most paradoxical of all English facts, namely that it is not really a 'subject' in the traditional sense at all. Perhaps this 'content' myth is the fallacy behind all the others, that English, like certain other subjects, is little more than a body of factual knowledge to be transferred from teacher to pupil, this factual knowledge being dependably concrete (and lending itself naturally to syllabus planning, textbook systematising and examinations) and ranging from the twenty-five, or fifty-seven, figures of speech, to author's dates, to the mythological references in the ninth book of *Paradise Lost* to Shakespeare's grammatical eccentricities and the rules governing subordinate clauses.

Grammar and the content fallacy

It is when we turn to the vexed question of grammar that the 'content' fallacy becomes most striking. Originally grammar was promoted in the battle against nineteenth-century illiteracy, since it was believed that only with such knowledge could a pupil begin to read and write effectively. This belief continued (has it completely disappeared now?) in the early decades of the century, but was increasingly supplemented by other corollaries, one being that English must after all be academic, examinable and respectable because of its considerable body of grammatical facts which were not only patently 'there' but no easy matter to master. The number of grammars published each year rose steadily between 1900 and 1920, when, due not so much to the 1921 Report itself as to the spate of thinking and writing on the subject that the Report triggered off, there was a sudden sharp drop.

As well as improving the use of language, grammar was also seen at the beginning of the century as being an excellent 'mental trainer' according to the Transference theory, that is, it was believed that its rigorous 'logic' would strengthen all the mental faculties and promote lucid and analytical thinking generally (for the same reason whole pages of *Paradise Lost* were learnt by heart to 'train' the memory). 'We teach grammar . . . to train the reasoning faculties and the judgment' write Roberts and Barter in 1908, and in a *Journal of Education* article (April 1907) Stewart Robinson maintains: 'I have no belief that grammar teaches correctness of speech or writing; but I claim for it a place . . . as a training of mind' (which is a good example of the grammarian's determination to get one in the end). We find the idea expressed as late as 1928 (see 'The Teaching of English' by J. H. Arnold in the *Journal*, July 1928) and there is evidence to show that some teachers in the thirties still upheld the theory. Indeed, the belief lingered on when both Transference and Faculty theories had long since fallen into disrepute, its advocates presumably feeling that an indefinable aura of benefit hung around the tough and abstract details of grammar which – in some vague emotive way – they believed to be of value to their own teaching if not to the pupils.

The type of grammar work done in schools before 1920 was, frankly, nasty. Fairly typical is Mary Hyde's *Practical English Grammar*, 1905. Here twenty-seven pages are devoted to the parts of speech, one-hundred-and-fifty-one to the subdivisions and inflections of those parts, and thirty-three to analysis in a step-by-step advance which is clearly meant to carry the reader along line by line. When parsing pronouns, the pupil is required to give class, antecedent, person, number, gender, case and syntax. Little tables abound containing such things as 'whoever – whosoever – whomever – whomsoever' and the language is laid out in neat procrustean boxes. W. Williamson's 1902 *Junior English Examination Papers* gives an idea of junior secondary standards. 'What are Correlative Conjunctions? Write three sentences to illustrate;' 'Show for what reason French Relatives are less ambiguous than English Relatives;' 'Give the present participle and past tense of: lain, bereft, strewn;' 'Conjugate fully the verb "to be".'

Parsing was a favourite, of course, and had all the respectability of classical method; the Latin novice was required to parse his way through an inflected jungle of carefully contrived sentences, and the pupil of English could benefit equally by doing the same with his own language. There are times, however, when the textbook writers seem to be inspired by a passion for ciphers rather than grammar – witness the parsing lay-out recommended by J. Mushet (*Exercises in English*, 1912):

> 'I *had rather go* home this way, *please*'
>
> had:— Verb. defect. intrans. – act. subj. past indef. sing. 1st – agreeing with 'I'
> rather:—Advb. of degree, old comp. form – mod. 'had'
> go:— Verb, strong, intrans. – act. infin. pres. – dep. on 'had'

please:—Verb, weak, intrans. impers. – act. subj. pres. sing.
3rd – agreeing with 'it'.

F. J. Rahtz's *Junior English* (first published in 1908 and still going
strong in its 38th edition in 1946) is thorough on tabular analysis
and the parsing of Shakespeare, with the requisite number of little
tables ('drive – drivest – art   driving – wilt   drive – hast   driven –
wert driving') getting, eventually, to composition writing via several
hundred exercises on (1) words (2) phrases (3) clauses (4) sentences
simple (5) sentences complex or compound (6) paragraphs – with
plenty of reproduction and outline expansion thrown in for good
measure. This walk-before-running approach, though mistaken, is
satisfyingly neat and makes a strong appeal to tidy minds; what we
find in numerous early textbooks is the 'walking' stage (of clause and
sentence construction, for example) expanded to the point where
pupil and teacher alike forget where it is all supposed to lead. One
will not learn to play a tolerable game of golf or cricket by standing
in a corner of a field for four years energetically practising the full
range of swings and drives; the swinging practice (and it has its
place) is only worth while as a means, not as an end, and the real
action can only begin on the field proper or at the first tee. In any
case, it is probably quite wrong to think of a pupil's use of English in
terms of separate, practisable units each of which can be exercised
in isolation; here perhaps is another of the false analogies which has
been accepted by English theorists including examiners.

Above all, composition was almost entirely absorbed by grammar
work, so that a book labelled 'Composition Study' would invariably
devote 150 of its 200 pages to the parts of speech, verb conjugations,
parsing, etymology and analysis, finally ending with points on sentence and paragraph construction and with a list of suitable essay
topics ('Might is Right. Discuss'; 'Why has the sugar trade in the
West Indies fallen off?'; 'A Stitch in Time Saves Nine'; 'Garden-
ing'; 'Your favourite Mother in fiction'; 'Is War an Unmixed
Evil?'; 'All's Well that Ends Well'; 'The Life Story of a Lump of
Sugar'; ''Tis better to have loved and lost . . .'; 'Wind').

There were even distinct stages at the level of composition proper;
having graduated from sentences the pupil would probably begin
the serious work of writing with synthesis exercises (joining two or
three sentences into a continuous passage), thence move to the kind
of outline expansion already described, thence to solo compositions
using model passages as a basis, finally launching out into an
independent essay in the required objective, formal 'adult' style.

The preface to W. J. Gwillam's *Grammar Combined with Composition*, 1901, partly explains the rationale behind this grammar-
composition link. According to Gwillam teachers are now able to
combine grammar and composition where before they had to be

treated separately; since grammar is clearly far more important (because without it composition cannot be started) teachers will naturally devote the great majority of their time to it. Many teachers of course did just this, though the very questionable premiss that grammar is the necessary basis for writing was not questioned. True to his lights Gwillam's own book offers fifty-nine pages of grammar, one devoted to composition.

There were some ingenious exceptions to this dull tradition – for example using pictures, sometimes even coloured pictures, as a basis for writing, the children 'writing the story in the picture'. The illustrations used in composition books were usually small black and white prints based on steel engravings representing a variety of scenes and situations; a large stag stares into the distance; two children blow bubbles from clay pipes; a boy in a Norfolk suit climbs a rock face; an enormous eagle is suspended against a lake background; a little girl in an enormous hat flies a kite; and a stylish King Canute stands at the edge of the sea. (See David Salmon's *Exercises in English Grammar and Composition*; Thomas Nelson's *Picture Essays*, 1907; Lewis Marsh's *Picture Composition*, 1910 or G. H. Green's *Composition for Junior Forms*, 1915.) There were even attempts to ginger up grammar (as in Edith Hastings's *Exercises for Parsing in Colour*, 1906, with its green nouns, red verbs, yellow adjectives and blue pronouns), and a rather splendid book is C. H. Maxwell's *Composition for Schools and Colleges*, 1904, which gets straight down to business by giving lists of pre-packaged ideas suitable for inclusion in the standard off-the-peg essays of the day (he includes 'Good Manners', 'Chinese Characteristics' and 'An Explosion in a Coal Mine'). Under 'Mud', for example, he suggests that the writer attend (a) to its nature (b) to its origins (c) to its uses (d) to Egypt, which is a triumphant testimony to its permanent benefits.

In short, composition was – and remained for several years – very much a poor relation; as late as 1920 it had still not found an unquestioned place in English work outside the preparatory courses for the Certificate and Matriculation examinations, as the English Association's Pamphlet No. 43 (1919) indicates ('Its right relations with the teaching of Spelling and Grammar are even now by no means determined'), and when it was practised it was along the imitative-reproductive lines sketched above. Indeed the pupils wrote compositions as a means of showing off their acquired grammar as much as for anything, extending the exercise 'Write three sentences to show the correct use of the following' into a slightly longer form to include paragraph and construction skills generally. 'Composition' was merely a testing device, the proof of the grammar pudding, and the idea that pupils would have something personal to say in these circumstances seems hardly to have been considered.

The difference is a subtle one and still needs to be clarified by every teacher. Is written work set to encourage pupils to *communicate*, or is it demanded as a means of assessing the mechanical facilities of the writers? The answer is that both aspects are working simultaneously (or should be, the situation in 1910 was that they were not) and that teachers must be aware of the interraction between the two and be quite sure in their minds as to what exactly it is they want from this class, at this point in time, with this specific piece of written work. Failure to get the situation clear will produce either a drifting back and forth between the poles of rigid, exercise-based formalism and 'spontaneous' easily achieved fluency-without-accuracy, or a permanent settling down at one of these extremes.

'Content' in the first decade of the century was generally supplied to the writer beforehand, even down to the separate sections of each paragraph; it was not the content that teachers were interested in. As one can see from a study of the composition textbooks of the time, every essay title carried its own set of expectations, the polite responses which the adult world took for granted and which children were required to learn along with the correct syntactical procedures. One fed the particular stimulus into the child ('Spring', 'A Stitch in Time') and waited for the correct set of responses to appear on paper. With older pupils who had learnt the routine one could quite simply give them the essay title and leave the rest to them. Small wonder that some teachers were uncertain as to the value of composition work or its place in their teaching.

This disregard for originality or creativity was almost universal and even had overtones of the 'original sin' notion. Children, left to themselves, could not possibly have anything of the remotest significance to say, and would merely reveal the empty childishness of untrained, primitive minds, neither civilised nor sensible. 'It should be remembered . . . that imagination grows out of imitation', writes James Welton, 'There is no value in letting the children simply produce the riotings of untrammelled fancy.'[17] Roberts and Barter believe that 'To lay too great a stress on the original and imaginative treatment of the subject-matter results in formless, chaotic exercises which provide no discipline at all in clear and logical sequence of thought.'[18] To allow children to express their 'immature and borrowed views' is positively dangerous. Left alone, they 'are unable to draw together their floating fancies, and they produce too often . . . a tangle of incoherent marvels'.[19]

A book such as Margaret Macmillan's *Education Through the Imagination*, 1904, was a remarkable exception to this tendency, where perhaps for the first time in the century the term 'creative imagination' is used in relation to children's work in this country, and where the critical need to foster imaginative expression is emphasised. Her omission of any reference to possible 'creativity' in written work is highly significant (she writes of children's music, painting, drama, modelling work and science) and would seem to indicate that such work was not envisaged at all at this time. We find her taking what is in effect a Romantic view of the child ('The child's Imagination is allied to that of the primitive man . . . It is allied, too, in some degree and at certain moments to that of the Seer'[20]) which is interesting as an anticipation of later creative developments and their theoretical basis in the ideas of Romanticism, though the Recapitulation theory is also implicit in her remark.

Philip Hartog in his *The Writing of English*, 1907, also took an unconventional line, requesting that children be allowed in their compositions to have opinions and ideas of their own, and freedom to express their personal feelings, indeed reminding teachers that it is the child's *right* to do so; '. . . there is one supreme thing for the teacher to remember. He must admit unquestioningly the right of each child to have an opinion of his own in dealing with his subject. If the subject has been properly chosen the child will have a right to an opinion of his own.'[21] Hartog also reminds teachers that all children can talk enthusiastically and fluently enough when they have something they really want to say; let the composition teacher create this kind of situation and then let (not make) the children write on the topic in the way that occurs to them, working to their own best standards, and without having the adult standards of the teacher imposed from the outset. In fact, Hartog is reintroducing into composition work the idea of communication and is beginning at the right end of the stick by trying to get children into situations where they are eager to communicate (first), dealing with the manner of that communication second.

The Writing of English is an excellent book, putting grammar firmly into perspective, encouraging children's silent reading for enjoyment, and showing how writing can be entertaining, personal, absorbing and natural. P. B. Ballard in 1939 (*Teaching and Testing English*) praised it highly, noting a gradual adoption of the 'Hartog approach' over the years. The fact is that excellent though the book undeniably was for 1907, its influence was extremely slow in gaining ground, and even in 1939 general practice had not completely caught up with it. But then, had all the first-rate English method books had immediate and universal influence, the development of the subject and its teaching would have been rather different.

Notes

1 The paper is reproduced in an Appendix of Stephen Potter's *The Muse in Chains*, 1937.
2 *The Rise of English Studies*, 1965, p. 64.
3 See E. M. W. Tillyard, *The Muse Unchained*, 1958.
4 See R. W. Rich, *The Training of Teachers in England and Wales during the 19th Century*, 1933. Also *Education 1900–1950*, the Report of the Ministry of Education for 1950, p. 82.
5 Board of Education, *The Teaching of English in England*, HMSO, 1921 (hereafter referred to as 'the 1921 Report'). See also the Board's Report, *The Differentiation of the Curriculum for Boys and Girls in Secondary Schools*, 1923.
6 J. H. Fowler, *The Art of Teaching English*, 1932, p. 2.
7 *Op. cit.*, p. 183.
8 *Op. cit.*, pp. 24–5.
9 *Op. cit.*, pp. 21–2.
10 The 1921 Report, pp. 214 ff.
11 *The Teaching of English Composition*, 1909, p. 28.
12 *Op. cit.*, p. 50.
13 See the 1936 *Year Book of Education*, p. 586; see also G. A. N. Lowndes's *The Silent Social Revolution*, 1937, p. 160.
14 *Teaching the Mother Tongue*, 1921, pp. 69–70 (1926 edn).
15 *Principles and Methods of Teaching*, 1906, p. 151 (1929 edn).
16 *Op. cit.*, p. 20.
17 *Principles and Methods of Teaching*, 1906, p. 180.
18 *The Teaching of English*, 1908, p. 157.
19 E. Covernton, *The Teaching of English Composition*, 1909, p. 27.
20 *Op. cit.*, p. 12 (1923 edn).
21 *Op. cit.*, p. 60.

C

Chapter two   1900-20
Progress or paralysis?   Some voices in the wilderness

Social implications: the Revised Code mentality

A consideration of the particular fallacies which were operating at the beginning of the century can take us quite close to the day-to-day details of classroom English teaching. What must not be forgotten is the extent to which the attitudes and practices of teachers are determined by wider, social influences which bear upon education as a whole. For example, we cannot appreciate the full significance of those 1900 Elementary School Schedules without understanding the 'philosophy' (crude and undeveloped as it may have been) of the elementary school as conceived by society at the time. The fact is that the 3 R's spirit of the Revised Code was still very strong, that elementary education was still seen by many as being a charitable gift to the 'lower orders' (what was needed by such children was 'useful', practical knowledge – grammar for example, or a clear, unimaginative prose style – which would fit them for their clerical/artisan stations in life) and that the following sentiments expressed in the Cross Commission Report still represented the views of the majority of people: 'Care must be taken lest in attempting to raise too much the standard of education the country might defeat the object for which education was given, namely, that manual labour in which so many children must be occupied afterwards.' Elementary teachers, trained or not, were required to accomplish their humble missions in life with a proper regard for their useful but inferior status; the elementary schools did not lead naturally to a further stage in education, but were largely, *sui generis*, institutions for the artisan class while the real business of the nation's education went on in the private or grammar schools. Something of the spirit of the elementary schools at this time can be gauged from H. C. Dent's recent survey of education, 1870 to 1970. Professor Dent was born in 1894, and he records this of his elementary schooling:[1]

I became a pupil in a public elementary school in 1900, some years after the last remnants of Lowe's Code had been officially removed, and I can testify from personal experience that the spirit inculcated by that Code was still very much in evidence in the attitudes and actions of both teachers and pupils. With relatively rare exceptions . . . teachers and taught were sworn enemies. The latter resisted by every means known to them (and some of those means were extremely unpleasant) the desiccated diet of irrelevant facts the former persisted in pressing upon them; teachers retaliated with incessant applications of corporal punishment, impartially inflicted for crime, misdemeanor or mistake.

The subsequent development of English teaching, particularly in the elementary schools and to a lesser extent in the secondary schools, is greatly dependent upon the gradual erosion of these nineteenth-century views and the slow but persistent growth of a more liberal (in both the political and cultural sense) attitude to the nature and function of education, and on this matter it is impossible not to mention the name of Matthew Arnold. Arnold's fight against the Revised Code mentality and its 'commercial theory' of education was prolonged and bitter; he insisted that the purblind 'vocational' obsession of the Code was a brutalising influence upon the nation. The schools must humanise (introduce all children to great literature, especially to the finest poetry, for example, and not for its grammar and allusions but for its spirit and beauty), they must be concerned with 'culture' and nothing less. The *whole* of society is implicated – every child in a course of humanised studies leading to individual growth and accomplishment within a common bond of civilisation. 'The poor require culture as much as the rich; and at present their education, even when they get education, gives them hardly anything of it' (*Literature and Dogma*); it is vitally important that the whole community 'be united by the strong bond of a common culture' ('The Popular Education of France').

Behind the educational myopia lies, for Arnold, social and political myopia; it is the rigid social division and inequality within the nation that is at the root of the schools' divisions into haves and have nots. His cultural ideal was also a political ideal – culture 'seeks to do away with classes'; 'the men of culture are the true apostles of equality'; the humanising process can unite 'the whole body of English society'; 'Man is civilised when the whole body of society comes to life with a life worthy to be called *human*, and corresponding to man's true aspirations and powers.'

As we shall see, the growth of a more liberal attitude in the schools is to be a slow and gradual process; not until after 1918 can the practical application of even part of Arnold's philosophy be seen to any great extent in the elementary schools, and it is an interesting point that where it is to be found there is usually an emphasis upon imaginative (i.e. 'creative') as well as upon 'intellectual' development in the young pupil. (The point should be remembered when creative, self-expressive attitudes to teaching are encountered before 1920.) This is not to maintain that opponents, say, of self-expression in composition are thus automatically unsympathetic to Arnold's views, but it remains a fact that those who come to take the strongest stand on the importance of rigorous formal grammar and on the importance of no-nonsense 'practical' written communication at the expense of everything else are adopting, however tenuously, something of the utilitarian position which distinguished the narrow vision of the Revised Code. It is the tentative movements towards creative English teaching, especially in the first two or three decades of the century (in seeking to cultivate the whole personality of the child and encourage individuality), that are nearer, consciously or not, to the spirit of Arnold.

New Board initiative 1902–10

An important document in the theoretical movement towards a wider concept of education was the Board of Education's 1904 Regulations for Elementary Schools. The Introduction to these Regulations includes (and the influence of Morant is clear): 'The purpose of the Public Elementary School is to form and strengthen the character and to develop the intelligence of the children entrusted to it . . .'; children should be introduced to literature and history, and should develop 'a taste for good reading and thoughtful study'. The Regulations, while retaining the 'reading' and 'writing' requirements of 1900, omitted the 'English' or grammar section for elementary schools and at the same time made a four-year course in language and literature obligatory in all State secondary schools within the grouping of 'literary' subjects. The distinctive feature of this 1904 Code was that it left head-teachers under their new employers, the LEA's, a much freer choice in curriculum decisions, although far too many schools were exceedingly slow to exploit the new possibilities which lay open to them for the curriculum generally and for English in particular.

If we follow the Board's Regulations for Elementary Schools through 1905 and 1907 to 1908 we see that increasing emphasis is laid on the importance of *silent* reading as opposed to the reading aloud which had earlier been the sole test of reading competence as measured by the Board's inspectors; where the 1904 Code refers only to reading aloud, in 1907 we find: 'In the higher classes silent reading should be the rule rather than the exception . . .' As for grammar, the 1908 Regulations actually lay down that '*If given*' instruction should be confined to the higher classes – though what happened in the actual classrooms was another matter.

The 1906 Regulations for Secondary Schools go further than those of 1904 by recommending the kinds of books that the Board would expect pupils in their schools to be studying ('The following scheme is intended to indicate in rough outline the kind of form in which a four-year course in English should be submitted by a Secondary School seeking the Board's approval of the same'). The scheme is worth quoting, if only as evidence of what children were being given at this time.

YEAR I (*Age 12–13*)

Texts: Poets. English Ballads   Longfellow (shorter poems)
               Macaulay's *Lays*   Cowper (shorter poems)
               The Ancient Mariner Patriotic songs and lyrics

Texts: Prose. *Robinson Crusoe*
               Stories of heroes (Greek, Roman, Scandinavian, Arthurian)
               Tales from the *Faerie Queene*
               Gatty's Parables from Nature

YEAR 2 (*Age 13–14*)

Texts: Poets. Longfellow (longer poems, e.g. 'Evangeline')
               Scott (e.g. 'Lady of the Lake')
               Patriotic poems (e.g. *Lyra Heroica*)

Texts: Prose. *The Pilgrim's Progress*
               Selections from *Don Quixote*, Froissart, Malory or *Gulliver's Travels*
               Prescott. Selections from *Peru* or *Mexico*
               Scott (e.g. *The Talisman, Ivanhoe, Quentin Durward*)
               Morris *Story of the Glittering Plain*

YEAR 3 (*Age 14–15*)

Texts: Poets. Simpler poems from one or more of the following: Milton, Gray, Wordsworth, Tennyson, Arnold *or* from selections such as *The Golden Treasury*.
               Shakespeare (*Julius Caesar, The Merchant, As You Like It*)
               Morris (selections from *The Earthly Paradise*)

Texts: Prose. Macaulay. Biographical Essays.
               Biographical sketches of Great Characters, e.g. Charlemagne, Alfred, Sir Thomas More, Queen Elizabeth, Raleigh, Cromwell, Frederick the Great, Dr Johnson, Washington, Napoleon or Nelson.
               Voyages and Travels, e.g. selections from Hakluyt, Purchas, Dampier, Anson or Cook.
               Scott (e.g. *Waverley, The Antiquary, Old Mortality*)

YEAR 4 (*Age 15–16*)

Texts: Poets. More advanced poems from Chaucer (e.g. *The Prologue*), Shakespeare, Spenser, Milton, Pope, Wordsworth, Tennyson or from selections such as *The Golden Treasury*.

Texts: Prose.

Shakespeare (Histories, Comedies, or easier
Tragedies)
Plutarch's *Lives*
Kinglake *Eothen*
Borrow *Lavengro*
Ruskin *Sesame and Lilies*
Frowde selected short studies
Modern prose Comedies (e.g. Goldsmith and
Sheridan)
Selections from British Essayists (e.g. Addison,
Lamb, Goldsmith)
Macaulay Essays, or selected chapters from
The History
[The strong Historical bias is much in evidence here.]

The 1904 Regulations can also be said to have transformed the
training college English courses – and this again due very much to
the personal efforts of Morant, who was directly responsible for the
relevant wording. The training college students must be given a
'wide and liberal' education, in which the study of literature, if pursued properly, can be a vital humanising and educative feature. The
factual, textbook-memorising approach must give way to close and
sensitive reading of texts themselves; 'The time devoted by the
student to textbooks dealing with literature, however exact and complete, is little more profitable than that devoted to verbal and
grammatical commentary, if he is thereby prevented from access to
the works of great writers . . .' Two 'kinds' of texts will now be
introduced, those for detailed study, and those for general reading,
and students will be able to make their own choices from the
general reading list.

In 1900 the Certificate syllabus had been: (men and women, 2nd
year) (i) a composition (ii) for exact and detailed study, *Henry VIII*
and Milton's *Paradise Lost* I and II (iii) for style and subject matter,
Leigh Hunt's *Essays* and *The Tempest*. ('Exact and detailed study'
meant close attention to grammatical and linguistic features, figures
of speech and allusions.) The 1904 syllabus is now (i) history of the
language (ii) for detailed study, *Coriolanus* and a dozen Bacon
Essays (iii) for general reading (scheme 1) *The Tempest*, selections
from the Book of Isaiah, Macaulay's 'Essay on Bacon', Frowde's
English Seaman, Scott's *Kenilworth*, Kingsley's *Westward Ho*, *The
Golden Treasury I*, and Tennyson's *The Revenge*. By 1911 this had
been extended even further, bringing in a far better selection of
authors, e.g. (i) for detailed study, *King Lear*, Burke's *Reflections on
the Revolution in France* (ii) (A), for general reading, one of: *The
Golden Treasury*, *The Oxford Book of Verse*, *The Paradise of English
Poetry*, *English Lyrics from Chaucer to Poe* (B) some of: *Romeo and*

Juliet, Cymbeline, Antony and Cleopatra, The Taming of the Shrew;
Milton's *Comus, Arcades, Lycidas* and sonnets; Pope, *Essay on Man*
I and II; White, *Natural History of Selborne*; Gibbon *Auto-
biography*; Jane Austen, *Emma*; Scott, *Old Mortality, Rob Roy, A
Legend of Montrose*; Byron, selected poems; Dickens, *Pickwick* and
Dombey; Thackeray, *Pendennis*; Mrs Gaskell, *Cranford*; Trollope,
The Warden; and Arnold, *Essays in Criticism*. In fact from 1905
until the mid-twenties, when the universities caught up with them,
one can say that for scope, variety, correct priorities and proper
study attitudes, the training colleges were offering some of the best
English courses in the country.

The Board's first *Handbook of Suggestions* in 1905 devotes nine
and a quarter pages to English (compare the forty-seven pages in the
1927 edition) and is distinctly disappointing. The value of 'repetition' or reproduction – rewriting stories and accounts read or heard
at second-hand – is repeatedly stressed, and the emphasis with
regard to composition work is almost entirely on the imitative 'how'
of rules rather than on the 'what' of content; 'The advance made [in
composition skill] should be in the mode of presenting the subject
rather than in the subject itself.'[2] Ability to clause-analyse poetry is,
the *Handbook* claims, essential to its appreciation and understanding,
in fact clause analysis is the key to the understanding of any English
which the pupil finds difficult. Although the majority of the section
is devoted to a discussion of grammar no concrete modifications or
advances emerge from its erudite but rather vague generalisations.
In its desire not to dictate, the *Handbook* has too often in the past
taken an excessively vague or understated line where clear recommendations would have been perfectly compatible with the spirit of
advice rather than direction which the system embodies; the effect
has often been – certainly as far as English teaching goes – that
teachers have been able to read pretty well whatever they wanted to
read into some of the suggestions, and advance or remain rooted in
the *status quo* as the mood took them. Grammar should not, the
1905 *Handbook* claims, be taught to children before the age of seven
and should not then be pushed further than the child 'feels the need
for it' (?) but in the end it must be seen as being necessary and
desirable, and should be given as a natural basis for composition
work and reading work throughout the school.

On the question of elementary reading material the *Handbook* is
less conservative. There is clearly a great need to get a wider range
of reading material into the schools, to give the children not only
snippets and extracts but whole stories, to get teachers reading more
to their classes, and to try and encourage literary 'taste' with a more
liberal approach to suitable subject-matter (and here the *Handbook*
is on much more constructive ground).

The main basis for elementary school reading was the 'reader' (not to be confused with the first infant primers). These readers, which continued in use well into the twenties as the principal source of story material for many pupils (and which were still being published in the thirties) were invariably produced in five, six, or seven books, carefully graded for each standard. The passages of prose were interspersed with poems, and it was not uncommon for the extracts to be illustrated by coloured as well as by black and white pictures. A brief appendix would contain grammar points and exercises.

A survey of the most popular readers published between 1900 and 1930 shows that the established format changed hardly at all, with the various publishing houses (Dent, Blackie, Macmillan and Chambers in particular) producing sets of books that were to all intents and purposes identical to each other. The first and second books in the series would consist largely of little animal stories, tales with a distinct moral element, or of pieces providing 'useful' information; the senior books would present abridged or simplified extracts from suitable novels (such as *Gulliver's Travels, Pickwick*, or *Robinson Crusoe*), these extracts running sometimes to twenty or thirty pages in the final book. Dent's *Temple Readers* (I–VII) appeared in 1901. Book One contains stories, one or two sides in length, such as 'The Fox and the Grapes', 'Tom Thumb', 'The Babes in the Wood' or 'How Ducks Swim'. Book Two continues with animal stories, 'Jack and the Beanstalk' and 'Beauty and the Beast'. Book Three includes simplified extracts from *The Swiss Family Robinson*; Book Four contains abridged bits of *Gulliver's Travels, Uncle Tom's Cabin* and *Masterman Ready*. Oliver and Boyd's *Excelsior Readers* (I–VI), 1907, are very similar. Here 'The Three Little Pigs' and 'The Two Frogs' (Book One) give way to abridged *Lorna Doone, The Mill on the Floss* (Book Four), *The Last Days of Pompeii, Ivanhoe, Tom Brown's Schooldays* (Book Five), and *Quentin Durward, Gulliver's Travels, Eothen*, and Lamb's tale of *The Merchant of Venice* (Book Six). Chambers's *Effective Readers* (1909) include extracts from *The Mill on the Floss* (Book Three), Kingsley's *Heroes* (Book Four), *Lorna Doone, Silas Marner, Vanity Fair, Tom Brown at Oxford* (Book Five), and *The Monastery, Pickwick*, and a scene from Shakespeare's *Richard II* (Book Six).

Coming up to 1915 we find Macmillan's *New Senior Class Readers* (I–IV) including abridged *Robinson Crusoe, Pickwick, Gulliver's Travels, Cranford* and *The Talisman*, and even by 1936–7 the pattern has changed very little (see, for example, Macmillan's *New Modern English Readers*, 1936 or the ULP *New Foundation Readers*, 1937). During the thirties, however, it is possible to see an increasing tendency to depend less on the use of abridged fiction and to give passages of interesting factual material instead ('The Motorcar', 'Seaplanes', 'Indian Tales', 'The Story of Printing') in all the books – an indication that pupils were now doing their fictional reading in the novels themselves (abridged or not). If the term 'reader' has a 1900 sound, its persistence as a school textbook (indeed as a school *course*) must not be underestimated. The reader could be said to take care of the literature side for many schools, with no necessity to look further. The Board of Education's 1928 Report, *Books in Public Elementary Schools*, makes the disturbing comment that some elementary schools are still depending solely upon the use of a set of readers to present literature and prose stories to their pupils in the traditional way (reading round the class).

In 1910 the Board issued its eleven-page *Circular 753* ('The Teaching of English in Secondary Schools') to supplement the usual Regulations and 'to give suggestions and guidance to teachers, by setting forth aims to be followed and errors to be avoided'. This is a much more positive document than the 1905 *Handbook*, and the Circular begins by anticipating George Sampson's (1921) point that 'Every teacher is a teacher of English.' 'The teaching of English in a school is not, and cannot be, confined to the hours definitively set apart by the time-table for the subject. Practically every lesson throughout the school is incidentally an exercise in speaking, reading, or writing English.'[3] (In other words, it is a misconception to approach English as a 'subject' in the normally accepted sense – the Board is half-way to the truth.) The fact is that in the schools English is not only being treated as a watertight unit, but is being taught by any member of staff who can be induced to 'take a few periods' to fill in time, and the Board can only conclude that in far too many secondary schools English is not taken seriously, and would be taken even less seriously if the Secondary Regulations were to be modified. (The Circular omits to mention the fact that in many schools 'grammar', 'composition' and 'literature' were all being taught to the same class by different members of staff.)

As regards the teaching of literature, the Circular makes a number of good comments. The teaching of literary history must give way to the actual reading of texts; only then can real knowledge and genuine appreciation grow (the remark seems so obvious that one can only gape in bewilderment at the then widespread practice of centring the literature courses on textbooks of literary history). 'To teach a pupil who has read very little Shakespeare and no Marlowe to repeat from a textbook statements about Shakespeare's debt to Marlowe is not merely useless; it propagates intellectual dishonesty in one of its most insidious forms.'[4] This kind of approach is encouraged, the Circular goes on, through the habit of certain examination boards of setting a period of literature for study (and, they might have added, by the often generalised and superficial examination questions that were all too frequently set on those periods). At the same time (and the Circular is characteristic of the pre-1920 period here) the texts chosen for study must (a) have real literary merit, and (b) be difficult enough to demand 'genuine effort' from the class – in other words, the pupil must come up to the standard of the text which will be chosen uncompromisingly for its 'merit' (*Religio Medici, Past and Present, On the Beautiful and the Sublime*) or go under, a principle which, though admirable in theory, made much School Certificate literature hopelessly unsuitable for its aspirants.

The Circular also insists that texts should not be chosen simply because they happen to supplement the history course, and it severely criticises editions of texts and textbooks of the 'classical format' type. As for grammar, a good basis must be laid down, but at the same time 'it should not bulk largely in the regular school teaching of English, and it should not be isolated from Composition and Literature and made into an abstract exercise. Whole lesson-periods should not be systematically given up to formal Grammar . . .'5

In its insistence on a proper approach to literature, the Circular was in fact expressing the opinion of a growing number of teachers who were showing increasing dissatisfaction with the exclusively historical-biographical-grammatical approach. Articles demanding 'real' literature study had already appeared in the *Journal of Education* (see the issues of March 1902, February 1903, April 1903, April 1907), all making much the same points. There can be little doubt that some extraordinary things were being done in the name of literary study, even by those with the best intentions, and that even where teachers were able to rise above Milton's prefixes or Scott's family tree the attempts at 'appreciation' could take some bizarre forms. In a leading *Journal* article ('A model literature lesson', August 1908) one Ethel Dawson suggests the study of Tennyson's 'Break, break, break'; after the appropriate readings, she recommends the following questions to search out the pupils' most sensitive responses: '(i) Give derivation and etymology of the word "break" as used in the poem. (ii) Scan the line "Break, break, break" and compare the metrical effect of "Ding, dong, bell". (iii) Discuss the influence of geological strata on poetry. (iv) Express in good prose the thought that the poet would fain have uttered, and indicate the reason of his disability.'

It is quite impossible to suggest the extent of the influence which Board publications such as the *Handbooks* or the Circulars had upon teachers in the actual classroom; in the absence of other, detailed method material it is probable that the early *Suggestions* exerted considerable influence. In its editorial comment on the 1910 Circular the *Journal of Education* stated that the publication was one of the most valuable that the Board had yet put out; 'If the principles laid down in the circular . . . are carried into practice, nothing short of a revolution will take place in the curriculum of secondary schools' – and this because although a not insignificant body of opinion is now (1911) prepared to accept English in secondary schools, there is no agreement on aims or methods in its teaching, and the Circular does something to supply the deficiency. This kind of comment must have influenced many teachers, even though the secondary schools were less likely, with their different historical background, to follow the Board's every hint in the way that the elementary schools might be expected to. As far as elementary teachers were concerned, the first twenty years of the century saw a continuing abject dependence on 'official' pronunciations in the old Code manner when in fact the Board itself was anxious that schools should at least make some gestures of independent thinking and when HMI's, no longer the awe-inspiring judges of the past, were doing their utmost to encourage teachers to think for themselves. Thus the 'suggestions' (merely) aspect of the *Handbooks of Suggestions* was probably interpreted in much too authoritarian a way, and we are justified in assuming that they were closely read. The fact remains that many of the bad teaching habits which the Board attacked continued to thrive long after official sanction had been given for their demise, although this may have been partly due to the vagueness, referred to already, of some of those pronouncements. Certainly each successive edition of the *Suggestions* is invariably followed by a new spurt of method and textbook publishing, often with prefatory references to the Board's most recent comments, though whether this stemmed from the writers' desires to be up to date and 'relevant' for financial rather than educational reasons is impossible to determine. Sometimes these textbooks broke new ground in an original and valuable way, giving practical classroom flesh and blood to the Board's theoretical skeleton. One such textbook was Lewis Marsh's *Combined Course of Literary Reading and Composition*, 1907, where a new approach to grammar and language work generally is attempted, and where the term 'Direct Method' appears. Marsh notes the 1905 *Handbook*'s emphasis on the importance of writing from models, and produces a (secondary) textbook consisting of extracts of poetry and prose (from writers such as Scott, Dickens, Longfellow, Shakespeare, Shelley, Milton or Lamb) each two or three sides in length, which form the basis for exercises in grammar, figures of speech, paraphrase, simple comprehension, and written work, the 'directness' lying in the first-hand use by the pupils of reasonably long pieces of English instead of working with the usual contrived, sentence-based exercises. Marsh is still concerned with such things as analysis and parsing ('Pick six adjectives from the passage and use them in sentences of your own', 'Analyse the second and third sentences in para. two' or 'Fill in the gaps in the following sentences using words from the passage') but at least he is trying to keep the grammatical elements in a written communicative context. The composition work is predictably imitative, with detailed outlines provided for each topic and directions such as: 'Write a short account of the incidents in the passage' or (after a passage on Spring) 'Write a short essay of about twelve lines in praise of the month of May referring to: flowers, streams, conclusion.'

This 'method' was to become popular in the second decade, but it must be said that although this was regarded as being something of a new approach in English teaching it was firmly rooted in the imitative fallacy – as, for example, C. Rooney's *English Composition from Models*, 1911 ('The work will, it is hoped, meet with the approval of teachers who favour the Direct Method . . .') eloquently testifies. Here the essay models provided (Lamb, Hazlitt, Bacon, Macaulay, Addison) are to be servilely copied or reproduced.

Another popular Direct Method textbook was F. Pickles's *Composition Through Reading*, I–II, 1913–14, which is also based on model extracts with follow-up exercises in grammar, reproduction and composition. In his Foreword Pickles writes:

No number of humdrum exercises in Grammar and Composition will make a good writer. There must be a systematic study of the work of the master-craftsmen . . . In other words, the tyro in sentence-making cannot do better than follow the example of his fellow students in the kindred arts of Drawing, Painting, and Sculpture, and *imitate* with care and constancy the work of the Great Masters.

The fallacies persist: grammar

Between 1910 and 1920 a gradual development in the subject continued, though English was still having to justify itself to many critics, not least among them the supporters of the classics many of whom refused to accept it as a potentially liberal, humanising study. In 1917 Nowell Smith can still write of the continuing 'belittlement and even distrust' of English at school level[6] – the irony being that as long as English teachers continued to borrow the teaching methods of their classical opponents they kept literary studies at a level which begged hostile criticism. It is strange that for so long 'classical' methods persisted in English teaching. R. S. Bate in a thorough study of secondary English in 1913, *The Teaching of English Literature in Secondary Schools*, can write:

while the reformers have seen that the mechanical drudgery of learning Greek and Latin grammar has not led, as a rule, to a knowledge of the languages, and so have abolished the Classics, they have, unfortunately, left us the methods

which made the study of the Classics unfruitful; and the very
men who have taught Greek and Latin without sympathy,
intelligence, or insight, have been permitted to apply the same
methods to English Literature.

... just as the first railway carriages were built like the stage
coaches which they displaced, because it did not occur to
anyone to build them otherwise, so we have been content to
teach literature as though it were Latin and Greek.

Bate's book is doubly interesting since he himself is obviously a
'Classic' well versed in and deeply committed to classical literature,
yet convinced that the time has come for English to assume the
liberal role which the older studies must now yield.

At the same time – or was it the same thing? – the worst kind of
grammar study persisted. An horrific little book is R. B. Morgan's
A New English Grammar for Junior Forms, 1912 (Prep. school
juniors, eight to thirteen years) which was sufficiently popular to get
itself reprinted ten times before 1928. Morgan manages to out-
grammar Latin (no mean achievement), turning the English language into a complex system of points, tables, diagrams, lists and
subsections as involved as the most involved of chemical formulae –
the whole being an attempt to do for English what all respectable
school Latin grammars have done for Latin. The book is in fifty-
two detailed sections, devoted to sentences, phrases, parts of speech,
cases, analysis, inflections, tenses, plurals, parsing, function etc.;
questions include: 'What is an auxiliary verb? Name as many as you
can'; 'What is an adjectival gerund? Distinguish it from a present
participle'; 'What is a verb phrase? A verb of incomplete predica-
tion? A complement? Give five examples of each'; 'Write out the
third person singular, future imperfect, indicative, passive of –
trouble, obtain, choose'; 'Write down in columns five nouns of (i)
masculine gender (ii) feminine gender (iii) common gender (iv)
neuter gender.' The verb 'to throw' is tabulated as 'am thrown', 'art
thrown', 'hast been thrown', 'wast being thrown', 'wilt have been
thrown'.

Other books in this mould include F. W. Bewsher's *Exercises in
English*, 1914 ('Underline any relative in this passage and also its
antecedents'; 'substitute adverbial phrases for all the adverbs in this
passage . . .'); J. S. Norman's *English Grammar*, 1918; J. S.
Chalmers's *The Primary School Grammar*, 1918 ('Analyse: "His
listless length at noontide he would stretch, and pore upon the
brook that babbles by"'); and Alfred West's *Elements of English
Grammar*, 1893, revised 1918 ('Show that in the following sentence
there is Pleonasm – "Traveller, from whence comest thou?"';
'Write the genitive case in the plural of the feminine form corresponding to "bachelor", "nephew", "gander", "sultan", "fox",

"peacock" . . .'). And as if the linguistic benefits conferred by grammar were not in themselves sufficient reason for its study, there was always the 'mental training' gambit; 'The inclusion of English Grammar in the school curriculum can be amply justified on the ground that it affords valuable mental discipline, and that it can be used as a means of developing clear and logical thought' (English Association Pamphlet No. 37, 1917).

In the face of this one or two individuals were doubtful that grammar knowledge was in any way connected with actual written competence. In the *Journal of Experimental Pedagogy* for 1912 (Vol. I, No. 3) Professor J. A. Green suggests that grammar knowledge does not improve written expression, and he indicates that it might be as well to try and find out through research exactly what the connection between the two is, and in the light of that take a hard look at what goes on in schools. When research did get under way some time later it tended to confirm Professor Green's suspicions, though considering the magnitude of the topic it is surprising that only small-scale investigating has been done on a local rather than on a national level. The correlation between grammar knowledge and written ability has been shown to be very low, or even nil (see below) but if this is the final word on the subject it would be helpful to have the conclusion embodied in a piece of major research taking in the whole country and schools at both junior and secondary level.

The year 1911 saw the final Report of the Joint Committee on Grammatical Terminology, originally set up in 1908 to bring some kind of order to the confusion then existing in grammar teaching (with no agreement among teachers on descriptive terms let alone on the desirable content of grammar courses) and to establish a common approach to English, Latin and foreign language grammar. The complicated nature of the Committee's final agreed basis indicates the appalling complexity that must have existed before, but the Committee presents forty recommendations concerning such things as sentence types (now to be simple, complex, double or multiple), gender (not to be emphasised), and analysis, which provide teachers and textbook writers with a common set of terms.

Before assuming that grammar was now reduced to a decent and manageable minimum, the reader should have a look at a book such as Alfred West's *Elements of English Grammar* (1893), which was completely revised in 1912 to meet the recommendations of the Joint Committee; the 'decent minimum' reveals itself over three-hundred pages in what (to the modern reader) is as detailed a coverage as anything in the late nineteenth century. It is true that West's original edition needed the publication of a separate 'Key' to guide the reader through, so a cutting back has occurred, but one feels that modification could have gone slightly further in 1912 – perhaps reducing the three-hundred pages to fifty.

The Committee made no reference to the desirability of grammar teaching, obviously assuming that it would be universally taught as a matter of course at both elementary and secondary level, and it is not to the Committee's credit that it deliberately gave new impetus to the mistaken belief that detailed English grammar was necessary to every pupil if only as an indispensable help in learning modern foreign languages. This, as we shall see, provided a last-ditch excuse for those who were beginning to waver over the matter and question the practical effects of grammar on ability in writing and speaking, and kept grammar teaching in its early pedantic form going that much longer. Perhaps grammar did not improve writing as dramatically as had been assumed; perhaps it did not promote logical thought – but how could Herr X or Monsieur Y teach German or French to pupils who didn't even know a gerund from a participle or how to deal with the analysis of compound sentences ? – particularly when that German and French was approached as bookishly, grammatically and artificially as the English was ?

Liberal advocates: Edmond Holmes, Montessori and 'activity'

Edmond Holmes's *What Is and What Might Be*, 1911, has already been referred to, and it can be said that no more vigorous and outspoken an attack on the narrow-minded, utilitarian pedantries of the continuing Revised Code attitudes was voiced in educational publishing between 1900 and 1920. The influence of the Code ('As an ingenious instrument for arresting the mental growth of the child, and deadening all his higher faculties, it has never had, and I hope will never have, a rival') doggedly persists in the elementary teachers' refusal to take an initiative in developing the curriculum, in the obsession with visible 'results' and examinations (an obsession Holmes traces to the Western World generally), in the obtuse Victorian 'original sin' delusions which still influence many teachers, and in the utter inability of educationists to distinguish 'knowledge' from mere 'information', 'education' from 'lower orders usefulness'. He makes it clear that he is not attacking the teachers, who are simply fulfilling the role which society expects of them: 'No one knows better than I do that the elementary teachers of this country are the victims of a vicious conception of education which has beyond it twenty centuries of tradition and prescription, and the malign influence of which was intensified in their case by thirty or more of Code despotism and "payment by results".'[7] But the fact remains that the true aim of education – inner 'spiritual' growth – enters their scheme not at all, and the child is starved of activity and made to sit passively in mechanical obedience, 'helpless, apathetic, and inert', the victim of the teacher's (and society's) delusion that he must be innately disposed to wrongdoing and stupidity. Thus in composition work, Holmes goes on, there is an exaggerated concern for the external 'results' – handwriting, spelling, grammar, lay-out – and a total disregard for personal expression; 'The teaching of composition in the ordinary elementary school is too often fraudulent and futile. *Indeed there is no lesson in which the teacher's traditional distrust of the child goes further than in this*[8] (my italics).

Now although Holmes nowhere refers to Arnold by name, there can be no question of his being considerably influenced by Arnold's ideas; he insists that education must 'civilise and humanise', he uses the term 'anarchy' in Arnold's sense, and some lines from 'The Grande Chartreuse' are quoted near the end of the book. One feels, in fact, reading *What Is and What Might Be* that Arnold could not have done better himself. Holmes also makes a number of 'sociological' points which go to the heart of the social class problems underlying the sorry educational scene and which relate directly to Arnold's own comments on the matter. There would be an incalculable gain to the nation, Holmes maintains, if 'the rank and file of its children' could be raised by a genuine education based on 'self-realisation'; intelligence is not, nor has it ever been, the exclusive property of the middle class. 'The dream, then, of leading the children of England – the children of the "masses" as well as of the "classes" – into the path of self-realisation, is not so widely impracticable as to convict the dreamer of insanity.'[9]

The one area where Holmes's comments and criticisms might not have applied would have been in the infant sections of the elementary schools. It has frequently been said that changes in methods of teaching and class organisation in this country have often originated in and permeated upwards from the infant school, and that the last fifty years have witnessed a gradual leavening, first of junior, and recently of secondary teaching attitudes by the spread of 'active', pupil-centred practices from the infant level. It is certainly true that the 'English' work of the infant schools (stories, poetry, acting) is invariably seen to be in advance of 'junior' English before 1940 in terms of the range of books used, the emphasis on reading for pleasure, the need for self-expression in talk and movement, and the activity of the children. If the elementary pupil of eight-plus before 1920 was expected to sit silently in his desk and learn grammar, his younger brother or sister in the infant class was enjoying a far more liberal day. 'Fantasy' was always tolerated in the new school arrival, and it is all to the good that gradually over the years educationists have come to uphold the importance of fantasy, 'play', imagination and imaginative expression for all children, adolescents as well as infants. It is no coincidence that the post-1945 creativity movement is to a great extent based on the theories of psychologists who have worked with very young children, Maria Montessori, for example, or Susan Isaacs.

The work of Maria Montessori was already becoming known in England by 1910 (see Anne George's translation of *Il Metodo della Pedagogica Scientifica* as *The Montessori Method* in 1912) and according to the 1932 *Year Book of Education* her influence had extended into most State infant schools by 1919.[10] Discussing the rise of child-centred psychology and teaching theories, P. B. Ballard asserts in 1925: 'Whatever may be the defects of her system it is quite certain that the movement towards individualism in the school has received its greatest impetus and its greatest inspiration from Dr. Montessori.'[11] Subsequently she was to be referred to favourably by a number of English method writers, and although she was not directly concerned with older children's composition work in a 'creative' sense, what she has to say about young children's drawings is very relevant to a creative approach to writing. In writing, as in drawing, the child must be left free to express what he wants to express, and the writing (like drawing) should not be led up to with a lengthy succession of walk-before-running exercises (the parallel will be obvious to any present-day English teacher):[12]

> There can be no 'graduated exercises in drawing', leading up to an artistic creation. That goal can be attained only through the development of mechanical technique and through freedom of the spirit. That is our reason for not teaching drawing directly to the child. We prepare him indirectly, leaving him free to the mysterious and divine labour of producing things according to his own feelings. Thus drawing comes to satisfy a need for expression, as does language . . .

In any case, as noted above, infant 'English' tended to be far more lively that junior work at this time, irrespective of the Montessorian influence. We find infant teachers being told to read a wide range of stories, nursery rhymes, fairy tales, legends, animal adventures and poems to their children; great importance is placed on free discussion between teacher and pupil, with plenty of activity in mime or recitation (see, for example, the appropriate sections in Roberts and Barter, *The Teaching of English,* or in W. J. Batchelder, *Notes on the Teaching of English*).

Another important influence on English work was the publication in 1911 of Harriet Finlay-Johnson's *The Dramatic Method of Teaching*. Briefly, this method worked from the assumption that children between seven and eleven years learn better when they are active, happy, and free to express themselves, and rather than sit passively and have the facts of history or literature pumped into them they should be allowed to engage actively with the subjects through improvised drama and mime. The factual source materials they will get from books and from the teacher, but the final realisation and absorption of those facts will be through a dramatic method

D

(this technique applies, of course, to the events of history or to the stories and plots of plays, poems or novels). This in a time of silent classrooms, fixed desks and passive pupils was obviously something of a novelty, but although *The Dramatic Method* was an important book for younger pupils, the general implications of the Finlay-Johnson technique were not realised for many years. The remarks of Arnold Smith (in his *Aims and Methods in the Teaching of English*, 1915) suggest the real significance of the Dramatic method: 'Of experiments in connection with the teaching of English none is more striking than the attempt to teach children by getting them to dramatise scenes from literature and history'; 'The experiment is indeed revolutionary, for it presupposes an attitude of mind on the part of the teacher which is repugnant to old-fashioned ideas of discipline ... and it aims at something which to the teacher of twenty or even ten years ago would have seemed mere foolishness.'[13] (And clearly remained so to many.)

English and the Recapitulation theory

While 'activity' was gaining respectable psychological ground, the time-lag that invariably operates between theory and accepted class-room practice continued. The theory that seems to have had most influence on English method writers in the period 1910-15 was the Recapitulation theory of Stanley Hall with its 'Culture Epoch' additions (Hall's *Adolescence* had been published in London in 1908). We can find a reference to the theory in its application to English teaching as early as 1902 in the (American) *The Teaching of English in the Elementary and Secondary School* by Percival Chubb (New York, Macmillan) where the nine- to thirteen-year-old is seen as still being at the 'epic phase' of civilisation with a consequent appetite for romance and heroism. It is in Smith's (1915) book that the full implications of 'recapitulation' for English appear. Smith points out that pupils should be given reading matter which is suitable to their abilities and tastes; the basis of any course of literature must be 'psychological' and the pupil 'should be recognised for what he is: a being who is repeating in little the history of the race and harking back, at each step, to bygone generations at various periods of racial history'.[14] The practical result of this is to recommend for the nine- to thirteen-year-olds such material as Norse, Greek and Arthurian legends, Malory, ballads, epics, *Ivanhoe* etc. and to encourage 'communal' composition (composition where all members of the class can contribute something to the group effort) since 'the child is genetically at the stage of the race when a kind of composition was practicable which is alien to modern civilisation – a kind of communal composition ... created, enjoyed, embellished and orally transmitted by the community.'[15] (See also

Ethel Tant on the Culture Epoch theory, the *Journal of Education*, September 1917: 'Both the child and the primitive man delight in hearing as well as telling tales.') As time has passed teachers have forgotten the 'racial' *raison d'être* for this and have merely gone on recommending ballad and mythic material to this age group because of the 'good yarns' involved; whether this kind of material is as suitable as is sometimes supposed is questionable (or, at least, ought to be questioned); once remove the anachronistic psychological prop and the whole theory totters, although as late as 1931 the Hadow Primary School Report is convinced that a great many teachers still hold the Recapitulation theory.

In fact, by 1915 such reading material had become commonplace in the schools; Roberts and Barter (1908) recommend the following texts for elementary pupils: the stories of Beowulf, King Arthur, the Mabinogion; Norse legends, Greek myths, the *Odyssey*, and the tales of Robin Hood. In the English Association's Leaflet No. 14 ('The Early Stages in the Teaching of English', 1910) we find similar recommendations, together with such ballads as 'Hind Horn', 'The Wreck of the Hesperus', 'Sir Patrick Spens' and 'Young Lochinvar'. Batchelder's lists (1913) are very similar, and the standard material included in the readers of the time also tended to the mythical-legendary for the middle standards.

Grace Bracken in *The Teaching of English in Secondary Schools for Girls*, 1924, gives the theory a new twist by suggesting that children's prose style develops from the initial 'crudity' of the Anglo-Saxons to the polish and 'maturity' of the nineteenth-century masters (again this curious fixation on the nineteenth-century essay and on the incomparable merits of writers such as Carlyle or Ruskin) and that teachers should choose suitable model passages for the pupil to study and imitate appropriate to his or her stage of development. What also emerges from Grace Bracken's comments is that 'recapitulation' was for many teachers conveniently synonymous with 'imitation' – the pupil, crude and uncivilised, submitting to the need to master the developmental phases and accepting at each phase the controlling and directing hand of the successful all-knowing adult.

Progress in attitudes to writing: O'Grady, Greening Lamborn and Finch

Nevertheless, 'activity' in the self-expressive sense was becoming increasingly respectable. Particularly in composition work there was a move away from the formal essay as a device merely to test grammar knowledge towards the idea that the essay could be a form of personal expression. Articles and letters demanding an imaginative rather than a mechanically impersonal approach to writing were appearing sporadically in the *Journal of Education* (February 1906, 'A neglected aspect of composition' by E. M. White; January 1907, 'English' by Arthur Burrell; April 1907, 'The teaching of English in schools' by Stewart Robinson; July 1914, 'English composition' by G. E. S. Coxhead). These made the obvious points, already expressed by Philip Hartog, that writing must be personal, that children are not totally devoid of inventiveness, and that oral expression can help written expression. Coxhead writes: '... self-expression is the goal of composition, and since there is a self in everyone it is the function of composition to bring it to adequate expression.' At the same time a number of extremely good books on the theory and practice of composition appeared between 1910 and 1920. We find E. T. Campagnac, for example, in his *Lectures on the Teaching of Composition*, 1912, actually writing (after describing how children like to make things): 'We may encourage this creative gift of children in the medium of writing' and 'We must find space and time for our pupils to do what they like, to be artificers and creators on their own account.'[16] In his *Notes on the Teaching of English* W. J. Batchelder reports (with evident excitement) the success he has had with 'oral composition' work in standards III and IV – the children actually making up a story themselves, through discussion and pooled suggestion, before writing it down. He seems to feel that he has to defend the whole business; the results (of course) were 'crude and disconnected', the whole thing 'inconsequential', but he sticks to his convictions and reprints one of the stories with: 'This exercise in imaginative composition is given *in extenso* because it is an actual example of what our country children can do when their interest is fully aroused.'[17]

A most remarkable composition textbook (for its date) was Hardress O'Grady's *Matter, Form and Style*, 1912, and this manual marks a new departure in textbook publishing by omitting grammar work completely and adopting a 'craft', practical approach to writing. The pupil is taken, not through clause analysis, parsing, figures of speech and sentence construction but through a study of various styles of writing (descriptive, emotive, satiric, persuasive) based on (1) his own attempts in these styles (2) the reading of good examples taken from the writings of professionals. O'Grady presents his pupils with prose passages which they must read and compare for effectiveness of presentation, trying their own hand at the technique (including short stories) with a list of good follow-up assignments. The book is extremely important because it rejects the wretched grammar-composition link, and insists that writing is learnt by writing and that the best way to proceed is to manoeuvre pupils into the writing situation first and show them what they are doing (in stylistic not grammatical terms) afterwards. The difference between this and the imitation-of-models approach which was going strong at the time is that O'Grady's first concern is with original and fresh writing from the pupil, who works at his own level and uses the model to get the spirit of satire or persuasion rather than a collection of hollow phrases or superficial tricks of expression. To quote O'Grady in his Preface: 'I have felt that many methods of teaching were doomed to failure because they took the component parts of a subject first, each part separately, so that the pupil could "not see the wood for the trees". Whereas it would appear more human and humane to get first the creative act, and then shape the thing created.'

Some indication of the speed with which developments in composition teaching took place can be gauged from the fact that O'Grady is still being enthusiastically recommended as an 'advanced' thinker by method writers in the 1920s and '30s.

Arnold Smith, however, sees in 1915 the imminent collapse of all repressive methods, and his optimistic assumption that 'repression' has now entirely given way to 'expression' is encouraging even if a little premature. His own views are certainly commendable; as far as English studies go 'The pupils should not be passive recipients of information, but should be active in their desire to know, and should wish to apply their knowledge practically, *either in creative work of their own* or in the solution of the great problems of human life which are the subject of literature'[18] (my italics). Pupils should be writing their own plays and their own poems, Smith goes on – he almost certainly has Caldwell Cook's first *Perse Playbooks* in mind – and their composition work should always be 'an expression of their own individuality'. He believes that grammar work is still important (analysis, for example) but is anxious to get it into its right place as the servant of written expression, not the master. He suggests that the following authors and texts would be suitable for a secondary school course: eleven to twelve years, Kingsley's *Heroes*, *Sohrab and Rustum*, an anthology of lyrical poetry; twelve to thirteen years, Malory, Lamb's *Tales from Shakespeare*, *The Idylls of the King*; thirteen to fourteen years, *Spectator* selections, *As You Like It*, *The Golden Treasury*; fourteen to fifteen years, Shakespeare's Roman or history plays, Thackeray's *English Humourists*; fifteen to sixteen years, Shakespeare's tragedies and comedies, Chaucer's *Prologue*, English prose selections (all these unexceptional by 1915 standards).

Smith's reference to the need for secondary pupils to write their own poetry is an important one. It is around this time (1914–16) that the idea of poetry writing as a normal and accepted part of school English for all pupils – as opposed to the merely classically imitative exercises of the senior forms – begins to take a tentative hold. E. A. Greening Lamborn in *The Rudiments of Criticism*, 1916 (chapter 10), makes a strong plea that elementary pupils be allowed to write their own poems. Lamborn's approach to poetry generally (and his book is intended as a discussion of the basic qualities of 'poetry' for training college students) is somewhat overdone in its generalised emotive tone: 'All of us, for example, see dimly, as a half-blind man sees a light, beauty in a hill or a cloud or a primrose; but the poet sees it as a radiant glow that moves him to cry aloud with delight . . .', and he tends to adopt the 'Wordsworthian'(?) stance of seeing children as 'natural seers' and thus 'natural poets', but he has some very important things to say about writing in schools. He rejects the formal elementary school 'style' imposed upon the children by their adult teachers; 'To write brightly and picturesquely is far better than to write merely grammatically'; 'he [the teacher] may write a grammatically correct essay, but the children's, if they are given a free hand, will be much more interesting and attractive, because their ideas and their style are fresh and unconventional, however inaccurate.'[19] Lamborn's claim is that children must be allowed to write 'original' verse, though the term requires some qualification; he advocates, for example, a strongly imitative approach, with pupils copying the styles and structures of well-known poems. Also, he begins with a detailed study of prosody, the pupil completing exercises in scansion and metre and filling out given metrical frameworks. As a result, the children's poems which he reproduces at the end of the book are often extremely artificial and stilted.

On the Model of Browning's 'Rabbi Ben Ezra'

The little birds are gay,
And little lambs do play,
The snowdrop bends its small white head so sweet,
The sky is blue and clear,
The dew lies like a tear,
The thrush sings merrily and little lambs do bleat.

The hedges are all green,
The swallow can be seen,
And April showers fall upon the ground,
The daisies show their heads,
Above their grassy beds,
And buds are coming out, and flowers grow around.

(Boy, 13 years)

April

Which month brings us the fresh'ning show'rs?
  Who makes the grass shoot on the hill?
Who brings us now the pretty flow'rs?
  'Tis you, 'Tis you, April.

Who makes the birds build in the tree?
  Who makes the moss grow by the rill?
Who owns of Spring the charming keys?
'Tis you, 'Tis you, April.

Who brings the yellow buttercup?
  And the primrose and the daffodil?
Who makes the buds of trees shoot up?
'Tis you, 'Tis you, April.

April, you bring us joy and sun,
  You brighten up our land with flow'rs,
You make the hare begin to run,
  And O, those helpful show'rs.

(Boy, 10 years)

Despite the somewhat forced style of his examples, Lamborn's principal argument and his actual selection of pupils' work for publication are extremely important in the development of school English; and this, remember, in a book intended for students in training colleges.

Perhaps the best of all the composition method books published between 1910 and 1920 was Robert Finch's *How To Teach English Composition*, 1919.[20] Far from having dated, this book (in two small volumes) could be studied with advantage by all English teachers today, and not merely from the point of view of theoretical interest but in terms of practical classroom work. The book was very favourably reviewed by *The Times Educational Supplement* ('This is an excellent guide to a persistently mistaught subject, and should be read by every teacher who sets an essay') and it is with the appearance of Finch's book that we can say that composition as it is understood today can be seen to establish itself. So far, Finch writes, composition has largely been a disaster:[21]

A superior being comes before us, and bawls out a list of
'subjects' or writes them down in frigid silence on the
blackboard. Here they are: 'Wool'; 'A Stitch in Time Saves
Nine'; 'The Capes of Scotland'; 'The Rabbit'. We are to
choose one of these inspiring themes, and we are to descant
upon it for the space of forty minutes . . . The coming forty
minutes we know will be forty minutes of unmitigated
purgatory.

Composition, he goes on, will only be valuable where pupils have something to say, and they will only have something to say where their interest is engaged. The teacher must therefore pick subjects which are certain to be interesting, talk them up with the class into something which is really absorbing, throw out a few hints as to the different ways the subject might be tackled, then let the pupils work out their own versions. The written work must be original – not copied, imitated, reproduced or falsified in an attempt to sound ten years older, but be the pupil's own individual expression. Poor work, where the writing comes slowly and unenthusiastically in short, plodding sentences, is as much the fault of the teacher as of the children; the teacher who cannot make suitable subjects interesting, or get children involved in topics, cannot expect to get writing which is lively and worth reading. Written work should cover every aspect of style and form; let children describe objects – an ornament, a flower, a toy; write on 'How to make a cake', 'How to make a rabbit hutch', 'How to mend a bicycle'; let them write animal fables, short stories, magazine articles, newspaper reports and plays; let them write real letters and answer real advertisements; let them use 'scientific' prose to describe simple processes, and figurative prose to make sensitive and imaginative descriptions of scenes, people and personal experiences. The teacher should develop a 'themes' approach, providing the pupils with stories, poems and vivid prose extracts relating to, say, homes, mystery and imagination, holidays, railways, etc., with the children writing something on each. As for grammar and exercise work, this must come afterwards, arise out of the pupils' actual writing, and relate, not to ideal and hypothetical needs, but to the mistakes that are actually being made. There is no point in teaching grammatical material to children before they are ready to use those structures; when they are ready the teaching can be done quickly and efficiently. Like Caldwell Cook, Finch rejects the idea of a series of graded skills going on and on year after school year in an attempt to 'prepare' the pupil for writing – that writing stage never, in fact, arriving. However, he agrees on the basic grammatical minimum laid down by the Board of Education and maintains that all secondary pupils must know the parts of speech and be able to clause analyse.

Finch also advocates the writing of poetry by all children, and this not through a detailed study of prosody, but by imitating simple metrical forms (ballad form, or couplets) which shall serve as frame-work for the child's own material. He takes rhyme for granted and implies that suitable diction along 'o'er', 'e'er', and 'yonder' lines is desirable, but insists that once the pupil gets the hang of things he should be encouraged and allowed to produce entirely original work on his own. Chapter 17 in Volume I of his book is interesting as being a selection of original poems by children thirteen to sixteen years from Hornsey School. These are in strict rhyme, are strongly patriotic and reminiscent of Watson and Noyes, but are none the worse for that.

All this sounds very 'modern', and certainly this is a most impressive book for 1919. It may well be that many of its ideas were not so staggeringly novel for the time as they may at first appear – our post-1950 advances are not so original as we like to think – but certainly the Finch approach to written work did not immediately become universal practice in the schools of this country, which was a great pity. In many grammar schools the old formal essay grind was to continue for many years, though Finch's methods were entirely suitable for work at all secondary levels, and despite his emphasis on a wide range of good writing the idea that acceptable English can only be the style of the formal essay along 'The Capes of Scotland' line took many more years to fall out of favour.

Caldwell Cook

The other outstanding writer on English teaching from this time was H. Caldwell Cook, and of Cook it is no exaggeration to say that in some matters English teaching has only caught up with him in the last fifteen years, and that the 'Play Way' – whatever else it may have been – was undoubtedly an inspiration as an approach to the business of pupils' writing. Some of the results of his methods at the Perse School had already been published as early as 1912 when the first *Perse Playbook* had appeared, and five others followed by 1917. These books contained the plays, stories, sketches and poems written by his pupils, and – and this is the important feature – were published by Heffer's as anthologies in their own right. The work of the senior boys has, not surprisingly, a strong classical and very 'literary' flavour, and nearly all the poems have the strict metre and 'poetic' vocabulary ('oft', 'doth', 'hath') of the minor poets of the late nineteenth or early twentieth century, all the more incongruous from the pens of thirteen-year-olds, but as Cook stated, and indeed proved, 'Quite seventy percent of our secondary schoolboys . . . can write creditable poetry, and all you have to give them is permission.'[22] The following, from the second *Playbook*, are reasonably representative.

O! my laburnam, when the summer comes,
And thou my lilac too, come show thy face,
Because the garden looks so dark without thee.
For thou laburnam dost light up the lawn,
And thou sweet lilac wilt the garden fill
With thy sweet fragrance, and when thy petals fall
The garden lawn with them is littered over.

(Boy, 12 years)

In the lovely cool of a summer eve,
When the hot sun is setting on the hills,
'Tis then that peaceful calmness reigns supreme;

While the trees rustle in the gentle breeze,
And the long grass is wet with evening dew.
Now the reflection of the setting sun
Shows beautiful in some slow flowing stream,
And his last rays shine blood-red through the trees.

(Boy, 12 years)

Others are a little less professional:

Cloud, O cloud, I love thee,
Streaming across the sky;
Cloud, O cloud, I love thee,
Thou art brilliant to the eye.

And thy great and powerful flight
Doth to our dark hearts bring light;
Rush across the sky with great might,
Then cloud, O cloud, I love thee . . .

(Boy, 12 years)

From his Introductions to the separate *Playbooks* one can compile a programme of Cook's basic theories. In the Introduction to the first we find: '1. Proficiency and learning come not from reading and listening, but from action, from *doing* and from experience. 2. Good work is more often the result of spontaneous effort and free interest than of compulsion and forced application. 3. The natural means of study in youth is play.' In the second book he asserts that real education 'demands freedom of expression and every opportunity for the exercise of originality'. Prose composition is not a science to be learnt *but an art to be practised* (in a sentence Cook has defined the twin peaks of English method) and a child will learn to use the English language by using it – not by completing grammar exercises. He has some perceptive comments on grammar teaching:

The craze for English grammar, which is not yet a thing of the past, can be explained in several ways: (1) Teachers from old habit look upon English as though it were a foreign tongue (2) With the use, under the direct method, of conversation and free composition, the time formerly available for the study of grammar is somewhat curtailed; and so the English lessons, if we are not watchful, are to be used as an additional training ground for the formal studies which are necessary in the other languages taught (3) English teachers sometimes have no real notion of what they want to teach in English; and so, as a child who does not know the use of a plaything, they devote their attention to pulling it to pieces (Introduction to the fourth *Playbook*).

Endless exercises as a preparation for writing (leaving no time for writing) are virtually useless, and in any case put the cart before the horse; does grammar knowledge improve writing? Cook asks; does an obsession with technical correctness achieve its aims? 'My contention that preoccupation with technique is preposterous is not merely the expression of opinion. To *labour* in the early stages for precision in punctuation and spelling, in sentence construction and the arrangement of matter, and to draft one's syllabus on a hierarchy of these things is beyond all doubt to begin at the wrong end of the stick' (Introduction to the fourth *Playbook*). Pupils should go in at the deep end – write stories, accounts, descriptions, plays and poems – with the teacher's task being to stimulate, encourage, provide a stream of ideas, finally standing back to allow the pupil to deal with things in his own way. This is the way to competence in writing and to a heightened appreciation of other writers; 'The final appreciation in life and in study is to put oneself into the thing valued and to live there *active.*'

In the fourth *Playbook* the following writing topics are suggested for younger pupils: at eleven years, stories on such themes as witches, tales of enchantment, ghosts, desert islands, shipwrecks, robbery, treasure and animals; at twelve years, medieval themes (attending to such topics as heraldry, castles, tournaments and falconry) with factual research supplementing imaginative composition. Cook uses islands as a starting-point for a whole course of imaginative thinking and writing, the children creating their own detailed, labelled, self-contained fantasy world which can be developed in a great number of fictional directions. (The self-contained fantasy world is, after all, at the heart of some of the finest and most popular of children's literature – C. S. Lewis's Narnia, Tolkien's Wilderland, or the island of *Treasure Island* itself, for example – and it is clear that this kind of invented world can be a potent source of fulfilment fantasy for children.) The drawing of islands, and the writing of stories about them became quite a chestnut in the composition repertoire after 1920, but Cook has his finger on a vital element in the child's reading or writing – let him create his own imaginative world, then enter it and extend its possibilities in whichever direction he wants.

It is also to Cook's credit that he was not afraid to attack the established secondary attitudes of the time over the question of literature; he is not happy with some of the texts which are consistently recommended for study in the schools:[23]

Why grind through the shoddy 'Marmion' and 'The Lady of the Lake' . . . Why do so many teachers of English know by heart, in spite of themselves, such rubbish as Goldsmith's 'Mad Dog', Southey's 'The Battle of Blenheim', Campbell's 'The

Battle of the Baltic' . . . and the sickliest perpetrations of
Tennyson . . . though many of us would be at a loss even to
quote the Dawn Songs of the Elizabethans, the incomparable
lyrics of the 17th century, or even Blake's Songs of Innocence?

Cook's beliefs were expanded into a more compact manifesto in
The Play Way, published in 1917. 'Play', by which he means the
involvement of the child in intense, self-absorbed activity, is the
ideal learning situation; in play the child is both active and keenly
interested, and it is where we, as teachers, can create a 'play' situation
that we are most likely to influence and teach children. (Cook does
not mean physical rampaging, children can play with intensity and
absorption with little or no movement; the activity is as much
mental as physical.) 'To do anything with interest, to get at the heart
of the matter and live there active – that is Play.'[24] Once again the
whole emphasis is upon pupils engaging actively in reading, writing
and discussing. They must make – in the 'play' situation – their own
stories, plays and poems. Again the deep-end approach is assumed,
they write first and consider the appropriateness of what they have
written in the light of short story technique, or poetic technique or
journalistic technique, afterwards. The customary approach to
composition work by teachers is again rejected:[25]

> They teach, in fact, little else in early composition but the
> minor technicalities of framework and punctuation. The very
> existence of English *verse* composition is rarely acknowledged
> in the schools of England today; the writing of poetry is never
> practised consistently as part of the school course of study. But
> in their middle-school lessons on *prose* composition, teachers
> bring in the full apparatus of technical instruction far too early.
> What with the making of frameworks and outlines for essays,
> paraphrase and precis, notes to write on the figures of speech,
> and chapters to learn on the elements and qualities of style,
> such as Brevity, Perspicuity, Lucidity, Vivacity, Frigidity,
> Sublimity and many another Pomposity, the wretched pupil has
> not the mind to write any prose of his own real making, nor
> the time to do it if he would.

Of course, it is true that Cook was dealing with pupils much
above the average (a point made at the time, but which has perhaps
been made too much of – the critical factor here being not so much
the quality of the pupils as the personality and forcefulness of the
teacher) but his influence on English teaching was still substantial.
He is praised by the 1921 Report, and obviously exerts some
influence – though not so much as one might wish – on subsequent
Board of Education pronouncements, as well as being eulogised by
a number of method writers. For accuracy's sake, however, it should

be made clear that a strong element within the profession rejected his ideas for something like twenty years – or at least paid them lip service while following traditional paths. In 1943 D. A. Beacock published his *Play Way English For Today* (with the 1944 Education Act and the imminent secondary school reconstruction with all its attendant curriculum problems very much in mind) in which he allowed that some of Cook's theory had come to be accepted in school English teaching, but adding that his influence was not yet universal and that play-way methods could still be adopted with advantage in many schools. Beacock has few reservations about Cook's importance ('a man whose experiments have laid the foundation for much of the progressive work in the teaching of English in our schools today') which, if not an overestimation of Cook's work, is rather an underestimation of many other writers in this field, but he is undoubtedly correct in re-emphasising the relevance of the Cook method to secondary teaching, 'academic' or 'non-academic'. ('A judicious seasoning of Caldwell Cook's methods may be just what is required to give that element of interest and originality which can so easily be lacking in Certificate forms.')

Dorothy Tudor Owen and the psychology of expression

One other book of note from this 1915–20 period was Dorothy Tudor Owen's *The Child Vision*, 1920, which includes reproductions of children's paintings as well as of their written work. She also makes a plea for genuine imaginative writing by children which can in itself promote 'inner' growth and learning; composition, she believes, is an art which can be of enormous value to the child as a means of clarifying, ordering and heightening his inner life as well as being a satisfactory outlet for expression. But as long as composition is treated as a mechanical, imitative exercise in vapid platitudes this real function will not be touched.

Dorothy Tudor Owen, in fact, represents an interesting transition in the development of composition theory; having moved from composition as a mere testing device for grammar knowledge and language skills to the idea of composition as an exercise in which pupils can express themselves personally and idiosyncratically to their own communicative satisfaction, we are now entering the deeper level where written expression becomes a way in which the child can order, sort, come psychically to terms with and 'realise' his inner (perhaps haphazard) feelings and emotions, and by so doing promote mental or personality growth. The technicalities of punctuation, spelling and so on are of secondary importance in the expressive structuring process which writing now becomes ('the first object of lessons in composition is to help children to realise their own impressions and express their own ideas'). She herself uses the art teaching analogy: as long as children are made to copy or imitate (in writing or in drawing) the process is superficial and has no personal significance for them; this has been realised with regard to art teaching, but not in composition teaching, where the method used is still overwhelmingly that of 'drawing from copies'.

Children must not imitate, but how 'original' can we expect them to be? Her answer is a good deal more sensible than some of the post-1950 answers which have come from extreme creative advocates. We cannot expect children to be original in the same sense that the creative artist is original; 'All we ask is that his images [the child's] shall be his own . . . those which he has derived from his natural experience, and that his words shall be an attempt to convey to others these images which have originated out of his own experience.'[26] She is also sensible in maintaining that the way to imaginative perception is not so much through fairy-tale fantasy as through a heightened and more sensitive perception of the real world; children must be encouraged – indeed trained – to see their world more accurately and in meticulous but sympathetic detail; attention to the here and now, to colours, textures, sounds, shapes, light effects and patterns, will bring the child writer to the accuracy and sensitivity which will allow him to place scenes and feelings with confidence and originality. She does not ignore such matters as the clarity of presentation, paragraphing, good spelling and accurate grammar, but (like Cook) insists that these must not be allowed to occupy the priority position. 'It will be wise, perhaps, to leave the whole question of spelling, handwriting, and punctuating undiscussed. The primary attention of the children should be concerned with expressing the meaning of their images with all the details which give it significance.'[27]

This is progress indeed; already by 1920 the (psychological) creative theory is appearing in a rudimentary form; already the bridge between Margaret Macmillan and Marjorie Hourd is visible. How was Dorothy Tudor Owen's book received? Probably with interest by some elementary teachers, but its impact upon secondary English was probably negligible. *The Times Educational Supplement* reviewer considered it likely that the majority of readers would put the book down after the first few pages, but added that this would be a mistake since 'The book deserves to be widely read and widely used.' Good theory is all very well, but what matters is good workable method at the level of the classroom, and the creation of that requires experiment and a disregard for the restrictions of established habit. Advances in teaching tend to be of the nature of modification and adaptation of existing practices rather than being sweeping new advances brought in overnight from scratch. Admirable as these creative ideas may have seemed to some teachers, the gap between them and existing teaching methods must in many cases have been so wide as to make an attempt to implement these new ideas quite impossible. At the same time the view of society generally regarding the nature of education was still such that innovation of Dorothy Tudor Owen's kind was largely unacceptable; the spirit of the time is much more accurately expressed in a letter to the *Educational Supplement,* April 1920, where the correspondent considers the pitfalls attending the developments in English teaching, and adds: 'it is hardly necessary to mention the possibility of excessive and precocious stimulation of the emotions, a danger all the greater now that we aim at making our pupils re-create the poem for themselves.' The advance which does occur in the subject is in fact much slower, and is a matter of gradual accretion rather than revolution.

School poetry 1900–20

One such example of gradual modification was in the approach to the reading of literature, particularly of poetry, where the range of material was now widening around 1920 to include more modern (i.e. contemporary) poets. The tendency at the beginning of the century to over-estimate children's capacity was nowhere more obvious than in poetry; a very popular anthology, for example, many times reprinted (and still being recommended in the 1930s) was J. C. Smith's *A Book of Verse for Boys and Girls,* 1908. In three parts, this anthology was intended for children from about seven years upwards; the Preface to Part I indicates that this part 'is meant for children who have just learnt to read' and even allowing that the poems can be read to children (rather than their reading them for themselves) the inclusion of such Blake pieces as 'The Little Black Boy', 'A Dream', 'A Cradle Song', 'Reeds of Innocence' or 'The Echoing Green' is an indication of the kind of over-estimation of smaller children common at this time (the subsequent parts, for children only slightly older, are for the most part made up of Romantic and seventeenth-century lyrics and the minor poems of Milton).

The two standard anthology favourites until well into the twenties were *The Golden Treasury* and W. E. Henley's *Lyra Heroica* with its glowing sentiments (and at least 68,000 copies sold between 1891 and 1917) 'To set forth, as only art can, the beauty and the joy of living, the beauty and the blessedness of death, the glory of battle and adventure, the nobility of devotion . . .' (Preface). Henley's own poems 'Pro Rege Nostro' and 'Last Post' set the tone nicely:

What have I done for you,
England, my England?
What is there I would not do,
England, my own?

An examination of poetry anthologies intended for children, 1900–30, reveals a monotonous consistency that is quite extraordinary – so much so that the content of any new anthology produced can be predicted with almost 100 per cent accuracy. Broadly there are two main approaches to children's poetry: to offer standard 'classics' from the Elizabethans, the Romantics etc., or to descend into a world of whimsy and sickening sentiment with a multitude of twee 'fairy' poems ('What does little birdie say . . .', 'Where did you come from, baby dear?', 'The woods are full of fairies', 'Oh, who is so merry, so merry, heigh ho, As the light-hearted fairy? heigh ho' and so on – see for example Elizabeth Spooner's *Poetry for Little Folks*, 1900; L. Thomson's *Poetry for Junior Schools*, 1909; Chambers's *Progressive Poetry for Juniors*, 1911).

The 'classical' poems considered to be suitable are sometimes surprising, but once established their pattern remains unchanged. The following will be found in any and every anthology from 1900 certainly until well into the mid-thirties, even later: Isaac Watts's 'Cradle Song'; Wordsworth's 'We are Seven', 'Daffodils', 'Westminster Bridge', 'To the Cuckoo'; Blake's 'Cradle Song', 'The Little Black Boy', 'The Tiger', 'Reeds of Innocence', 'The Lamb', 'Sweet Joy', 'The Echoing Green'; Hogg's 'A Boy's Song'; Scott's 'Young Lochinvar', 'Lullaby of an Infant Chief'; Longfellow's 'Hiawatha'; Cowper's 'John Gilpin'; Keats's 'Meg Merrilies', 'To Autumn'; Shakespeare's songs and lyrics; 'Sir Patrick Spens' and 'Chevy Chase'; Tennyson's 'The Brook', 'Sweet and Low', 'The Owl'; Macaulay's 'Horatius'; Browning's 'Ghent to Aix', 'Home Thoughts'; Newbolt's 'Admirals All'; Byron's 'The Destruction of Sennacherib'; Shelley's 'Ode to the West Wind', 'The Skylark'; Gray's 'Elegy'; Allingham's 'The Fairies'; Southey's 'The Inchcape Rock'; Stevenson's 'The Lamplighter'; Anstey's 'Wreck of the Steamship Puffin'. (See Longman's *Junior School Poetry Book*, 1902; W. H. Woodward, *A Book of English Poetry*, 1904; S. E. Winbolt, *English Poetry for the Young*, 1904; A. P. Graves, *Poems for Infants and Juniors*, 1910; Macmillan's *Children's Anthology of Verse*, 1913; S. Maxwell, *Poetry for Boys*, 1914; *The Cambridge Book of Poetry for Children* (edited by Kenneth Grahame), 1916; Ruth Fletcher, *The Children's Poetry Book*, 1920; R. Ingpen, *Choice of the Best Poems for the Young*, 1922; L. and U. Littlewood, *Simple Poems for Boys and Girls*, 1922; Alice Meynell, *The School of Poetry*, 1923; H. Strang, *One Hundred Poems for Girls*, 1925; A. W. Bain, *A Poetry Book for Boys and Girls*, 1927; A. Le M. Simpson, *Young Pegasus*, 1930; Guy Pocock, *A Poetry Book for Boys and Girls*, 1933; J. A. Stone, *Take Your Choice*, 1949.)

A third development was the introduction of contemporary poetry into pupils' anthologies. Stevenson, Newbolt, De la Mare and Masefield had themselves become children's 'classics' by 1920, but it is also possible to see a deliberate attempt to bring modern poets into the schools in anthologies such as The English Association's *Poems of Today*, 1915 (including work by Belloc, Binyon, Brooke, W. H. Davies and Yeats), L. D'O Walters's *An Anthology of Recent Poetry*, 1920 (including Belloc, Brooke, Chesterton, Alice Meynell and W. H. Davies), Richard Wilson's *Junior Modern Poetry*, 1922 (Eleanor Farjeon and J. Elroy Flecker) or H. B. Elliott's *Gems of Modern Poetry*, 1922 (Binyon, Alice Meynell, Eden Phillpotts). A conviction that may sound odd today but which underlay the attitude of editors, compilers, and publishers alike (and which helps explain the consistency in anthology publishing) was that any anthology for children ought to present a representative cross-section of the history of poetry – hence the somewhat unhappy selection of 'suitable' material from the works of the great English poets of the past.

The most used prose 'classics' in the elementary schools 1910–20 included the Greek and Norse legends, *Alice*, *The Coral Island*, *The Water Babies*, *The Heroes*, *The Rose and the Ring*, *The King of the Golden River*, *Uncle Tom's Cabin*, *Robinson Crusoe*, *The Last of the Mohicans*, *Tom Brown's Schooldays*, *Ivanhoe*, *Westward Ho*, *Treasure Island*, *Lorna Doone*, *The Mill on the Floss*, *The Arabian Nights* and *Pickwick* – although younger pupils would meet these in abridged 'reader' form. The pupils in the higher standards were expected to read Dickens, George Eliot, Shakespeare or Scott unabridged.

Secondary English 1910–20

In the secondary schools expectations continued extremely high with regard to literature, and the Higher Certificate examination courses were exhaustive. The English Association's Leaflet No. 8 ('Types of English Curricula in Girls' Secondary Schools', 1909) outlines a number of existing study schemes. At St Paul's Girls' School the 1907–8 syllabus included: Form IV (thirteen years): Shakespeare, *Julius Caesar*; Milton, *L'Allegro* and *Il Penseroso*. Form Lower V (fourteen years): *Spectator* Essays; Wordsworth, odes and sonnets; Macaulay's History. Form VIII (seventeen years) – in preparation for the Higher Certificate: the period 1625–1700; *Paradise Lost* I–IV; Sir Thomas Browne's *Hydriotaphia*; Bunyan's *Holy War*; Shakespeare, *Coriolanus*; and Old and Middle English set books.

A breakdown of all the schemes given in the Leaflet shows that for 1907–9 in the London girls' schools the following texts and authors are the teaching favourites: at fourteen, Lamb (essays); *The Spectator*; *The Golden Treasury*; Scott's novels and poems; Milton's Minor Poems; Macaulay; Spenser (*Faerie Queene*); Coleridge;

Tennyson; Southey; and Stevenson. At fifteen, Shakespeare; Spenser; Milton; Hakluyt; Chaucer; Malory; Bacon; Addison; Tennyson. At sixteen, Shakespeare; Milton; Wordsworth; Scott; Pope and Burke. By far the most popular authors, in the sense of being most used, in all schools at all levels are Shakespeare, Milton, Scott, Tennyson, Bacon, and the eighteenth-century essayists.

The Examination Boards varied slightly among themselves, but until the early 1920s it was customary for a Higher Local (or Certificate) English course to include the study of a period of literary history, perhaps a century of literature, as well as of special authors and Old and Middle English. For example, the Cambridge Higher Local syllabus for 1905 included a special study of *The Tempest*, Byron selections, Carlyle's *Past and Present*, and Tennyson's *In Memoriam*; the period 1797–1858; and Old and Middle English. The 1920 syllabus shows little change: special texts – *Macbeth*, *Paradise Lost* I–IV, Browne's *Religio Medici*, and Dryden's essays; the period 1625–1700; and Old and Middle English. The Oxford syllabuses are very similar, except that two periods for study could be undertaken – e.g. for 1919 special texts, *King Lear*, *The Merchant of Venice*, *King John*, Burke's Speeches; the periods 1550–1637 and 1625–1700.

Sixth-form English was clearly meant to involve spectacularly extensive reading, though one can only conclude that pupils merely learnt very little about a great deal – a suspicion which is strongly supported by the continued popularity of the potted literary textbook (each author getting half a page and three useful remarks) and by the often easy and generalised nature of many of the examination questions. The following question from the 1908 London Matriculation paper is typical: 'Round the dome of the reading-room in the British Museum are inscribed the following representative names . . . Addison, Bacon, Browning, Byron, Carlyle, Caxton, Chaucer, Gibbon, Locke, Macaulay, Milton, Pope, Scott, Shakespeare, Spenser, Swift, Tennyson, Tindale, Wordsworth. *Write a couple of lines about each*, taking the names in chronological order.'

The first reports on the School Certificate reorganisation after 1917 made just these points; that with candidates being expected to cover two hundred years of literature to answer such questions as 'Give the titles, dates and plots of six novels by X' genuine literary study was impossible. No wonder little primers such as J. Logie Robertson's *Outlines of English Literature*, 1905 (nine hundred years of literary history covered in 164 pages); D. Campbell's *First History of English Literature*, 1905 (still widely used in 1920); W. T. Young's *A Primer of English Literature*, 1914; or E. M. Tappan's *A Brief History of English Literature*, 1914, were so popular. Young devotes twenty-three of his small pages to the Romantic poets; Wordsworth gets five pages, Southey one, Coleridge three, Scott one, Byron two, and so on. (We should not mock his splendid generalisations, he was fulfilling what was obviously a desperate need on the part of the examination candidates.)

Another feature which suggests a tendency to superficiality in upper form study was the popularity of books of 'selections', or secondary anthologies, which attempted to give representative extracts from the major writers perhaps over a period of a century and which were clearly used as a substitute for a real reading of those authors. *Readings in English Literature*, edited by E. W. Edmunds and F. Spooner, 1908, was one such; here, in the nineteenth-century volume, Dickens is represented by twelve pages of *David Copperfield*, Thackeray by ten pages of *Vanity Fair*, and George Eliot (for some reason) by five pages of *Amos Barton*. Another example is H. N. Asman's *Selections from English Literature*, 1911, where (in Volume II) Ruskin is given two pages of *The Seven Lamps of Architecture*, two pages of *Sesame and Lilies*, three pages of *Stones of Venice*, and Jane Austen is represented by two pages (seemingly chosen at random where the book fell open) from the middle of *Pride and Prejudice*. (Poets fared a little better, though not much, being chopped about unmercifully so as to get everybody in.)

R. S. Bate in his *The Teaching of English Literature in Secondary Schools*, 1913, confidently offers a hair-raising three-year sixth-form course which in effect covers every single major work in the language from Beowulf to Browning, including (whole or in part) *The Anglo-Saxon Chronicle*, all *Beowulf*, *Piers Plowman*, Layamon's *Brut*, *Havelok*, *Sir Gawayne and the Green Knight*, most of Chaucer, Malory, *The Faerie Queene*, *Gorboduc*, ten Shakespeare plays, the Metaphysical poets, Jacobean drama, Milton, Pope, Johnson, Dryden, Swift, Addison, Steele, Smollett, Fielding, Jane Austen, the Romantic Poets, *et al*. Incredible though this may seem today, Bate's scheme is not far removed from the kind of sixth-form work that did go on before 1920; though obviously we are back in the world of short 'representative' extracts, material from composite Histories, and absurdly over-simplified criticism. Undoubtedly, far too much was attempted in the examination courses, with pupils being consistently over-estimated throughout the secondary school both in their capacity for sheer reading and in their critical-appreciative abilities (the modern thirteen-year-old would probably not take too happily to Macaulay's History, Burke on the Beautiful and the Sublime, or to *Religio Medici*). The Boards came to realise this themselves, and undertook a considerable pruning of courses after 1921, though with little modification of the by now standard authors. Despite such modification we still come across remarks such as that by Grace Bracken in *The Teaching of English in Secondary Schools for Girls*, 1924, to the effect that by the time girls are thirteen or fourteen they should know 'some five or six' Shake-speare plays well, having begun (with *Hamlet* and *Macbeth*, say) at eleven.

After 1915 there was an increasing dissatisfaction with the impracticable nature of sixth-form courses in literature, and a move-ment, albeit gradual, away from the generalised reproductive kind of examination question towards questions that required genuine appreciative responses from the candidates. In the lower, first examination forms there was also a growing tendency to approach literary texts as literature and not merely as grammatical or rhetori-cal springboards. Increasingly pupil and text are being brought together without any ulterior motive beyond pleasure and know-ledgeable appreciation. In his chapter on English in *The New Teach-ing*, 1918, John Adams indicates that there has been a gratifying improvement in literary studies in recent years; 'When it comes to English Literature we find that the radical difference between the old teaching and the new is that we have passed from books about books to the books themselves.'[28] The kind of study that depends wholly on a reading of generalised textbooks, the student com-mitting to memory such statements as 'Keats was essentially a sensuous writer' or 'Wordsworth was the most philosophical of poets' without having read a line of either, was at last giving way to more satisfactory attitudes, though the difficulty of balancing 'facts about' and 'appreciation of' has remained a thorny problem for all subsequent students and teachers of literature.

In 1915 *The Lesson in Appreciation* by F. H. Hayward (an LCC Inspector) was published. This sets out to give school poetry study a proper basis. It is clear from Hayward's remarks that the idea of discussing a poem at any length with the members of a class (elementary or secondary) or of asking whether the children in fact *liked* it, and if so why, was a rare event at this time. Hayward demands that poems be seen – like pictures or musical compositions – as artistic wholes; the teacher should first read poems to the class without stopping to discuss every line ('Reading or reciting *to* a class is even now a rare thing in English schools . . .'[29]). After such a reading or readings, discuss the poem with the pupils with a view to getting them to articulate their impressions, however simple. Which lines or images do they like? (Here is 'an almost uncharted region of educational investigation'.[30]) After discussion, during which the teacher will unobtrusively lead the class to see the qualities they themselves have over-looked, there will be a final reading. This will end the important, appreciation stage. If now the teacher wishes to go on to exercises in paraphrasing, vocabulary, figures of speech or analysis, and Hayward indicates in no uncertain terms that such exercises are of secondary importance, then he may do so, but must realise that such follow-up work has little or nothing to do with the real business of coming to terms with the poem. Hayward has little time for the pedantic mysteries of scansion and makes, for 1915, an extremely enlightened remark to the effect that 'The genius of English poetry at its best will never be understood so long as classical notions of syllabic length or even of mere poetical stress hold the field.' He also remarks (and the problem still baffles some student teachers) that the Herbartian principles of lesson organisation (introduction, development, application) are simply impossible of application to a poetry lesson and do considerable harm to poetry study at school level.

Of course, examination English also meant language as well as literature, and the Junior Local or First Certificate examinations were much stronger on the language side. The Oxford and Cambridge Locals had been operating since 1858 (the Joint Oxford and Cambridge Board since 1873) and by 1900 the London Matriculation paper was also being used as much as a leaving Certificate as an entrance examination. If we look at the Junior Locals spanning the years 1885 to 1930 we find a surprisingly consistent, stiff obstacle course in clause analysis, parsing, punctuation and paraphrase, with a formal essay included either as part of the paper or separately. The essay subjects are predictable: 'Bores', 'The Rivalry of Nations', 'Rustic Sports', 'The Delights of a Country Life', 'Chivalry', 'The Evil That Men Do Lives After Them', 'The Charm of Poetry', 'The Novel as an Instrument of Reform', 'Every Man is the Architect of his Own Fortune', 'Early Rising', or 'Wild Flowers'. In 1920 the Oxford Junior Local candidates were required to write on 'A Railway Station', 'The Story of a Grain of Wheat as told by itself' or 'Hobbies'; to analyse

When years had passed on, by that still lake-side
The fisher looked down through the silver tide,
And there, on the smooth yellow sand displayed,
A skeleton, wasted and white, was laid . . . etc.

to paraphrase 'Forward the Light Brigade . . .'; and punctuate short passages. (This being not so very different from the 1885 paper, nor from the 1940 one, for that matter.)

Not surprisingly in the wake of the examinations streamed a host of drab textbooks, all claiming with scholarly modesty to be the gateway to examination success, and all depressingly similar in format – textbooks such as J. D. Rose's *Elementary English Grammar Through Composition*, 1912; G. Ogilvie and E. Albert's *A Practical Course in Secondary English*, 1913 (reprinted nine times by 1926); J. C. Nesfield's *Matriculation English Course*, 1914 – all following a 'word-phrase-clause-sentence-paragraph-essay' progression. Like the chicken and the egg it is debatable whether the nature of the examinations produced the type of textbook, or vice-versa; certainly the influence was not all one-way, and the conservatism of the book writers cannot be wholly exonerated on the grounds that 'given the exam there was nothing else they could do'. It is perhaps more accurate to say that both the nature of the examinations and the nature of the textbooks depended on the common misconceptions arising out of the 'content' and 'grammatical' fallacies which were still strong; the same kind of thinking lay behind each. It certainly seems astonishing that major publishing firms were content to go on reproducing what in effect were different versions of the one basic book year after year for half a century or more, particularly when those books held only a tenuous link with English teaching proper.

If we turn to the Higher Certificate papers we will find further confirmation of the fact that whereas the Boards took their language very seriously and exacted stringent standards, they were (intentionally or not) much more easy-going over literature. For example, the 1905 Cambridge Higher papers, which are representative of the time, include: 'Select from the plays of Shakespeare an example of (a) a tragedy or (b) a comedy. Show from a short account of the play chosen why it is called a tragedy or a comedy.' 'Explain briefly the following terms: Euphemism, the Augustine Age, the Romantic Movement.' The Oxford, Cambridge and London Boards are all running true to this type at this time; roughly their questions can be sorted into such broad categories as: 'Write brief notes on ten of the following (books or authors)'; 'Name five great poets in x century, and say what you know about them'; 'Discuss the life of z, and say something about his works' – perhaps, as already suggested, an inevitable approach in view of the extent of fifth- and sixth-form courses with their rote memory material.

Then as now many people were quick to point to the damage which they believed examinations were doing to English literature; '. . . what the examiners require is too often not real knowledge, training or cultivation of mind, but simply the memorising of comparatively useless facts' (Carpenter, Baker and Scott 1903); '. . . the influence of examinations on writing and on thought-training is, in the main, an evil one' (Philip Hartog, 1907); they 'have been indirectly responsible for much bad teaching' (Roberts and Barter, 1908). Although the teaching of literature is becoming more sensitive in the second decade of the century 'there are still many schools where literature is taught in the manner in which geography used to be taught – as a mere collection of more or less interesting facts; and the system is perpetuated by the nature of the examinations for which these schools prepare their pupils' (R. S. Bate, 1913); 'in addition the examinations have encouraged the very worst kinds of textbooks' (Arnold Smith, 1915).

In 1919 the Secondary School Examinations Council, which had been set up in 1917 'for the better organisation of examinations in

Secondary schools', published its report on the July 1918 'First' school examinations. By and large the investigators approved the papers of the various Boards (Oxford, Cambridge, Oxford and Cambridge, Bristol, Durham, London and the Joint Northern) but made several recommendations. For example, they thought that the essay topics set tended to be too abstract, and indicated that subjects should be included that would allow of *imaginative* treatment; also, that there should be no separate test of formal grammar, since skill in this would reveal itself in the candidates' general standard of English. A précis, they maintained, should be an essential feature, and reproduction exercises, though valuable, 'may possibly give undue advantage to merely verbal memory' and should be dropped. On the literature papers they indicate that set books should be further limited in number, and that intensive study of a few texts rather than a generalised skimming of several dozen should be the rule; 'The difficulty is to avoid questions that encourage the reading of manuals of literary history or the reproduction of lecture notes, instead of first-hand acquaintance with great authors. The scrutiny of scripts showed the Investigators that this difficulty had been surmounted in some cases but not in all.'

In 1921 the Council reported on the Higher Examination (of July 1920) and here criticised even more strongly the superficial knowledge shown by the candidates. Evidence of genuine close reading was a rarity. Two sound comments were made in the report: 'Questions inviting recollection of manuals or lecture notes are above all to be deprecated' and 'The Investigators were unanimously of the opinion that Anglo-Saxon and Middle English before the time of Chaucer are not suitable subjects at the school stage.' The Old English was in fact dropped soon afterwards by those Boards who still included it.

The 1914 Suggestions: *progress 1900–20*

The other 'official' publication which had appeared since 1910 was the second, 1914, *Handbook of Suggestions*, with English sections that showed a tentative desire to keep up with the times. There are now twenty pages devoted to English, and the generalised vagueness of 1905 has been replaced with a little more detail. The *Handbook* notes that in 'junior' classes children are still often limited to only one or two readers a year when there should be an abundant supply of books including 'Fairy tales, legends and myths, stories about animals . . . adventures and experiences of children'. On composition the *Handbook* is now, most significantly, referring to the 'invention' as well as to the reproduction of stories, and to the need for children to be left free to experiment in their writing; 'the teaching of composition . . . consists, not in shielding a child from every danger of mistake, but in enabling him gradually to correct his errors for himself'; 'For these reasons a skilful teacher will generally allow children, even in the early stages of written composition, to compose independently and freely.'

In the senior classes emphasis must be placed firmly on silent reading for pleasure (as opposed to the traditional assumption that reading skill must be synonymous with skill in reading aloud); specific books are now recommended, including *The Water Babies, The Heroes, Robinson Crusoe, Masterman Ready* and *Tom Brown's Schooldays*.

Composition in the senior classes will involve some formal essay work, using models, but it is much more important that pupils be exercised in describing the experiences, sights, sounds and feelings associated with their everyday lives; the key word in these 1914 *Suggestions* is 'imagination' (cautious and conservative though their 'imaginative' directives may be), which is certainly an advance on the term 'repetition' which dominates the 1905 section.

On grammar teaching, however, there is not only no change from 1905 but a hardening of attitude; the *Handbook* is prepared to admit that much grammar teaching has been 'superfluous', but having got that sop out of the way, it proceeds to re-occupy the old ground with a vengeance; not only must formal grammar ('This indispensable knowledge') be taught, but it must be taught separately as an isolated discipline in its own right, and not just as a supplement to reading or writing. Clearly there had been a movement away from grammar teaching since 1905, and some observers were convinced that relaxation had gone too far.

In conclusion it can be said that some remarkable advances had in fact come about in English teaching theory between 1910 and 1920. John Adams clearly believes that his choice of title, *The New Teaching*, for his 1918 book is not over-optimistic, and in his Introduction to that book he lists the following as being symptomatic of the gradual change which is taking place in educational thinking – that the elementary schools are at last beginning to rise above their former narrow conception of education; that it is now recognised that the pupil must play a much more active part in the learning process; that it is accepted that pupil-centred modifications must be made to the subjects taught; that the individual pupil is now seen as being the learning unit rather than the class as a whole; and that it is now recognised that the pupil has the right 'to do things in his own way within reasonable limits'. To these also could be added such features as the growing influence of psychological discoveries and new theories on education (including new attitudes to the nature of individual learning), the increased expertise and sense of professionalism among teachers, the increasing subject-consciousness at secondary level (with the formation of various subject associations) and the growing demands of society for more and better education.

Cautious as the advances may have been since 1900, progress had been made, and if 1918 saw the end of much of the old order, it also saw the beginnings of a new spirit in teaching. The decade after 1920 is characterised by rapid and widespread advances both within the field of English method thinking and within education generally, and it is no coincidence that these advances were paralleled by equally widespread social and political transformations. With the changing social order is to come a changing concept of education as a whole and of English as a part of that whole.

Notes

1 *1870–1970: Century of Growth in English Education*, 1970, pp. 18–19.
2 *Op. cit.*, p. 27.
3 *Op. cit.*, p. 5.
4 *Ibid.*, p. 10.
5 *Ibid.*, p. 4.
6 *Cambridge Essays in Education*, 1917, p. 108.
7 *Op. cit.*, preface.
8 *Ibid.*, p. 130.
9 *Ibid.*, p. 274.
10 *Op. cit.*, p. 137.
11 *The Changing School*, 1925, p. 195 (1929 edn).
12 *The Advanced Montessori Method*, 1918, Vol. II, p. 304.
13 *Op. cit.*, p. 34.
14 *Op. cit.*, p. 21.
15 *Ibid.*, p. 160.
16 *Op. cit.*, p. 51.
17 *Op. cit.*, Vol. I, p. 124.
18 *Aims and Methods in the Teaching of English*, pp. 15–16.
19 *Op. cit.*, p. 140.
20 In two volumes; Finch was English master at Hornsey County School.
21 *Op. cit.*, p. 16.
22 Introduction to *Playbook* No. 2, 1912.
23 *Playbook* No. 5, 1915, pp. 33–4.
24 *Op. cit.*, p. 9 (1919 edn).
25 *Ibid.*, pp. 297–8.
26 *Op. cit.*, p. 8.
27 *Ibid.*, p. 91.
28 *Op. cit.*, p. 64.
29 *Op. cit.*, p. 70 (1929 edn).
30 *Ibid.*, p. 86.

The 1921 Report

The decade 1920–30 is dominated by the Board of Education's
(Newbolt) Report *The Teaching of English in England* (HMSO, 1921),
whose 360 pages, excluding appendices, is the most detailed and
exhaustive investigation of the subject by Board or Ministry to date.
The Committee members included Sir Henry Newbolt (Chairman),
Professor C. H. Firth, Sir Arthur Quiller-Couch, George Sampson,
Caroline Spurgeon and John Dover Wilson, and with its aim 'To
enquire into the position of English in the educational system of
England' it covered English studies from infant school to university
level, and is still a fascinating document to read fifty years later.

The investigators make clear from the outset their belief that
English can and must become the centre of the genuine liberal
education which British schools must work to establish, especially
(and considerable regret is expressed at their passing) since classical
studies are no longer central at secondary level. This fact, however,
regrettable or not, must be faced, and although the Report goes to
considerable lengths to soften the blow, it insists that the classicists
bow to the logic of events and yield – what they have already yielded
in practice if not in theory – the centre of the literary stage to
English.[1]

> for English children no form of knowledge can take precedence
> of a knowledge of English, no form of literature can take
> precedence of English literature: and that the two are so
> inextricably connected as to form the only basis possible for a
> national education.

And this is not merely to offer English as an alternative to the
classics, but to uphold it at all school levels as '*the true starting-point
and foundation from which all the rest must spring*' (my italics).

This is the ideal, but what of the reality? Despite some improvements in the status of the subject since 1900, the investigators found
that it was still regarded in many schools as being unimportant,
trivial and 'irrelevant'.[2]

> From the evidence laid before us it became speedily clear that
> in many schools of all kinds and grades that part of the teaching
> which dealt directly with English was often regarded as being
> inferior in importance, hardly worthy of any substantial place
> in the curriculum, and a suitable matter to be entrusted to any
> member of staff who had some free time at his disposal.

This, in fact, is their chief complaint (and, as we shall see, the

Report itself simply as a report does a great deal to remedy the fault) that English is not regarded seriously enough, is not subject to serious curriculum studies aimed at establishing an original form, content and methodology appropriate to it, and is not seen as being of real importance to all pupils. Even where teaching has been undertaken on a more consistent and responsible level there has been the tendency to distort the subject in the strangleholds of classical method. 'The old classical system is still responsible for a warping of method in the teaching of English, for a futile application of time-honoured forms, as e.g. the rules of prosody . . .'[3] Too often the lesson in literature has become merely a lesson like so many others – a period in which to impart the maximum amount of 'factual' information to the pupils; this is *not* the way to approach Literature: '. . . we are strongly of opinion that in dealing with literature the voyage of the mind should be broken as little as possible by the examination of obstacles and the analysis of the element on which the explorer is floating' – what is required is not the 'chemical analysis' of the water, but an appreciation of its 'sounds and colours' (the metaphorical language of the Report is often everything it should be).

In the elementary schools the teachers are still afraid of their post-1902 freedom; still assume that 'English' is synonymous with 'grammar'; and have still not clarified their aims, merely seeing English as they see arithmetic, 'a specific and limited subject, or worse, as a collection of detached subjects'. (It was in 1921 in his *English for the English* that George Sampson identified the following separate, timetabled 'subjects' which could be found in many elementary schools: oral composition, written composition, dictation, grammar, reproduction, 'reading', recitation, 'literature', spelling, and handwriting.) Despite the severe and crippling restrictions of the old codes, it seems that teachers as a group prefer to know exactly what they are supposed to be doing, and are less happy when left free to find their own way, however beneficial such freedom can be to their pupils if put to thoughtful and imaginative use – an accusation which, in 1971 as in 1921, will not be so very far from the truth with regard to the less adventurous majority.

The Report is not satisfied with the qualifications of many teachers who are involved in English work. The 1920 returns showed that there were over 30,000 uncertificated, and over 11,000 supplementary teachers in the elementary schools, many of these never having had any education themselves beyond the age of thirteen; 'To the question "What proportion of the students who pass from College with Certificates every year are really qualified to take English with a class?" the answer given by the English Section of the Training College Association was "Certainly not more than one-third." '

Elementary school children have not been given the opportunity
to read enough literature, the Report goes on, although there is now
an increasing movement towards presenting classes with a wider
range of enjoyable reading matter; speech training has been grossly
neglected; and composition has been largely a mechanical drudgery
producing perfunctory or artificial writing, with little effort to foster
the creative impulse.

This is good, sensible comment, but it would be wrong to assume
that the 1921 Report was necessarily in the forefront of current
method thinking. Gently progressive though it may have been in
many respects, it was not quite that, indeed much of the comment
on composition work, for example, was only a re-statement of what
Philip Hartog (complimented at some length in the writing section)
had advocated in 1907, and which writers such as Robert Finch or
Caldwell Cook had emphatically overtaken and passed by 1920.
Perhaps by reason of its 'official' nature the Report chooses its
words a little too scrupulously; a typical example of this kind of
caution comes in the section on secondary written work. If 'creative'
composition can be encouraged with benefit in the elementary
school it should be approached *very warily indeed* in the secondary
school, where reproduction should be a regular exercise ('Imaginative subjects, too long neglected, are today sometimes used to
excess'). What the Secondary pupil really needs, according to the
investigators, is constant practice in constructing, writing, revising
and reconstructing single paragraphs – which is to practise the construction of the formal essay in miniature (and which has been
standard procedure since before 1900). In the same way, while verse
writing is recommended, the investigators clearly see the exercise
almost wholly in terms of applying and extending a knowledge of
prosody and its more sophisticated techniques, and not as a medium
for genuine 'self-expression' – an attitude which is simply a
throwback to the classical fallacy, all the more ironic in that
the Report is anxious to create for English a new, non-classical
study approach.

With regard to external English examinations, the investigators
are very much of the opinion that the examinations have had a
beneficial influence on the subject. What they mean is that the
examining of English (language and literature at first and second
Certificate levels) has made it an official part of the timetable and
helped promote its study at a serious level (the point remains valid
after 1921; whatever harm the examinations may do to English
teaching, to stop examining would be to guarantee a serious – in the
case of literature perhaps total – neglect). Like the Examinations
Council, the Report insists that in studying for examinations the
first consideration must be the set text, not literary history or background knowledge generally, and that in answering questions what

should be required from the candidates is evidence of first-hand knowledge and appreciation of their texts.

As for the study of Old and Middle English for Certificate examinations, the Report is not very favourably disposed to the practice, and offers as an alternative scheme a study of the development of the English language from Chaucer down to modern times. But with regard to Old English degree studies, although the usual remarks are made (to the effect that the philological bias in English degree courses was an unfortunate product of the circumstances attending the setting up of the first university schools) the cautious conclusion is that (a) the emphasis on Old English has been excessive (b) it must be kept in proportion (c) it nevertheless remains a valuable and important study (though not necessarily for *all* degree candidates) which must not be allowed to fall into neglect.

An entire chapter (chapter 9) is devoted to the knotty problem of grammar, and here the witnesses' opinions differed more than on any other topic, with an extraordinary range of views being expressed. P. B. Ballard is quoted, for example, as a leading opponent of formal grammar teaching:[4]

> I have convinced myself by an extensive enquiry that in the elementary school formal grammar (a) fails to provide a general mental training, (b) does not enable the teachers to eradicate solecisms, (c) does not aid in composition, and (d) takes up time which could more profitably be devoted to the study of literature. During the last fifteen years English composition, both written and oral, has steadily improved in the elementary school, and this improvement has taken place concomitantly with a declining attention to grammar and an increasing attention to literature.

At the other extreme from this comes the argument of a witness such as Mr J. E. Barton, headmaster of Bristol Grammar School, who claims that:[5]

> Immense harm has been done by the well-meant discouragement of formal grammar in the elementary schools . . . Grammar can *not* be satisfactorily 'picked up' in the course of learning Latin or French. Grammar drill, of the simpler kind, with analysis, should be universal . . . The official discouragement of formal grammar has sacrificed absolute accuracy in the old grammatical sense, without securing in return any real knowledge of literature.

The Report tries to find a way out of the impasse with a little deft sleight of hand. The fact is, it goes on, that Messrs Barton and Ballard and their followers are really saying *the same thing*; the confusion arises because they mean something different by the term 'grammar'. Dr Ballard is attacking the *old*, traditional, pre-1900 grammar; he is not of course implying that all grammar work should be abandoned. Again, Mr Barton is not suggesting for one moment that this traditional kind of grammar teaching be resurrected; no, he is merely saying that *some* grammar has to be taught. This is not, in fact, what either witness means, but the Report has its own path to follow and it is most sympathetic to precisely this kind of compromise approach (which in the end, not surprisingly, leaves the situation unresolved and therefore largely in the hands of the traditionalists). Of course, the old grammar grind must go, but we cannot abandon all grammar work; after all (and the investigators are now giving another lease of life to the 'foreign language' fallacy) without a good knowledge of grammar the pupil will have considerable difficulty when studying modern languages. 'Grammar of some kind, then, should be taught in either the elementary or the secondary school, or in both.'

The Report then goes on to complete its second sleight of hand. The old Latin-based grammar is now obsolete; there is no advantage in pursuing that kind of language study because there is now a new and more important grammar (a 'pure' grammar of function rather than of form) emerging – a grammar which reflects the structure of human thought itself (they have Jespersen's work in mind). So far so good, but it appears that this 'pure' grammar is to be reached through the usual parsing and analysis treadmill, and despite the Report's insistence that the kind of grammar taught must relate to these universal thought/language functions, it leaves the practical classroom *status quo* virtually unchanged, with teachers (in the absence of more detailed information) advised simply to 'go on teaching grammar'.

The Report concludes with 105 recommendations covering the whole range of English teaching; these include:

[elementary schools] 3. That every teacher is a teacher *of* English because every teacher is a teacher *in* English . . . 4. That speech training must be undertaken from the outset and should be continued all through the period of schooling. 8. That oral work is the foundation upon which proficiency in the writing of English must be based. 12. That if literature is to be enjoyed by the children it must be entrusted to teachers with a love of it. [secondary schools] 20. That the pupil should be made familiar with a body of fine poetry . . . 21. That during the period 14–16 the study of English should not be subordinate to that of Science or of foreign languages. 22. That during the period 16–18 some study of the growth and development of the English language would be preferable to a course in Old English. 27. That throughout the Public Schools

English Literature should be regarded as entitled to a place in the regular school course, and not be relegated to spare time. [teacher training] 44. That it is desirable that the standard in English required for admission to Training Colleges should be raised . . . 45. That the Syllabus in English for the Final Examination of students in Training Colleges should indicate that Reading, Recitation and Phonetics are essential features of the study of English. [universities] 56. That in every University, 'Schools' of English Language and Literature should rank as at least the equal of any Arts 'School'. 61. That in a School of Honours in English Literature, weight should be given to knowledge both of Anglo-Saxon and pre-Chaucerian English Literature, and of the 'Mediterranean' literatures . . . 62 That before the post-graduate period English language should be taught on humane lines, philology and phonetics occupying a subordinate place. 65. That candidates for Honours in English should not be compelled to take Anglo-Saxon, but allowed to offer as alternatives Middle French or Mediaeval Latin. 67. That English should be a qualifying subject in all matriculation examinations. 79. That the endowment of an English Chair should be at least equal to that of any other humanistic Chair in the same University. [grammar teaching] 84. That the grammar taught in schools should be *pure* grammar . . . [examinations] 88. That the examination system should be applied as widely as possible to the power of 'communication' in English. 89. That examinations in English for scholarships to Secondary Schools should be tests of this power rather than tests in grammar, analysis and spelling. 93. That an examination on set books should leave the teacher of literature as free as possible to draw up his own syllabus and adopt his own methods. [drama] 96. That as soon as children are old enough they should attempt to dramatise familiar ballads, stories or fairy tales, or famous historical incidents . . . and [libraries] 102. That every Elementary School should possess its own library.

It is perhaps unfair to expect this Report to be anything but carefully progressive, though evidently the work of the most advanced writers on English method since 1915 had not made a whole-hearted impact upon the investigators and witnesses. This is its main weakness, that in charting the development of the subject from 1900 it relies too much on 'official' (i.e. Board of Education) advances and ignores the contributions of talented individuals, many of whom had consistently left the Board standing.

Where the Report is of incalculable importance is in its insistence upon seeing English and English teaching in relation to the whole educational experience. It is here, in its attempts to formulate a philosophy of education – a total picture into which the subject and the manner of its teaching then fits – that it can be said to break entirely new ground, and there can be no question that in going for the total view as well as merely concentrating upon a revision of the separate elements making up English ('reading', 'writing' etc.) the Report creates a precedent in English method thinking that cannot be over-estimated.

English has been found by the investigators to be getting shoddy treatment, and the fault lies partly within the schools, but the Report is also quite prepared to follow the line of cause and effect into society generally and see that wider and more sinister influences are involved.[6]

> The inadequate conception of the teaching of English in this country is not a separate defect which can be separately remedied. It is due to a more far-reaching failure – the failure to conceive the full meaning and possibilities of national education as a whole, and that failure again is due to a misunderstanding of the educational values to be found in the different regions of mental activity . . .

Thus the Revised Code mentality still exists, partly because teachers are unadventurous and conservative, partly because society insists on thinking (still) in Code terms with regard to education.

Not surprisingly we find the Report taking a very strong Arnold line, to the extent of quoting him on several occasions, and paraphrasing his arguments on others, and the investigators are united in their earnest desire that all children should receive a humane, liberal and broad education of the kind Arnold advocated, based on the language and literature of their country. English must be the key to this proper education and, taught in the right way, it can raise and unify first the pupils in the schools and later the nation in a way hitherto unimagined. The Report can still refer to the 'social chasms' which divide education; it quotes Arnold's remark that 'culture unites classes'; and it adopts that wider liberal stance that we have already noted earlier, maintaining that such an English-based education 'is the greatest benefit which could be conferred upon any citizen of a great state, and that the common right to it, the common discipline and enjoyment of it, the common possession of the tastes and associations connected with it, would form a new element of national unity, linking together the mental life of all classes by experiences which have hitherto been the privilege of a limited section.'[7]

There is no time for real English work in many schools, the investigators argue, simply because such work does not fit into society's current theories of education, those theories being 'the discipline theory', 'the utilitarian theory', the practical 'learning by doing theory', and the 'acquisition of many facts theory'.[8] What is required is not merely a new approach to poetry, or composition, or grammar, but a total new theory or philosophy which shall stress the importance of imaginative and emotional experience, the importance of the aesthetic and the creative, and the importance of civilised human relationships, while at the same time upholding the need for *every* child to receive the benefits of such an education.

The Times Educational Supplement took up this point in its editorial on the Report, 5 November 1921. Having noted that the Committee had made 'a masterly presentation of the case for a broad and humane education' attention is drawn to the 'sociological' problems which have been outlined in the investigation, and the comment is made: 'Our corporate life is not nearly so corporate as it might be'; 'The industrial classes still surely need to be protected against the educational "lie in the soul" which is that their schools should fit them primarily for manual or mechanical work.' That this matter was one of the Committee's first concerns is reinforced by Henry Newbolt's own remarks at an LCC lecture in 1922 where he commented, first, that the Report had broken all previous HMSO sales records, second that 'Education by means of English, if carried out in the schools of all classes of the community, would facilitate intercourse between all classes . . . and by diminishing class distinctions would make the nation more homogenous and a greater State.'

It must shock us today to find this Report in 1921 noting that 'There are still people in positions of influence who are inclined to regard a humane education of the lower classes as subversive of public order',[9] though it is good to find the opinion that Arnold's hopes for genuine poetry study in the schools have been fulfilled in some areas.

The 1921 Report, despite its equivocation over formal grammar teaching and its over-cautious approach to secondary composition work, sets its face emphatically against the 'utilitarian' concept of schooling and cannot be faulted in its realisation of the importance of English in any new humane scheme of education. What is also important, as noted already, is the very fact of the Report's publication at all. Here at last was an official, expert, and detailed account of English teaching which laid almost unlimited emphasis upon the importance of the subject and upon the responsibility and 'specialness' of English teachers, and – far from apologetically upholding it as an important 'extra' – insisted on page after page that English is central, the lynchpin, the discipline above all others that must dominate the education of the English school pupil. It is not that the teacher of English at all school levels is at last being recognised as being of equal status to his or her classical or mathematical colleagues, but that a real degree of superior status is being claimed for

F

him consequent upon his special responsibilities; his subject, his training, his expertise and his influence inside the school become matters of vital concern within the nation's educational system. In addition to this, the Report has much to say of importance concerning the practical aspects of methodology – stressing the need for genuine literary studies, emphasising the dangers attendant upon the 'classical', 'Old English' and general 'content' fallacies which were still influential in varying degrees, and insisting that teaching methods appropriate to and specifically designed for the unique nature of the subject be evolved as quickly as possible. With the publication of this Report in 1921 English ceased to be the poor and suspect relation; it had, in a very definite sense, come of age, and although it had yet to throw off several immature habits it was well set for the decades ahead.

New moves in speech work

Textbook and English method writers were not slow to follow the lead given by the Report with regard to specific features concerning English teaching which had been raised in its pages; indeed, during the years immediately following, it becomes almost a *sine qua non* to pay obsequious compliments to the Report in the preface to any textbook published – whether or not the textbooks in question followed the Report's recommendations or were in frank opposition to them (and for all the change in content, format and tone of many of them the Report might not have been published at all).

One point which had been raised and referred to in some detail was the lamentable absence of oral work in the schools. Not only was little or no opportunity given to pupils to practise speech work through conversation, discussion, or dramatic activity, but the rule that children should for the most part be completely silent while working in the classroom was still generally upheld, and it is tempting to wonder whether the rather stilted and artificial style of much of the children's formal writing was due in no small degree to a lack of opportunity to develop or practise oral fluency.

Attitudes had been changing in certain thoughtful quarters after 1915, and teachers were tending to give more time to what was called 'oral composition', or directed class discussion leading to the formulation of 'composition' material which could either lead on to writing or be an end in itself. John Adams includes such oral composition work in his list of significant advances in English teaching in *The New Teaching*, 1918: 'Oral composition is now begun at the earliest stages in school . . . Matter is provided that naturally provokes questions and counter questions, and draws answers sometimes from the pupil, sometimes from the teacher. The interest in such talks is centred not on the form of speech, but on the subject-matter . . . As the lessons proceed, pupils should be encouraged to make more or less consecutive statements . . .'[10] 'Directed' was the key word, since the pupils were usually required to speak in turn, formulate their answers in complete, formal sentences, and finally copy out the resulting composition from the blackboard, the final version being as much the result of the teacher's editing and rephrasing as of the children's contributions. Some schools were encouraging more spontaneous dramatic work, but these were certainly in a minority before 1920.

After 1920 additional emphasis was laid on oral work of a freer kind. W. S. Tomkinson in *The Teaching of English*, 1921, breaks new method ground by devoting a long section of forty-four pages to speech exercises, and goes to some lengths to assert the value of spoken competence for all English work. Too many children, he claims, are leaving school virtually inarticulate because they have never been encouraged to speak up, speak out, or speak freely. This situation is not helped by the universal assumption that the most important form of communication must be the *writing* of English when in fact, for most pupils, it is speech that is most important in their lives (the Newsom Report is still having to make this point in 1963; *plus ça change . . .*). In any case, Tomkinson rightly asserts, it is only when speaking is accurate and fluent that writing will be good, and teachers would be advised to concentrate more on oral, less on written skills, in order to improve written expression generally. 'The insistence on writing as the main approach to composition, restricts the child to crawling after he has learnt to walk'; 'It is this consideration which has led the new school of English teachers to make a fresh approach to composition in the lower classes and to order their work on the sequence: Speech first; Writing second.'[11] Tomkinson includes in his speech activities: reading aloud by individual pupils, improvised dialogues, story telling, descriptions of objects or persons, lecturettes, 'chain' stories (the story line kept going by different pupils in turn), debates, mock trials, interviews and play acting.

George Sampson makes very much the same points in his excellent *English for the English*, 1921:[12]

It [pupil's oral work] ought to be the most successful feature of school work, simply because the interchange of views between teacher and taught is the staple of most good lessons; but it is very obviously not the most successful feature of school work, as any visitor will at once discover. Too often teaching is little more than the delivery of monologues by the teacher, the pupil's required contribution being dead silence.

E. A. Greening Lamborn in his *Expression in Speech and Writing*, 1922, actually devotes a quarter of his book to oral work. 'There is great need', he writes, 'to get back into written exercises the easy, natural fluency and simplicity of speech instead of the stilted, conventional phrases that a shallow and pretentious system has made customary in the schools'; 'Children write artificially because they have no opportunity to develop their language the natural way – through talking.'[13] His speech exercises also include talks, mock trials, mock elections (with speeches), debates and message-passing games.

George Sampson

Of course, George Sampson's *English for the English* is in its way almost as important a publication as the 1921 Report, for it is not just a very good method book but a method book which incorporates an historical survey of English teaching since the 1870s (as the Report does) and as such provides us with a further account of the development of the subject up to 1920. Sampson, for example, reproduces the Board's 1887 English Schedules for Elementary Schools – they differ hardly at all from the 1900 Schedules – and concludes:[14]

> Is it not pitiful? But why, it may be asked, should we turn to the obsolete schedules of the eighties? *Because those obsolete schedules still represent the spirit in which elementary education is understood by most officials and teachers.* The elementary school is still moulded after that pattern, the only difference being that it is moulded by the choice of the teacher instead of by the compulsion of the code [his italics].

Like the 1921 Report Sampson is concerned to put the present inadequate situation into social perspective. If the Revised Code spirit persists it is because no new vision has appeared to replace it. In a desire to check this unthinking drift, Sampson wishes to ask all teachers 'What are you trying to *do* with your children?' He wishes to establish a concrete, worth-while definition of the term 'education for life', and he wishes to bring home to the State the simple fact that although its schooling system is called 'education' it does not provide anything approaching a proper education for three-quarters of its children, being enmeshed as it is in the irrelevant vocational side-issues. The elementary schools all too often still see their role as that of producing domestic servants, clerks, office boys or factory hands according to the social class expectations and prejudices of forty years back; he points to the tragic lack of understanding between the various parts of the school system – secondary heads refusing to liaise with elementary heads, the contempt in which elementary teachers are so often held, or the practice in some grammar schools of keeping the scholarship pupils separate and isolated.

His answer to this unedifying confusion is quite simply to assert (1) that the elementary schools, which educate the majority of pupils, are the most important in the country, and (2) that English is the most important 'subject' in those schools. 'These two propositions depend upon an assumption that the purpose of the elementary school is really to develop the mind and soul of the children and not merely to provide tame and acquiescent "labour fodder" ' and he virtually uses Arnold's words (although he does not mention Arnold by name): 'The safety of the world and the future of civilisation depend upon the character and intelligence of the multitude . . . As long as the elementary school is the chief means of humanising the masses, it is the most important school in the country . . .'[15]

Also like the 1921 Report (and Sampson was a member of the Committee, which raises the interesting question 'Was his book influenced by the experience of the investigation and the line the Committee as a whole took over certain problems, or does the Report embody the thinking of *English for the English* where those documents are on common ground ?') – like the Report, he insists that the colossal potential of English as the one area of study that involves its pupils intellectually, emotionally and morally, has not yet received general recognition. 'No attempt has ever yet been made to give the whole English people a humane, creative education in and through the treasures of their own language and literature. The great educational reform now needed is to begin that universal education.'[16] But this can only come when the declining importance of classical studies is faced and accepted, when grammar is treated with sensible moderation, when literature is read as literature, and when teachers of English have the courage to abandon methods which seem safe because they are traditional, long-established, or conveniently cut-and-dried but which in fact are inappropriate and positively harmful to pupils and themselves alike as creative individuals.

What Sampson also grasps is the unique nature of 'English'; 'In plain words and in the ordinary sense, English is not a school "subject" at all. It is a condition of school life. The difference is important, for the failure of the elementary school to be a humanising influence on its products may be attributed in part to the mistaken efforts of the teachers in treating English as they treat Arithmetic . . .'[17] Compare the phrasing of the Report: 'The Elementary School might exert a more permanently humanising influence on its products if it were not for the mistake of some teachers in treating English as they treat Arithmetic . . .' There are a large number of other examples of verbal similarity, too many to be coincidental: *English for the English* appeared in August, *The*

Teaching of English in England in October 1921. Consider also Sampson's remark that 'education' has nothing to do with trade or livelihood – that it is a preparation for living not for *a* living, with the Report's comment: 'The fact that the majority of elementary school children will have to take up some form of manual labour, perhaps of unskilled labour, must not limit the kind of education they are to receive, for, as we have shown, education is a preparation for life, not, in the first place, for livelihood.'[18]

With regard to grammar teaching, Sampson is prepared to go further than the Report and take a stand very close to Ballard's. He does not advocate the total rejection of grammar work throughout the schools – certain points will present themselves for consideration as the pupils' writing advances – but he indicates that an extreme line against grammar is needed rather than moderation since the pro-grammarites are still very much in control. With this in mind he writes: '*It is impossible to have too little grammar at the elementary stage of education*' (his italics) and (of older pupils) 'The amount of practical help a boy will get in speech or writing from grammar is infinitesimal' – though having said this, the recommendation of any form of grammar work, and Sampson includes a good basis of it in his own textbooks, would seem to be something of an anti-climax at best, inconsistency at worst, though it would be churlish to split hairs over Sampson's good and liberal intentions.

There is in his book, perhaps even more than in the 1921 Report, a strong desire to see the establishment of a 'common' school (beginning at the elementary level) within the kingdom, a school which shall offer the best possible education to all children of any age group irrespective of their social backgrounds. Such schools may not yet exist, but what does exist, and it will be the key to future unity, is a common national culture based on the English language (the 'English' of the English). At the same time the social and political implications are clear: 'There is no class in the country that does not need a full education in English. Possibly a common basis of education might do much to mitigate the class antagonism that is dangerously keen at the moment and shows no signs of losing its edge.'[19] In his Preface he explains that he has, in the book, said nothing as to whether 'the present elaborate isolation of Secondary Schools from the main elementary high road, as shown by the difference in scale of building and equipment, in status and pay of teachers, in size of classes, and even in such trifles as length of school day, incidence of term, and duration of holiday is not a display of diseased class consciousness . . .' – a comment which is eloquent enough even if only made in passing.

English for the English is probably the best-known of all the pre-1940 English method books (a reprint has been issued recently) and certainly it is one of the best. At the same time it was not the *only* good method book to appear before 1925, and the almost total neglect of the 1921 Report in comparison with the attention which *English for the English* has received in recent years is rather a pity in view of the comprehensive and, for the most part, sound advice which that Report had to give over a much wider field. As far as the official commentators in 1921 were concerned, Sampson's book was a very miserable affair compared with the Report and both the *Journal of Education* and *The Times Educational Supplement*, while praising the Report to the skies, gave *English for the English* a very cool, not to say hostile reception in their review columns. The nature of those reviews is such, however, that one wonders whether the writers had the slightest idea what Sampson was really getting at (the *Journal* attacked him for 'being rude about Arithmetic' – presumably a reference to the first chapter) which makes their enthusiasm for the Report all the more suspect in view of the basic similarity of thinking in both publications.

Textbooks: progress in composition

Another feature which was gaining steady ground in schools after 1920 was the use of comprehension exercises to increase children's sensitivity and accuracy in silent reading. Since 1910 there had been an increasing shift from the old practice of reading aloud, often in chorus, by elementary pupils to a concentration on personal, silent reading (see the Board's 1914 *Suggestions*). There now came an increasing use of comprehension to check on the accuracy of this reading. The 'Direct Method' textbooks had included such exercises as one of the many possible follow-up activities to the study of particular passages, albeit in rather an 'allusion-hunting' manner, but now genuine comprehension-based course books began to appear, and along with them books on the theory of silent reading such as N. B. Smith's *One Hundred Ways of Teaching Silent Reading*, 1925. Richard Wilson's *Spoken and Written English*, 1925, was one such, or, slightly later, A. J. Coles's *Thought in English Prose*, 1930. Wilson also published an attractive series *Reading and Thinking*, 1926–7, which included not only comprehension work based on quite long extracts of prose and poetry, but also picture study with coloured reproductions of old master paintings (Titian, Rembrandt, Velasquez) with a brief description of each in an attempt to call pupils' attention to pictorial detail and atmosphere.

In 1930 E. F. Davidson, a former HMI, noted this recent progress of comprehension work in schools in his *Modern English Teaching* but added that despite the evident value of such work it was still under-estimated (or ignored) in many schools, and that teachers in their training were not being taught to read as accurately, closely, or sensitively as they should. (He adds the point that chorus reading aloud is still going strong in many Elementary classes.) The 'Direct Method' itself continued in the sense that textbooks in the by now familiar format were regularly published, but the method was increasingly becoming less novel as a wider range of reading material was introduced into the schools. The 'Direct Method' was not so much superseded as absorbed into the continually broadening field of English teaching, and the somewhat cramped nature of its approach was not modified to meet the new circumstances. Frederick Pickles produced another series of elementary school Direct Method textbooks in 1924 (*Reading, Narration, Composition and Drawing*, I–IV) again using prose and poetry extracts as a basis for grammar, comprehension, vocabulary and composition exercises. 'Composition is no longer a task, but a delight', he writes in his Foreword; the pupil is now free 'to soar away on the wings of his imagination and to let loose all his powers of self-expression' – admirable theory, no doubt, but the strongly imitative nature of the exercises set does not bear out the initial claims – 'Write out the story above in your own words'; 'Read the following. Give it a title and write a similar story of your own'; 'Make a story using the following outline', and each book has a rather nasty Appendix with the ominous title 'Grammar Made Easy'. (This model-based, imitative approach is to be seen in a large number of composition textbooks in the twenties – see as another example Amy Cruse's *A New Course of Composition*, 1925, which is well stocked with outlines for expansion.)

F. H. Pritchard's *Junior English Extracts and Exercises*, 1926, is also 'Direct Method' in approach with passages from Dickens, Scott, Stevenson and Thomas Hughes and questions such as: 'Give nouns that correspond to the following adjectives used in the passage . . .'; 'Supply the missing words in these sentences' (from the passage); or 'Put yourself in the place of Gulliver/Mr. Pickwick/Ivanhoe and describe what you saw.' In 1926 also Evans Brothers published their *Direct Method of Teaching English* in the well-known Kingsway series. This attempted to take the direct element a stage further and involve the young pupil not merely in the study of an interesting piece of writing but in 'real' situations in the classroom. These situations involve the teacher's manipulation of coins, matches, pieces of chalk, and furniture, together with the showing of pictures to the class, the pupils writing down what they see taking place in front of them. Once again the theory involved is excellent (the Introduction emphasising that children must be shown that writing is not 'special' but an instrument for everyday usage) with the actual practical details coming as something of an anti-climax (though the logical next step is to take the children *outside* the classroom and show them worth-while writing situations there).

There was certainly a stronger feeling among teachers now that writing should be made real to pupils and that the formal arti-ficiality of much written expression as encouraged for so many years was long overdue for thorough modification – by no means a new idea (as Hartog, O'Grady and Finch could testify) but now seemingly beginning to catch on with the profession generally.

Two books on writing from the twenties which merit special attention are Guy Pocock's *Exercises in English*, 1924, and R. T. Lewis's *Composition Through Story Writing*, 1927. Pocock's is a remarkable little book, and it anticipates many aspects of 1960s practice with its lively approach to composition. Like O'Grady's earlier, the theory behind the book (for pupils aged nine to fourteen years) is extremely simple: 'The best way, indeed the only way, to learn to write is to try to write.' Pocock then gives a series of amusing and entertaining assignments for children to write on: a picture of a hideous sea serpent, for example, with the direction 'Write about this thing. Treat it in any way you like'; a picture of a torn and shredded sail with part of a message on it ('Decipher and write a story on'); a picture of a man climbing a sheer cliff ('Write his adventure'); a map of an island ('Write a story about'). A separate section is devoted to the writing of stories or novels, and another to poetry writing. The approach of the book is also 'non-grammatical', that is, writing is something to be plunged into from the beginning, and although there are some vocabulary exercises which rely rather heavily on the 'fill-in-the-gaps-in-the-following' technique, the essential approach is one of craft not of step by step exercises.

R. T. Lewis offers a more ambitious scheme, a long imaginative adventure story written by younger secondary pupils over a term, with close project affinities. Beginning with selected readings from *Treasure Island* and *Robinson Crusoe* and carefully drawn island maps of their own, the boys sketch out their plots and chapter headings, and are referred to books on ship-building, voyages, ship-wrecks, piracy, coral islands, and the sixteenth- and seventeenth-century navy (Hakluyt, for example) where they can acquire authentic material to build up the details of their stories. Rough drafts are prepared, read aloud to the rest of the class, discussed, and revised. The scheme is extremely attractive, depending (as Lewis, invoking Caldwell Cook, points out in his Introduction) on the principles that where pupils are personally engaged they will write freely, and that where they can 'make' something of their own they will take pains and be thorough (Lewis vouches for his own success with the scheme).

Another lively, and at times comic, approach to writing can be seen in G. Y. Elton's *Teaching English*, 1929, which includes a large number of modest but engaging assignments of an ingenious kind: 'Write a story beginning: "Once upon a time there was a very large

policeman who was standing on top of a railing, balancing, because
...'" '; 'Write the diary of a drunk who is afraid of cows'; or 'Write
a story bringing in: Thirty zebras, two people of the name of
Johnson, an Easter Egg . . . and a sheet of green note paper.'
Along with this kind of liveliness went a growing feeling that only
by encouraging quantity and all the trial and error that that entails
will children be able to achieve a genuine level of quality – not the
carefully prepared, outline-based, occasional production of a few
self-conscious pieces of 'formal' writing, but constant and regular
practice on a more down to earth level. Through constant practice
the pupil will work himself out of many errors and into competent
expression (a firmly established view at present, and probably true).
'Copiousness will in time secure accuracy . . .'; 'the English teacher's
first concern is with quantity: he must secure a free and copious
outpouring of ideas. And everything that checks that outflow is
bad, whether it be grumbling or grammar' – these remarks coming,
not from an 'advanced' teacher of the sixties, but from Ballard in
1921. 'Increasingly', Greening Lamborn writes in 1922, 'the modern
teacher of English centres the child's attention on self-expression
and leaves handwriting, grammar, and spelling to improve incidentally and unconsciously.' Especially with younger children 'quantity
is more important than quality' (W. S. Tomkinson, 1921); 'the
younger children should be encouraged to write and to write
copiously' (George Sampson, 1921).

Creative advances: Nunn, Lamborn and Tomkinson

Creative attitudes generally had also received tangible encouragement from a book published in 1920, and reprinted no less than
thirteen times before 1930 – Percy Nunn's *Education: Its Data and
First Principles*. If the post-1918 period saw a new spirit in education, it is true to say that much of that spirit was concerned with an
emphasis on the individual pupil, and on individual (as against
class) learning, and Percy Nunn's book attempts to formulate a
philosophy of education based on the 'freedom', 'free development'
and 'expression' of the individual. *The Times Educational Supplement* devoted a long and very enthusiastic review to the book,
praising it highly (11 March 1920). 'As a treatise on the broad
principles of education it is indisputably the best that has appeared
for many years'; 'The author . . . allies himself with the developmental school of thought; and it must be admitted that the school
has stood in need of a defender of Professor Nunn's clearness of
thought and dialectical skill.' The review also relates Nunn's
thinking to a number of important predecessors: 'Those who regard
Mr. Edmond Holmes as a voice crying in the wilderness, Montes-
sorianism as a mere fashion of the hour . . . and the Playway as the

way to anarchy and incompetence, would do well to read what this book has to say.'

Despite the obvious connection between this kind of thinking and the growth of Arnoldian liberal attitudes, Nunn's tone is sometimes strongly Romantic in a way that Arnold's is not, and we have here an emphasis on free expression ('the infinite value of the individual person', 'free development of individuality', 'freedom of the child's self-creative growth') which is much more reminiscent of some of Rousseau's more cogent remarks.[20]

We must hold that a scheme of education is ultimately to be valued by its success in fostering the highest degrees of individual excellence of which those submitted to it are capable . . . We shall stand throughout on the position that nothing good enters the human world except in and through the free activities of individual men and women, and that educational practice must be shaped to accord with that truth.

Nunn also lays considerable emphasis on the importance of aesthetic experience and expression in education, and he laments the absence of such work in the school lives of so many children. He offers a slightly suspect theory to support the notion that human beings are naturally creative in the artistic sense, pointing to primitive man and asserting that once his tools had been made functionally efficient he went on 'instinctively' to decorate and shape them to make them beautiful.[21]

This doctrine has great importance for aesthetic education. It teaches that the power to produce beauty is not a gift grudgingly given by the gods to a mere sprinkling of fortunate beings; but an ability which, though varying in strength, like other abilities, from individual to individual, is yet as universal as the power to learn arithmetic. Let boys and girls make under conditions that stimulate the natural flow of energy, let their social milieu be free and humane, let them acquire by pleasant repetition the mastery that enables them to *play* with their materials – and beauty will inevitably appear . . .

Percy Nunn is referring to creative expression generally, though he includes written as well as artistic expression in his argument, but the two books specifically concerned with English teaching which may be described as being the most uncompromisingly 'creative' at this time were Tomkinson's and Greening Lamborn's. It is extremely interesting to see, between 1920 and 1922, a positive barrage of references to the need for 'liberal' education, to 'culture', 'Arnold', 'humanising', to the importance of the emotional and spiritual aspects of childhood growth, and to the need to educate for 'life' far beyond the short-sightedness of the school courses as at present constituted – see the 1921 Report, Sampson, Nunn, Greening Lamborn, Tomkinson. It is, however, with the last two that general liberalism and specific creativity in English, as we understand the term today, are most closely linked. Both writers are emphatically against grammar teaching ('The theory that parsing and analysis are a means of improving composition is as dead as the books in which it was propounded' (Lamborn); 'it is incontestable that the study of grammar does not ensure correctness in writing' (Tomkinson)); both advocate pupils' own poetry writing, both suggest the use of pictures and music to stimulate written work and written self-expression, and both see expression through English as being a way to personality growth for the pupil (and both, for that matter, refer to Arnold and his culture ideal).

Lamborn obligingly provided a Preface (written in 1920) to Tomkinson's book. In it he writes:

> The new ideal in the elementary schools is indeed the old ideal in the universities – an education not so much concerned with livelihood as with living. What is really new is the revelation of the importance of the emotional life and of the need to cultivate and enrich it by humanistic treatment of all our studies . . . to provide that 'culture of the feelings' without which, as John Stuart Mill discovered, all intellectual culture is in vain.

He takes this further in his own *Expression in Speech and Writing*: 'Our natural instincts urge us along the road of self-development, which is the meaning of life, and stimulate us to self-expression, which is the manifestation of life'; '. . . the development of personality is the most important object of education. It has been assumed that the individual exists for the state: we need to recognize that the state exists for the individual to fulfil himself in it.'[22]

All individuals have creative power and an instinct for beauty, he maintains, whatever their intellectual gifts or social background; hence the importance of encouraging creative written and spoken expression in all schools, if necessary to the neglect of all the 'factual' and 'useful' cargo which is usually loaded into pupils' heads. Tomkinson makes the further point that the industrial age has reduced the idea of education to a narrow and base one, while at the same time stifling, by its very nature, the instinct for beauty; it must therefore be the task of the schools, through creative teaching centred on the child, to 'right the natural balance of the individual which the machine and the factory have knocked wholly awry'. (Tomkinson also makes use of Percy Nunn's theory that man works instinctively to make the useful beautiful.) Above all, at the practical classroom level, both Lamborn and Tomkinson stress the overwhelming importance of spontaneous, fluent, self-expressive writing by the pupil.

Now no one will deny the good sense behind much of this (with the proviso that the pupils, while they are writing regularly, are also being corrected and guided – not left to perpetuate an endless round of inaccuracy) but along with these remarks goes another, new, but rather less palatable way of thinking which seems to characterise the really committed advocates of creativity at this time. We have already noted the tendency of some of those writers committed to 'self-expressive' principles to rely very much on a pseudo-Romantic approach of doubtful authenticity when discussing children's imaginative capacity, and to fall into emotive and careless definitions. It is rather surprising to find John Dover Wilson taking this line in his 1916 English Association Pamphlet 'Poetry and the Child', where, after the requisite references to 'The Immortality Ode', he goes on to make such remarks as: 'I would suggest that the relationship between the child and poet is far more intimate than has been generally realised . . .'; 'Poet and child belong to the same species, most teachers belong to quite another species, the "grown ups" .' Now, of course, what Dover Wilson and other humane men are trying to do is to get the teachers of 1916 to look again at children and recognise that they have voices, imaginative powers and inventive capacities of their own, and to allow these to be developed within a freer class situation – in other words the Victorian attitudes are limited and limiting and should be abandoned. What is disturbing is the extent to which advocates of the 'creative' child seem prepared to go to make their case, and along with the creative advances of the early twenties goes a rather unfortunate element of adulation and airy hyperbole with regard to children's capacities (an attitude tied in with a somewhat suspect theory of literature and with a sentimental approach to poetry) which is frankly unacceptable. W. S. Tomkinson strikes the note in some of his remarks on children's verse writing: do teachers realise how closely the child and the poet are related, taking 'delight in pictures', 'joy in music', ruled by 'the heart not the head'? Do they realise that the poet's expression – 'simple, sensuous, passionate' – is the expression of the child? but that whereas the poet creates beautiful works, the child 'creates himself' through expression.[23]

Greening Lamborn can be equally effusive. A teacher once showed him an unusual phrase in a pupil's exercise book, thinking it unconventional; 'and of course it is, as all genius is unconventional: it is the perfect epithet that would only occur to a poet or a child.'

It is not simply that *The Waste Land* was now published and that the new critics of the Richards-Empson-Leavis School were already deploying their forces to drive sentimental gush off the literary critical scene, but that such comments (and they gain momentum after 1945, some educationists seemingly claiming that children's poetry can stand the test of comparison with the best of adult poets' work) are simply untrue. Granted that the aim of such remarks in 1921 or 1922 was to gain for the child an opportunity to speak for himself, one nevertheless feels that in rejecting one false view the creative-Romantics were in danger of falling into another. Greening Lamborn's assertion that the natural spontaneity of children had long been unnecessarily and unfeelingly suppressed was a welcome shaft of light on a very gloomy scene, but as with all iconoclastic pronouncements it suffered the danger of going excessively far in the opposite direction.

J. H. Jagger (*Poetry in School*, 1928), while heartily advocating children's verse writing (and this is not the point), administers a dash of cold water to such sentiments, pointing out that poetry, real poetry, means toil, tears, unusual verbal skill, trained imagination and adult experience, and that children's productions must, in their very nature, be imperfect.

At the same time it is good to see method writers in the twenties continuing to recommend children's writing of poetry as a usual and necessary part of the English course – Guy Pocock, for example, in *Exercises in English*, J. H. Jagger in *Poetry in School*, or G. Y. Elton in *Teaching English*, although some of the advocates of the practice still seem to be rooted in the attitudes of the 'classical' approach. The IAAM in its 1923 *Memorandum on the Teaching of English* still sees pupils' verse writing merely in classical-imitative terms as a means of practising the techniques of prosody which have to be learnt in order to appreciate the technique of the poets studied in the literature lesson – this 'original' writing having no significance whatsoever beyond that.

Reaction: the progressives attacked

Despite these innovatory ideas the creative advocates remained, for a time at least, very much in a minority – and evidently in a despised minority at that. A far larger number of writers expressed the view that 'imaginative' work was going much too far, and insisted that the old ways were the best with their sound approach to the writing side through the imitation of 'good models'. The 1921 Report had tended to steer a non-inflammatory course, but the Board's 1924 *Suggestions for the Teaching of English in Secondary Schools* was less inhibited; teachers are encouraged 'within such limits as common sense suggests' to *permit* exercises in 'self-expression' but, 'except under the guidance of a teacher who is skilful as well as enthusiastic, their use in the class-room should be rare and occasional.'[24] Grace Bracken also in *The Teaching of English in Secondary Schools for Girls*, 1924, tells English mistresses that 'original narrative' must never take precedence over reproduction work, warning them that 'The danger of formlessness is here at its greatest.'

In 1927 H. A. Treble in *The Teaching of English in Primary Schools* directed a blistering attack on the new permissiveness, laying much of the blame at the feet of that popular teaching butt 'psychology'.[25]

> From psychology we have progressed by easy steps to the
> *pleasant*, the *easy*, the *self-expressive* . . . Education has come to
> mean mere drift, the casual development of instinct or intuition,
> the expression of a miniature self that has nothing to express.
> If we think for a moment on the subject with which I am to
> deal . . . we shall find a perfect example of the flabby
> superficiality that has ensnared us. Let the child express
> himself, we have argued, unfettered and unrestrained. Speech
> and writing shall interpret the innocent beauty of his
> imagination, his unconscious poetry, his ideals of life – forsooth
> – his natural art. So from a kind of illogical laziness of thought
> we have sunk deeply into the slough of sentimentalism.
> What of all this self-expression . . . Has it taught the child how
> to write a letter ? how to speak in intelligible sentences ? how
> to spell ? how to understand the simplest thing about language ?
> how to read a good book ? . . . It is doubtful.

No, writes Treble, 'We are always apt to over-estimate the capacity or quality of the child's mind' and composition must mean disciplined reproduction work and constant practice in sentence and paragraph building. (The *Journal of Education* reviewer, apparently recognising in Treble a kindred spirit, praised the book extravagantly: 'this common-sense, practical, yet highly stimulating work ought to find a place on the shelf of every teacher of English'; 'The writer is experienced enough *and fearless enough* to plead for the reinstatement of paraphrase as well as grammar . . .')

Treble's sentiments are repeated – somewhat more moderately – by G. Y. Elton in 1929 (*Teaching English*):[26]

> The teaching of composition today, in reaction against the
> dry-as-dust methods formerly general, is suffering from a
> conception of 'self-expression' which tends to foster
> emotionalism, introspection and self-thinking [*sic*]. Everybody
> nowadays accepts the doctrine of helping a pupil to develop
> and express his individual tastes and powers, but not many
> people (teachers or others) appear to realise that it's equally
> important to encourage him to get away from and despise the
> 'self-standpoint'.

E. F. Davidson (*Modern English Teaching*, 1930) is quite convinced that composition standards in the elementary schools are dropping as a result of the new attitudes; lessons in word-building, spelling, parsing or analysis are less frequently found and at the same time the writing of the older pupils, while being fluent enough, is increasingly characterised by 'muddled and slipshod expression, lack of punctuation, and faults of spelling'. Perhaps it is premature, Davidson goes on, to expect children of this age (twelve to thirteen years) to 'express themselves'.

These comments are interesting, if only because they suggest that definite changes were taking place in the schools, albeit much to the dismay of the traditionalists. No doubt the emphasis on technical perfection (paragraph construction and so on) was weakening; one hopes that the children were benefiting in other ways, in finding, for example, that writing could be real and even pleasurable. It is also interesting that the two schools of thought – the 'Classical imitative' of Treble and the 'Romantic expressive' of Greening Lamborn – were so clearly defined so early in the century. When today we argue for or against 'creativity' we tend to assume that our debate is the spearhead of current method thinking; in fact we are merely re-entering one of the oldest spirals in education and are adapting the impermanent experience of the present to the unchanging framework of the argument. What should give us pause for thought is the fact that by and large the creative advocates have had their way with the passing of time, not in a universal sweep, but slowly and piecemeal, so that the conservative-classical standpoint has itself moved gently but gradually farther to the 'left'.

It must also be evident that what Treble and, say, Greening Lamborn are fighting about is the concept of 'education' as a whole and how it should be defined. The 'Classical-Romantic' terminology is apt in that it directs attention forwards to the skirmishing which has gone on in English since 1945, but the basis of the conflict lies backwards in time in the Revised Code-Arnold battle which has already received so much attention.

What we seem to be witnessing in the reactions of a good number of writers in the late twenties (and, as we shall see, in the early thirties also) is an increasing tension between the 'vocational' view of education and the liberal, 'whole-personality' view, that tension arising because perhaps for the first time the liberal advocates are organising themselves into a coherent – and very articulate – group with a measurable degree of support from public opinion.

Davidson goes on, perhaps unfairly: 'self-expression, creative imagination, originality, are the watch-words of many. Fluency has been cultivated, but any attempt to discipline this fluency into form . . . has been deprecated.'

This concern for a possible decline in 'accuracy' also troubled Ballard, but his answer (in 1925, in *The Changing School*) is slightly different from Treble's or Davidson's: 'There is no charge that is more loudly and more persistently urged against modern methods of education than that they fail to produce accuracy', he writes. And has accuracy in written English declined? Well, perhaps it has slightly, but the standard of accuracy required up until recently has been excessively, even absurdly, high. Ballard is convinced that if, earlier, children 'were highly trained on a starvation diet' they are now 'modestly trained on a generous diet' and the change is all to the good.[27]

The fact remains that the period from approximately 1927 to 1932 is marked by a seemingly concerted attempt to stave off creative developments and keep to the straight and narrow of traditional English teaching – and that included a demand for a return to the most formal of formal grammar teaching. Reading the comments of the time one feels that grammar had never had such a good press: 'Fortunately, there is a revulsion from the idea that grammar is unnecessary. It has been proved that it is not enough to give children good literature to read, thinking that thereby they will imbibe correctness of expression . . .' (B. S. Colquhoun, 'The teaching of English in girls' prep. schools', the *Journal of Education*, July 1929); 'The old-fashioned elaborate methods of intensive study of English grammar are gone for good and . . . many teachers . . . have completely banished all grammar and syntax from their time-tables. It is now realized, however, that this won't do' (G. H. Crump, *English for Schools*, 1929);[28] 'It seems clear that the majority of teachers of English today are agreed that the reaction against the teaching of formal grammar has gone too far . . .' (review in the *Journal*, March 1933). *The Times Educational Supplement* printed a string of letters through 1927 and 1928 from correspondents lamenting the decline of 'real' grammar teaching, though the battle was not entirely one-sided; a characteristic of these letters is the minute, inordinately lengthy and savagely aggressive way in which the correspondents analyse the deficiencies of the previous writer's own grammar – which in itself is significant – and the *Supplement* also printed two front-page articles in 1931 (21 February and 9 May) strongly supporting grammar teaching, expressing dismay at its recent decline, and giving yet further support to the 'mental training' and 'foreign language' fallacies.

This phenomenon of reaction is an intriguing one; the 'proof' that B. S. Colquhoun mentions (that it is not enough to give children literature) seems almost certainly to have existed in the minds of like-thinking conservatives rather than in anybody's actual research. Given that the cause of the discontent was the rise of more creative English methods in the period 1918–22 (and that would cover the publications of Cook, Nunn, Sampson, Tomkinson and Lamborn) the anti-grammar rot would have had no more than one generation of schoolchildren to reveal itself. In 1928 the Board's Report, *Books in Public Elementary Schools*, includes the comment: 'It is probably true to say that for some time past the study of formal

G

grammar has been almost wholly omitted in many Elementary Schools' – though in using the word 'many' rather than 'all' the Report is keeping strictly to the truth. The number of new grammars published each year did decline after 1920, but the reprint industry remained active and it was not uncommon for a grammar published before 1910 to be reprinted ten or twenty times in the space of thirty years. It would therefore be quite wrong to assume that grammar teaching was literally on the way out by 1928 – in the secondary schools it was probably as strong as ever.

There were continued attempts to make grammar more entertaining (Isabel Fry's diagrammatic analysis in *A Key to Language*, 1925, is one such attempt to make grammar 'fun') but writers generally relied on the well-tried, exam-orientated formulae of parsing, analysis, figures of speech, sentence types, and formal essay construction in the by now standardised format of the 1890s. Typical books include R. B. Morgan and H. A. Treble, *A Senior English Grammar*, 1922; W. J. Weston, *English Grammar and Composition*, 1925; G. A. Twentyman, *Elementary English Grammar and Composition*, 1926; E. W. Edmunds, *A Senior Course of English Composition*, 1927; C. C. Boyd, *Grammar for Great and Small*, 1927; J. W. Marriott, *Matriculation English*, 1928; L. Oliphant, *A Matriculation English Course*, 1928; or C. Granville and A. Simpson, *A Four Years' English Course*, 1929.

The idea that 'composition' was only another term for 'grammar' was a very long time dying at secondary level, and despite the existence of good composition books, the 1921 Report, by sanctioning 'pure' grammar, had encouraged the continuation of the old ways of thinking. In addition the 1923 *Memorandum* of the IAAM, taking an uncompromising (and sadly stiff-necked) 'grammar school' line, set the secondary seal on the composition-grammar link-up. 'It is unanimously agreed', the *Memorandum* states, 'that from the earliest stages of the secondary school course some training in formal grammar is necessary and desirable' *because no pupil can improve his writing unless he knows grammar*, and indeed can improve only through a grammar approach. The *Memorandum* also helps to perpetuate the 'foreign language' fallacy, insisting, if all else fails, that grammar teaching is necessary as a basis for learning modern foreign languages.

To some extent these sentiments represent the 1921 Report's ambivalence over grammar coming home to roost. The IAAM *Memorandum* on English was produced, after many committee meetings and much professional consultation, to provide a sound, well-based and well-organised programme of English teaching for secondary masters in the light of the Report's recommendations, in fact the intention was to follow those recommendations as closely as possible. If the IAAM chose to interpret the grammar sections in the light of its own undoubted predilection for the subject, it was hardly surprising; the result in the *Memorandum* is to confirm the worst possible practices and keep the clock firmly at 1900. Another example of this can be seen in E. G. Browne's *Lectures on the Teaching of English*, 1924, which also quotes chapter and verse from the Report with proper enthusiasm, and then sails into as formal a scheme of grammar work as one could wish for.

B. L. K. Henderson in his 1926 secondary textbook, *The English Way* (subtitled, somewhat ironically, 'A Textbook on the Art of Writing'), takes an identical line to the *Memorandum* and speaks with the uncompromising voice of the past:

> The study of Greek and Latin having almost ceased in the schools, teachers of modern languages are finding daily that their scholars are destitute of that knowledge of Grammar which is requisite for reasonable progress in another tongue; and that there is a general absence of the *mental discipline* formerly provided by a grounding in the essentials of Latin Grammar (Preface; my italics).

An interesting document from the mid-twenties is the winning scheme in the *Daily Mail* Curriculum Contest of 1925. This was won by a Mrs Helen Dobson (the judging panel including several eminent educationists) with her curriculum for girls aged nine to fourteen years. Her reading scheme is predictable, ranging from myths and Longfellow at ten years to *Lyra Heroica* and Scott at thirteen years. But her grammar syllabus is even more traditional, with parsing at ten years and analysis from eleven years on:

9–10 years	*Literature*	'Hiawatha' and ballads.
	Reading	Folk songs, Fairy Tales.
	Composition	Simple records of things done.
	Grammar	The sentence; subject and predicate.
10–11 years	*Literature*	Myths (Greek, Norse, Medieval).
	Reading	A History book.
	Composition	Simple descriptions.
	Grammar	Parsing.
11–12 years	*Literature*	*A Midsummer Night's Dream.*
	Reading	Abridged Scott and Dickens.
	Composition	Character sketches.
	Grammar	Clause analysis.
12–13 years	*Literature*	*Lyra Heroica* and *The Golden Treasury.*
	Reading	Scott, Dickens, Thackeray, Lamb.

	Composition	Letter writing.
	Grammar	Parsing. Complex analysis.
13–14 years	*Literature*	Scott, Tennyson, *Twelfth Night,*
		The Merchant of Venice.

Just about the only thing which relieves the uncompromisingly traditional nature of this prize-winning scheme is the suggestion that the thirteen- and fourteen-year-olds could undertake a limited study of magazines and newspapers – a surprisingly progressive idea for the time – but one cannot fail to be depressed by, first, the jejune nature of her composition programme and, second, by the rigid division of the subject into separate, isolated segments.

The social context and the silent revolution

Of course, the grammar schools were less liable to any spirit of radical change simply because they existed in splendid isolation (the public schools excepted) as the coveted, eagerly sought-after gateway to the universities and the professions. If the Certificate examinations which linked the schools so closely to the universities exhibited a strikingly unchanging pattern over many years, the demand for those Certificates – and the career prospects which they implied – grew with an intensity which tended to sweep critical assessment of the nature and quality of the examinations aside. The predominantly middle-class group who benefited most from the grammar schools was content to leave the details of curriculum and subject content to the teachers and examiners and accept their judgment – as long as the university-sponsored Certificates continued to pour in. Acutely conscious of their role as guardians of 'academic tradition' the schools naturally tended to be conservative anyway; this conservatism is apparent in the reluctance to forgo the classics (and then to abandon classical methods in English teaching) to ease up on grammar work, and in the reluctance to change the canon of 'great authors' – Scott, Dickens, Bacon, Macaulay – set up according to Victorian taste and buttressed by all the weight of sparsely read genteel literary preference. The main pressures being brought to bear on the grammar schools through the twenties and thirties were more concerned with a desire for an extension of their benefits rather than with a desire to alter the nature of the courses which led to those benefits. The social stability and desirability of the schools ensured a relatively unchanging course of studies – including the grammar ritual, formal composition, and the familiar 'classical' authors. At the same time the uncompromisingly academic attitude of so many (graduate) grammar school teachers, whose status compared with elementary teachers, for example, was self-evidently high, also tended to work against change of any drastic kind and ensured – all kindly guidance and teaching skill accepted – that the subject must come before the pupil in the scale of pedagogical priorities. (Hence the predictably conservative views of the IAAM and the Association of Assistant Mistresses, even up to the 1950s.)

On the other hand, and despite the fact that the advocates of a more creative, self-expressive approach to English remained in a minority, social influences were at work on the elementary schools which were to have far-reaching effects in determining the nature and content of education for the nation's children. It is perfectly true that the Revised Code spirit was still strong in 1920, but considerable changes were to take place in the elementary schools by the 1930s, resulting as much from external (social pressure) initiative as from internal reform.

In the first place the post-1918 period saw a marked erosion of the old class barriers, and the growth of an egalitarian spirit which would no longer tolerate the idea of a restricted (in terms of provision) education in the grammar and public schools for the privileged minority and a 'special' (inferior) education for the majority in the elementary schools. The 'silent social revolution' was characterised by a vociferous demand for better education, including the provision of secondary education as a right, for all. At the same time, and despite the Depression, the nature of the country's industrial and economic development was making the need for a properly educated population increasingly apparent, and where education meant upward social mobility, there was naturally a growing interest taken in what the elementary schools were doing. *The Times Educational Supplement* in a 1926 editorial (24 July) comments on the keen interest which many working-class parents are now taking in the schools, their traditional indifference, hostility or ignorance of school matters, so-called, existing more and more in the minds of out-of-touch administrators: 'The working mother and father do take an interest and a steadily increasing interest' in their children's education, 'and this especially since the educational road has widened and shown a conceivable vista to the uneducated parents of educable sons and daughters.' The 1918 Education Act had made an attempt to improve the situation with its proposals for a raised leaving age and for better courses in the elementary schools, and all the time class numbers were dropping as more (and more trained) teachers entered the profession. The result was the slow but inevitable growth within the elementary system of a new attitude to education, which, coupled with the increasingly favoured pupil-centred/activity theories of the psychologists, effected a startling transformation in something like fifteen years. We have to wait until the 1950s before we find creativity as we understand it today operating in junior school English work, but the elementary school of the thirties and forties was already involved in project work (see, for example, Joyce Kenwrick's *Junior School Projects*, 1935), pupil-centred writing activities, and in teaching aimed at developing the individuality and expressive capacity of each child.

The ideal of many in the late twenties and throughout the thirties was to make the elementary school so good a school that all parents, irrespective of social class or financial advantages, would wish to send their children to it. We have already seen George Sampson's hope for a common school offering the finest education possible to all children, and increasingly in the years following (and particularly in left-wing political quarters) we find hopes expressed for the creation of a common (national) culture within the common school. In 1929 Stanley Baldwin wrote: 'One of the strongest bonds of union between men is a common education, and England has been the poorer that in her national system of schooling she has not in the past fostered this fellowship of the mind.'[29] And in a book such as L. P. Jacks's *The Education of the Whole Man*, 1931, we find a desire expressed for the uniting together of all individuals in and through a common, creative education, for 'The regeneration of man by an education adapted to his whole nature . . . conducted as the enterprise of the whole community'.[30]

The Hadow Report of 1926, while attempting to bring the problem of the inadequacy of secondary places to a head, and recommend secondary education for all, also insisted that the elementary schools must give 'a humane and general education' which will include 'an understanding of the body of human civilisation'. The Hadow Report (and it is surprising that despite the commendable overall views it takes of the educational scene the Report is sadly unimaginative when it gets down to the brass tacks of the English section) makes the point that elementary education is improving in quality, that improvements are keenly demanded by many parents, and that there is now a considerable body of public opinion which desires to break down the divisions between the different types of school in the State system and ensure that the nation makes full use of the talent of its young people. (Tawney was a member of the Hadow Committee, remember.)

In its advocacy of a genuinely humane education the Report makes W. S. Tomkinson's point:[31]

[On character formation] It is here especially that a national system of education may serve to elevate a nation. Great Britain, like other countries, but perhaps more than most, is passing through an era of industrialism. Industrialism has its grave effects on national life. It demands, only too often, a narrow specialisation of faculty; it produces, only too readily, a patterned uniformity of work and behaviour; and it may, unless it is corrected, infect the minds of men with the genius of its own life. Education can correct industrialism, by giving to the mind the breadth and the fresh vitality of new interests . . .

The Scholarship problem

The problem was, however, that despite the growing liberalism within elementary school courses, the demand for secondary education still vastly exceeded the number of places available. Thus the elementary schools were forced to prepare their brighter pupils for the scholarship examinations with an increased keenness and arid single-mindedness (as demand increased and competition grew) which effectively put paid to any wider educational concerns in the relevant standards. Thus a Revised Code dehydration was reintroduced, assuming it had ever been abandoned, which almost outdid the original in the strength of its application to the older children.

The complaints expressed in the columns of the educational periodicals at this time have a surprisingly, and depressingly, familiar sound. One elementary teacher wrote to the *Journal of Education*:

> The effects of the scholarship examination upon the organisation of junior schools are quite pernicious. Where the children are divided into A and B parallel groups, the former for the brighter, the latter for the more retarded children, only with the B group can anything like a true junior technique be developed . . . It is thus impossible to secure . . . the gradual awakening of a wide range of real interests; the cultivation of taste in music, art, and literature; and the slow germination of the corporate spirit.

A most significant feature was the fact that throughout the thirties the *Teacher's World* included an LEA Scholarship paper in its weekly (and otherwise determinedly cosy) pages, with answers and notes for the benefit of teachers.

One wonders how the present-day eleven- or twelve-year-old would cope with the kind of English Scholarship paper which was common in the twenties. A useful selection from the various LEA's can be seen in F. Potter and T. Bamford's *Scholarship English*, 1926, with questions such as 'Analyse the following sentence: "Blue doves I saw and summer light on the wings of the cinnamon bee" ' (Birkenhead LEA); 'Write down two words which have the same meaning as: costly, leap, weary, sorrow, nimble' (Sheffield); 'Analyse into subject, predicate, object and extension: "I to her cottage bent my way/Beneath the evening Moon" ' (Darlington). How would today's 'O' level candidates, let alone 11-plus candidates, manage such questions as these from Bolton in 1924?

1. Analyse the following sentence: 'My brother, whom you know quite well, told me he had met you in Liverpool today'.

2. Parse the first eight words in the sentence given in question 1.

3. Make sentences containing the following words used correctly – lain, chose, bared, rung, singed, worst, sail, borne, Briton, soared.

4. Give the meaning of the following prefixes and suffixes: de, contra, ante, non, vice, post, extra, ous.

5. Try to write from four to eight lines of verse of your own. Choose, as the title any topic suggested by Spring; for example 'Birds in Spring' or 'A Spring Morning' or 'Spring Flowers'.

6. Write an essay on one of: School games; Educational Opportunities provided in Bolton for young people; 'Where There's a Will There's a Way'.

(Though whether such questions have anything more than a very tenuous link with 'English' at all is another matter.)

One also wonders just how much influence a book such as P. B. Ballard's *Teaching the Mother Tongue*, 1921, had, where (in the most extended argument up to that date – eight chapters of it) he concluded that 'There is no more reason for thinking that the ability to identify parts of speech affects a child's English, than there is for thinking that the ability to identify molars affects the mastication of his food.' Ballard's views have already been quoted as given to the 1921 Report investigators, but his own book is so important to the grammar argument that further quotation is appropriate. He reviews the arguments in support of grammar teaching. Does it improve children's writing? No. The standard of composition work in the few schools where grammar is not taught is invariably better than that produced by 'formal grammar' schools – indeed grammar knowledge and composition ability have been shown to correlate as low as 0.3 in children. Does it help pupils to understand literature? No. Is it necessary for an explanation of a pupil's errors? No. Does it teach logical thinking? Perhaps, but so can mathematics, science, geography, woodwork – any subject on the timetable. The fact is that pupils acquire correct English, not through learning grammar, but through reading, listening, speaking, and absorbing what sounds right through constant usage within a lively and generous environment of good English. It may be that older secondary pupils will benefit from some instruction in grammatical function, but Ballard's conclusion is that 'Before the age of twelve the study of grammar is demonstrably premature. Between the ages of 12 and 14 the study of the subject is possible, but scantily productive' (a conclusion which later research investigations have agreed with; W. J. Macaulay, for example, in his Scottish investigation reported as 'The difficulty of grammar' in the *British Journal of Educational Psychology* in 1947).

Another document which took an equally no-nonsense view was The English Association's 1923 Pamphlet No. 56, *The Problem of Grammar*. Taking the 1921 Report to task for its wishywashy attempt to face both ways, the contributors lay into the supporters of formal grammar teaching with gusto. S. O. Andrew also considers some of the arguments that are customarily given to support such teaching, and he has no hesitation in rejecting the idea that grammar work produces good speech and writing. As for the foreign language fallacy, this is a nonsensical legacy from the old classical school, 'a heritage which has saddled us . . . with a collection of categories and terms many of which are meaningless in English grammar, and with incredible stupidities like the exercise of parsing uninflected words. Ulterior motives are always a danger to honest teaching; in this case they have given rise to a pretentious sham education . . .' One repeats, how much influence did such pronouncements have?

The Dalton Plan and 'content' attitudes

Before leaving this battle between the progressives and the traditionalists some reference should be made to the work done under the Dalton Plan scheme. British Dalton experiments were in operation by 1920 (see Helen Parkhurst, *Education on the Dalton Plan*, 1922; Evelyn Dewey, *The Dalton Laboratory Plan*, 1922, or A. J. Lynch, *Individual Work and the Dalton Plan*, 1924). Curiously, as far as English was concerned, the Dalton work recorded is very traditional in its content approach, despite the emphasis on pupil-centred 'activity' which the scheme embodied. The idea is that pupils work on their own, look things up, shape the direction of their individual work in the 'free' environment of the subject room, but study the by now standard authors such as Scott, Longfellow, Macaulay or Gibbon. A. J. Lynch reproduces a typical specimen assignment as it would be presented to a senior elementary pupil. The poem to be studied is Byron's 'The Destruction of Sennacherib', and the pupil is directed (i) to read the account of Byron's life on p. 36 of the Literary History (ii) to read the source passage in the Bible, 2 Kings XIX (iii) to read the poem straight through (iv) to read it through again using a dictionary (v) to mark the stresses in the first verse, and (vi) to find half a dozen similes. Finally a piece of comprehension work will be given to test whether the poem has been grasped.

Now the fact is that this kind of project work is extremely limited in its application to literary study, and the inevitable falling back on the factual fodder of dates, biography and 'content' allusions (figures of speech) is unavoidable in a situation where the pupil has to be given distinct, concrete things to 'do' with the poem. This kind of correspondence course approach does not work in literary study, and is particularly unsuitable when one is dealing with young pupils. As for language work, not only is grammar included in both Lynch's and Dewey's specimen assignments, but the study method (again unavoidably) is of the worst 'underline the nouns in the following', 'fill in the gaps in these sentences' style.

Such examples of the 'factual' approach to literature teaching were all the more retrograde for the early twenties in view of the fact that literature study was definitely becoming more pointed and relevant with an increasing emphasis on a more enjoyable if disciplined and sensitive kind of reading. The new tone is to be seen in F. H. Pritchard's *Training in Literary Appreciation*, 1922, where something akin to the 'practical criticism' method of today is to be found. Various qualities of good writing are examined ('unity', 'contrast', 'rhythm') with good illustrative passages for the student to read carefully and critically in an attempt to arrive at a reasoned and careful appreciation of their sense, style and tone. This approach is a great advance on the kind of reading that looks solely for unusual vocabulary, examples of pathetic fallacy, the number of stresses per line, or the author's use of classical prefixes. Robert Finch's *The Approach to English Literature*, 1923, is even better. Finch insists that the first thing teachers have to do is to get away from the wretched influence of the External Literature Examinations, with their deadening pressure to read texts in the worst possible way. The pupil cannot read an examination book for enjoyment, but 'must dissect it, criticise it, track down allusions, explain difficulties, and cram its literary history'. Literature after all is something to enjoy, and school children obviously enjoy reading such things as 'bloods' or trivial pulp fiction; if teachers were to start from *that* basis and nudge their classes from Sexton Blake to Sherlock Holmes, from the cruder versions of space fantasy to *The War of the Worlds*, or from the banal doings of some impossible comic school to *The Fifth Form at St. Dominic's* (and from thence to real literature) then a sound basis of genuine appreciation might be laid. Let children choose (within reason) the books they would like to study, and let them have opportunity to discuss books with the teacher, rather than imposing obscure texts upon them for prosodic or rhetorical disembowelment. As for poetry, Finch wants more poetry and less teaching: 'The poem should make its own appeal, and it should make it directly, without any intervention on the part of the teacher.' (Alexander Haddow – *On the Teaching of Poetry*, 1925 – has something very similar to say; teacher and class should work together in partnership to bring the poem alive on the page, not reduce it to an unwieldy mass of particular details where, finally, the wood is lost sight of amid the mass of grammatical and prosodic trees.)

Finch's remark about External Examinations comes as no surprise. The increasing dissatisfaction with the 'content' approach to literary texts meant that the friction between some teachers of literature and the public examinations system tended to become more acute – the examinations continuing to rely upon the easily assessable materials of 'facts' (many of those irrelevant to the real business of genuine critical reading) where more and more teachers wished to move into those areas of study and appreciation that are extremely difficult, if not impossible, to assess by formal examination. A significant book was A. J. J. Ratcliff's *The Teaching of English in Upper Forms*, 1926, which is a well-argued and sensible plea for more humanised literature papers (requiring personal responses at first-hand from the candidates rather than the regurgitation of memorised generalities) and warning that 'successful' teaching, in terms of examination successes, is not always synonymous with good literature teaching. Ratcliff's argument is based on the truism that literary study that does not produce some kind of personal engagement between the pupil and the spirit of the text he is reading is largely valueless, and is a fertile ground for boredom, insincerity, and negative, anti-literature attitudes. In July 1928 the *Journal of Education* included an article, 'The teaching of English', by J. H. Arnold, in which the writer suggests that advances in English teaching are being held back more by the examination system, with its fondness for the wrong kinds of questions on the wrong kinds of texts, than by anything else. Arnold wonders whether the universities who are responsible for the papers have the least idea what the average pupil, who will not necessarily end up in a university, is like in terms of reading and critical capacity – or whether, in fact, they care.

The texts studied in the secondary schools between 1920 and 1930 did not change much from those studied before 1910 (see also the consistency of the anthologised poets listed above). The favourite authors from the teaching point of view were still Scott, Macaulay, Ruskin, Bacon, Gibbon, Carlyle, Kinglake, Sir Thomas Browne, Burke, Shakespeare, Longfellow, Tennyson, Milton and Wordsworth. Standards remained uncomfortably high – for example, the Board's 1924 *Suggestions for Secondary Teachers* recommended, in Appendix III, such authors as Gibbon, Macaulay, Holinshed, Plutarch and Southey for thirteen-and-a-half-year-olds, and Burke, Plato (*The Republic*), Newman, Cicero, Thoreau and Gibbon at sixteen years – a list which, apart from its refusal to compromise on quality or difficulty, still has a marked classical-historical slant.

Elementary school pupils continued to read 'Young Lochinvar',

'Sir Patrick Spens', 'Hiawatha', 'The Brook', 'Daffodils', 'Horatius' and *The Golden Treasury* generally (although the publication in 1923 of De la Mare's large anthology, *Come Hither*, considerably widened the scope of poetic material for younger readers) and to read the prose of the nineteenth century. In 1928 the Board's Report, *Books in Public Elementary Schools*, noted the gratifying increase in the number of books to be found in the classrooms of some of the schools, but qualified this by adding that many schools had still a long way to go with regard to book provision. (Some, as we have seen, were still depending solely on the use of readers.) The Report includes the revealing statistic that over the country as a whole less than 1 per cent of the educational expenditure per child is going on books.[32]

Other Board publications 1920–30

Up to 1926 the Board had continued to issue regularly an 'official' elementary curriculum (intended as a *guide* to teachers) but then ceased the practice. It is worth quoting the final prescribed curriculum (for pupils aged seven-plus) as a further indication of the point which the Board had reached with regard to English teaching. The study course should include:

The English Language, including practice in speaking with clear enunciation, exercises in continuous oral narration, reading for information both silently and aloud, and written composition. Throughout the course the reading books used by the children should include pieces of literary merit, some of which should be learned for recitation. In the higher classes silent reading should be the rule rather than the exception, and the scheme of instruction should include a wide course of reading under suitable guidance, with the aim of creating a capacity for systematic study, and a taste for good literature. Instruction in grammar should be confined to the higher classes. If given, it should be directed to enabling the children to understand the structure of the sentences which they speak, read, or write, and the functions of the several words in those sentences, and should be as free as possible from technicalities.

In addition to its Codes, the 1928 Report on Books, the 1921 Report, and the 1924 *Secondary Suggestions*, the Board issued two new *Handbooks of Suggestions* in 1923 and in 1927. The English section of the 1923 *Suggestions* is – with a few alterations to isolated single sentences – the same as that for 1914, despite the fact that the 1921 Report had made many of the 1914 points inappropriate or simply redundant. The 1927 English section, however, has a considerable amount of new material over the forty-seven pages, particularly in the sections on 'Poetry' and 'Reading' which have been greatly expanded and three-quarters rewritten, and in the 'Grammar' section which has been shortened and slightly modified. A much wider range of poetry and prose books than hitherto is recommended (including A. A. Milne and Beatrix Potter for infants); emphasis is placed on the need to provide a wide choice of books for individual (private) reading in the classes; teachers are told to adjust their literature schemes to the pupils' abilities and tastes ('In literature the teacher's starting point should be the reading, however rubbishy, which his scholars are doing for their own amusement out of school'); and are told that that literature must be read in a spirit of enjoyment for its own sake.

The grammar section is distinctly better than that of 1914/23, but remains very conservative in view of the development of ideas on English teaching made by such men as Cook, Ballard, or Sampson, who between them make a very impressive case for the running down of the grammar side. However discreetly the 1927 *Handbook* may advance its views ('The teacher should be careful to preserve a sense of proportion. He should avoid obsolete and burdensome pedantries, such as detailed parsing on the lines of Latin Grammar, the multiplication of arbitrary rules ... Nor should he forget that grammar was made for language, not language for grammar'[33]) the fact remains that grammar teaching is still, as far as the Board *Suggestions* are concerned, a vitally important part of the elementary school curriculum. 'The intelligent study of language will necessarily involve some teaching of grammar' and pupils must be taught their parts of speech, the inflections of those parts, and – later – the analysis of simple and complex sentences.

What, after the abundance of method material published between 1914 and 1927, has the *Handbook* to say about the rise of personal, self-expressive attitudes to writing? The following passage makes it quite clear that the developments in this field are not wholly acceptable to the Board's Committee:[34]

> It is most desirable to exercise and quicken the genuine imaginative power in children ... But the term 'imaginative composition' has in recent years generally been used to signify not descriptions of reality which are alive with imagination, but exercises in invention, such as fairy tales or imaginary autobiographies, which illustrate merely the unrestrained play of the fancy and the love of make-believe. Such exercises are very useful when fluency still needs to be acquired, but after that stage their value is not great. They are at present very popular owing to the originality which they are supposed to show and the facility with which children produce them. But their merits are apt to be overrated ...

Notes

1   *Op. cit.*, p. 14.
2   *Ibid.*, pp. 9–10.
3   *Ibid.*, p. 52.
4   *Ibid.*, p. 279.
5   *Ibid.*, pp. 278–9.
6   *Ibid.*, pp. 4–5.
7   *Ibid.*, p. 15.
8   *Ibid.*, p. 53.
9   *Ibid.*, p. 60.
10 *Op. cit.*, p. 50.
11 *Op. cit.*, p. 14.
12 *Op. cit.*, p. 45.
13 *Op. cit.*, pp. 12–13
14 *Op. cit.*, p. 20.
15 *Ibid.*, p. 16.
16 *Ibid.*, p. 105.
17 *Ibid.*, p. 24.
18 *Op. cit.*, p. 60.

19 *Op. cit.*, p. 39.
20 *Op. cit.*, p. 12 (1956 reprint).
21 *Ibid.*, pp. 89–90.
22 *Op. cit.*, pp. 7–8.
23 *The Teaching of English*, p. 81.
24 *Op. cit.*, pp. 26–7.
25 *Op. cit.*, pp. 2–3.
26 *Op. cit.*, p. 6.
27 *The Changing School*, 1925, p. 240.
28 *Op. cit.*, p. 108.
29 Quoted by G. A. N. Lowndes, *The Silent Social Revolution*, 1937, p. 119.
30 *Op. cit.*, p. 30.
31 *Op. cit.*, Preface, p. xxiv.
32 *Op. cit.*, p. 66.
33 *Op. cit.*, p. 99.
34 *Ibid.*, p. 108.

Chapter four   1930–40
Reaction – old themes for new citizens

The Primary School Report

In 1931 the Board of Education's *Report on the Primary School* (the second of the Hadow Reports) was published, its terms of reference being 'To enquire and report as to the courses of study suitable for children (other than children in Infants' Departments) up to the age of 11 in Elementary Schools . . .' In its references to English work this Report is commendably positive. Every class must have its own library, stocked with a variety of books ('mainly story books, but they should be widely chosen. Care should be taken not to press upon the children books of a kind not likely to be attractive'); suitable books should be provided for (1) oral reading (2) individual, group and class study (3) silent reading for information and enjoyment (4) for reference purposes; and the principal aim of the teacher must be to get children reading fluently 'and with pleasure'. 'Literature, in the sense of prose and verse, read or learnt *for enjoyment*, has an indispensable place . . .' (my italics) and poetry study must cease to be a matter of grammar or hunting out 'allusions'.

The Report also includes an extremely important statement concerning imaginative creativity – a statement that does much to redress the reserved balance of the 1927 *Suggestions*. 'In scientific as well as in literary and artistic work, the young child's imagination is fully capable of taking considerable flights, provided only that what is to be imagined can be pictured in concrete form. Our witnesses were of the opinion that during this age period the exercise of creative as distinct from reproductive imagination should be cultivated . . .'[1]

This is entirely in the spirit of the Report's famous comment that 'the curriculum is to be thought of in terms of activity and experience rather than of knowledge to be acquired and facts to be stored'. What we also find in the Introduction is a very strong Arnold-liberal line, quite as strong as that taken by the 1921 Report, but here applied, by the terms of reference of this Report, to the elementary school situation as a whole. Considering the nature of its task – to recommend courses of study – the Committee declares that it has used the following general criterion: 'Is their [the pupils'] curriculum humane and realistic, unencumbered by the dead wood of a formal tradition, quickened by inquiry and experiment, and inspired, not by an attachment to conventional orthodoxies, but by a vivid appreciation of the needs and possibilities of the children themselves?'[2] Significantly, special gratitude is expressed to Cyril Burt and Percy Nunn for their material assistance in the preparation of the Report (Cyril Burt has a long Appendix on child development) – both these men being well-known for their advocacy of child-centred teaching and 'individualism' in the learning situation. The investigators insist that an essential feature of education at the primary level must be 'the enlargement of the individual's horizon by contact with other minds through literature' and that first and foremost the schools must 'civilise'. They note the progress that has been made in these respects in the twenties and are pleased at what they see; 'During the last forty years, and with increasing rapidity in the twelve years since 1918, the outlook of the primary school has been broadened and humanised.'[3] Formerly the elementary system was organised as a charity for the children of the labouring poor, giving 'appropriate' instruction consequent upon that role; now, in 1931, the Report can say that the elementary school 'is on the way to become what it should be, the common school of the whole population, so excellent and so generally esteemed that all parents will desire their children to attend it.'[4] The radical change in the social context of the schools has meant that where the children were formerly taught the 3 R's (and little else) they are now taught to *live* and are taught through their own activity and interests according to their individual abilities and rates of progress.

In view of all this it must not surprise us if we find the Report taking a comparatively enlightened and progressive view of English teaching. Its one blind spot (no surprise here) is over the question of formal grammar work and, to a slightly lesser extent, over written work in the higher standards, and here it adopts a rather ponderous and almost wholly traditional stance, which, if nothing else, reveals how deeply rooted in the national consciousness grammar has become. Written work must mean the 'formal' composition, with constant practice in narrative, exposition and description; it should also mean reproduction ('of . . . the sense and substance of a passage read to the pupils'), the last exercise being termed 'This useful practice'. Good writing can only come through pupils learning an 'irreducible minimum of pure grammar' (parts of speech, cases, analysis) and the Report notes with some concern the fact that grammar teaching has declined somewhat in the elementary schools, with the result that 'the teaching of English has become weakest on its formal side.'

One gets the impression that the investigators are anxious to preserve the teaching of formal grammar for no other reason than that such teaching is customary and ought to be kept 'just in case', since they are quite prepared to admit that 'speaking generally, pupils learn to write and speak correct English by imitation' (Ballard's point) and may receive only the most marginal benefits in their written expression from grammar exercises. (With this kind of remark we seem to have arrived at the point where advocates of

formal grammar are prepared to admit that the subject has no
practical value whatsoever, but that it must still be learnt in schools
because this has been the British tradition in the past.)

It is just possible that the remarks on imaginative work in the
Report also owed something to an extremely important book published in 1930, Susan Isaacs's *Intellectual Growth in Young Children*.
Here, in a description of her work with children between two and
ten years of age at the Malting House School, the author carefully
argues the importance of fantasy and imaginative play and expression
for children, both as a means of coming to terms with their world
and of developing and shaping their individual personalities.
Imaginative expression, whatever form it takes, is an indispensable
part of intellectual and emotional growth, and children must have
freedom and opportunity to indulge in such expression. Perhaps
significantly (in view of the real lack of development in written
method at the time) she nowhere refers in the book to the possibilities of written imaginative expression for older children, but she
does discuss free, creative work in art, drama, music and physical
education. What she has to say, however, is so relevant to post-1945
creativity in all English work, that passages such as the following may
justifiably be described as blue-prints for creative methodologists.[5]

> Psycho-analytic studies of little children . . . have also shown
> that in their free dramatic play, children work out their inner
> conflicts in an external field, thus lessening the pressure of the
> conflict, and diminishing guilt and anxiety. Such a lessening of
> inner tension through dramatic representation makes it easier
> for the child to control his real behaviour, and to accept the
> limitations of the real world . . .
> [Imaginative play] is a starting point not only for cognitive
> development but also for the adaptive and creative intention
> which when fully developed marks out the artist, the novelist,
> the poet.

The child, she insists, must be seen as a whole being in a whole
environment (he is not 'recapitulating' anything) and his expression
– though childlike – has an integrity of its own.

Further reaction: conservative misgivings

The truth is, of course, that the practical and wholehearted application of such statements to the business of English teaching are never
effected overnight (one recalls Treble on the despised psychologists)
and it took something like twenty years for the uncompromisingly
child-centred thinking of Susan Isaacs to find widespread and
generally accepted creative equivalents in classroom English technique. By and large English method continued to develop more or

H

less satisfactorily but slowly through the thirties, moving at its own unhurried pace, subject to its own rather mysterious laws, with a number of the fallacies doggedly persistent.

In 1932, for example, the Association of Assistant Mistresses issued its *Memorandum on the Teaching of English*, which is a most depressing document. The classical drums are still being vigorously beaten: 'Nothing has yet supplied the discipline given by Classical studies . . . The claim of the Panel is that for the majority today the study of English language and literature must meet this need.'[6] Old English still haunts the upper forms; '. . . the English course in the Sixth Form is properly balanced only if it includes a thorough course of linguistic study with a background of Old English.'[7] Good writing, the *Memorandum* stresses, is impossible without rigorous grammar study undertaken in and for itself. The reaction against grammar teaching has gone much too far, and the cult of 'self-expression' which has taken its place has proved to be a dangerous and irresponsible retreat from reality: 'to give children of ten no other exercise than freedom to cover many pages with the chatty and imitative outpourings which they call "stories" may result in a slovenliness that no later training can cure.'[8] The climate of thought in the Association can be further estimated from the Mistresses' Spring Conference in 1933, where the view was expressed that undergraduates reading for English degrees were spending far too much time on 'literary criticism' and other fripperies when they should be reading the Greek and Latin classics as the indispensable basis for 'real' English work (the view was 'welcomed by the Conference', see *The Times Educational Supplement*, 1 April 1933). The *Memorandum* includes a list of recommended books for use in girls' schools:

At 8–11 years – The *Alice* Books, *The Water Babies*, *Peter Pan*, *Black Beauty*, *A Christmas Carol*, stories by Charlotte M. Yonge, *Little Women*, *Prester John* and Stevenson's *Child's Garden of Verses*.

At 11–12 years – Kingsley's *Heroes*, *David Copperfield*, *Lorna Doone*, *Robinson Crusoe*, *The Pilgrim's Progress*, Scott's *Marmion*, and poems by Longfellow, Macaulay and Christina Rossetti.

At 12–13 years – *Silas Marner*, Scott's novels, *Great Expectations*, Essays by W. H. Hudson, Hakluyt and the poetry of Matthew Arnold, Scott and Tennyson.

At 13–14 years – Ruskin's *Ethics of the Dust*, *Cranford*, Scott, Dickens, Spenser's *Faerie Queene*, Keats' poems, Milton's Minor Poems.

At 14-15 years – More's *Utopia*, *Eothen*, Ruskin's *Sesame and Lilies*, North's Plutarch, Carlyle's *Past and Present*, *Pride and Prejudice*, Lamb's *Elia*, Macaulay's History, Chaucer's *Prologue*, *Paradise Lost*, the poems of Wordsworth and Coleridge.

For First Certificate Literature examinations the following are recommended by the *Memorandum* as being suitable for study: Bacon, Macaulay, Carlyle, Longfellow, Kinglake, Lamb and Hazlitt. For Higher Certificate: Burke, Sir Thomas Browne (*Urn Burial*), Arnold (*Essays in Criticism*), Bacon and Langland.

In short, these authors and texts remain unchanged from 1910 and before, as do many of the basic attitudes which the Association seems to want its members to adopt. Taking this 1932 *Memorandum* together with the 1956 *Memorandum* (which is also extremely traditional in outlook) one is justified in saying that the Assistant Mistresses Association (certainly as far as its official pronouncements go) has been perhaps the most conservative of all the professional bodies with regard to English method.

This reaction against the decline in 'standards' has already been noted at the end of the twenties, and here we may pick up the threads from Treble, Davidson and Elton. The early thirties continued to see a strong line being taken against the undisciplined aimlessness which some teachers believed had set in. A very firm stand is made by Herbert E. Palmer in *The Teaching of English*, 1930 (with secondary schools in mind):[9]

> Grammar must not be neglected; and this, of course, includes old-fashioned parsing and analysis . . . The newer 'Reform' methods (employed in the secondary schools as well as in the Primary) tend to omit the hard grind and make instruction so pleasurable and easy that insufficient is acquired. Grammar should be taught and handled from the very *lowest forms* upwards . . . [his italics].

Palmer is convinced that the ability to clause-analyse will cause children to write better than they would have otherwise: 'As a result of copious reading and essay writing they may learn to express themselves tolerably well; but unless the elements of Grammar have been mastered they will hesitate too long at a difficulty, or write an obscure or ungainly sentence . . .' He offers the following as original and valuable essay topics: 'The happiest day of my Life', 'Patriotism', 'A Country Ramble', 'The life of a cat or dog', 'A stitch in time saves nine', 'Reasons for War', and 'A visit to a picture-gallery'; he suggests that teachers might on rare occasions encourage their classes to write poetry 'if only to teach the primary laws of prosody and scansion'; he believes that 'a little elementary Anglo-Saxon' will do the upper forms a power of good; he upholds the links between English and history, recommending Macaulay, Froissart, Hakluyt, Plutarch or Carlyle, and maintaining that 'English literature and history, as far as possible, should be made relative . . .'; and his lists of texts suitable for school use are familiar, to say the least. In other words, whether he was doing it deliberately or not, Palmer has dug very firmly into the entrenchments of twenty years before and is offering his readers a splendidly conservative manifesto for the thirties; if the twenties were ushered in by writers such as Dorothy Tudor Owen, Ballard, Sampson, Greening Lamborn, Tomkinson and Finch, the thirties start with Treble, Palmer and the Assistant Mistresses – the pendulum returning upon itself in the most emphatic way.

Palmer's secondary sentiments are echoed in F. F. Potter's 1930 method book for elementary teachers (with pupils in the seven to eleven years range), *English in the Junior School*, though with slightly less conservatism. Spelling is being neglected, Potter maintains, and needs 'diligent attention'; the new, freer approach to composition is all right in controlled doses, but can soon lead to carelessness and must be kept 'within proper bounds'; the anti-grammar faction has made a good case (Ballard in particular), and the 'mental training' business may well be suspect, but 'some' grammar must be taught at this age level and language lessons will only be valuable if they contain 'a fair proportion of grammatical exercises' (Potter then goes on to offer his decent minimum which includes analysis).

Yet another expression of concern at the 'serious consequences' attendant upon the neglect of grammar is to be found in the 1933 *Year Book of Education* (the section in question being by H. V. Usill) which sounds warning notes as follows:[10]

> The modern tendency in the teaching of English has been directed towards the stimulation of the imagination and 'free' composition. Grammatical construction and punctuation have been attained, if at all, quite incidentally . . . The belief that spelling and grammar could be acquired incidentally through the medium of 'free' composition has proved to be unfounded. Without a groundwork of grammar, a child is left without a standard whereby he can correct his errors . . .

The conclusion of the *Year Book* section is that the chief fault of English teaching in 1932–3 is slovenliness in pupils' speech and writing due to a failure on the part of teachers to insist upon 'drill on fundamentals'.

Pritchard and the senior schools

Despite the evident sincerity of all this, the atmosphere generated by such sentiments remains dismally negative. The one ray of positive light in method writing at the beginning of the thirties was F. H. Pritchard's *English and the New Prospect*, 1930, intended (significantly) for the senior schools. Pritchard's efforts to find a kind of English which will work successfully with non-grammar school, mixed ability children in the top classes of the 'people's' schools anticipates much post-1944 thinking, and his basic principles have become more rather than less relevant as time has gone on. The teacher in the senior school can unite all his pupils, however wide their range of ability or background, in the reading of stories and poems – literature, *appropriate* literature 'is the common ground on which all may stand' (Pritchard is imaginative enough to interpret the 1921 Report's insistence that English become the centre of the curriculum as being a reference more to literature than to grammar). The unstreamed senior school situation (post-1944 read 'modern' situation) demands its own English approach and Pritchard takes several important steps towards providing it. Let the teacher read exciting and spirited narrative to the children – Dodd's fight with the pirates (*Hard Cash*, Reade), Jeremy Stickles in danger (*Lorna Doone*), the Flight in the Heather (*Kidnapped*), the chariot race (*Ben Hur*), Marmion's escape, Dantès' escape from the Château d'If, the attack on Newgate (*Barnaby Rudge*), 'The Red Thread of Honour' (Doyle). Let the pupils write about such incidents ('writing naturally and without restraint') in prose or verse, and let them also write stories, diaries, autobiographies, parables, fables, advertisements, plays or character sketches. In addition to this the job of the English teacher, according to Pritchard, is not just to hand out the figures and parts of speech and the tricks of analysis, and he is not rejecting the teaching of these, but to create 'awareness' in children, sensitive awareness of sights, sounds and experiences generally: 'The aims of all our work in English may be summed up in these two words – expression and appreciation.'[11]

Evidence suggests that Pritchard's views were shared by at least some senior school teachers; when A. J. Jenkinson made his survey of pupils' reading in 1940 he found that a much more realistic approach to literature work was being taken in the senior schools as compared with the grammar schools, with the inclusion of modern and less heavyweight texts for study chosen primarily for their appeal to this age and ability range and not because they happened to be part of examination tradition.

Textbooks: little change

Perhaps it was alarms such as those of Palmer or the *Year Book* that kept a steady flow of grammars and grammar-based textbooks in the by now fixed style coming throughout the thirties – the similarity of these to each other being exceeded only by their similarity to the textbooks of the first two decades of the century. A representative list could include: A. R. Moon and G. H. McKay, *A New English Course*, 1931; W. Kerr, *The English Apprentice*, 1932; H. Hothersall, *English Composition*, 1932; F. F. Potter, *Common Sense English Course*, 1932; L. Tipping, *Matriculation English Grammar*, 1933; T. V. Davies, *A Junior English Class Book*, 1934; R. W. Jepson, *English Exercises for School Certificate*, 1935; M. Alderton Pink, *An English Course for Schools*, 1935; A. F. and L. A. Davies, *A Modern English Grammar*, 1936; or E. E. Allen and A. T. Mason, *An English Grammar of Function*, 1939.

The grammar-composition link-up was carefully maintained, likewise the imitative approach to composition work. C. J. Brown in *The Writing of Prose and Verse in School*, 1931, uses model passages for the pupils (eleven to twelve years) to study and imitate, and R. K. Polkinghorne (*Easy Steps in English Composition*, 1931) actually reproduces short prose extracts for younger pupils to copy out to 'improve' their English.

Composition continued to be approached through a succession of separate, bitty exercises in filling out given outlines, paraphrasing filling in gaps in sentences, or literally copying from the textbook. Pupils continue to be 'prepared' for writing (very rarely doing any) with word-phrase-clause work of a comprehensive and detailed nature (E. J. Kenny, *An English Course for Juniors*, 1931; A. Huntley, *English Composition*, 1933; S. C. Glassey, *A Progressive Course in English Composition*, 1936).

Perhaps it is significant that two thoroughly good textbooks from this time (exceptions to these prevailing attitudes) have a Canadian and Australian background respectively. B. C. Diltz, *Models and Projects for English Composition*, 1933, is concerned with the craft of writing, that is, how best to construct a short story, a book review, a newspaper report, and he encourages pupils to find out by trying this kind of writing for themselves, comparing their achievements with those of the professional. Difficult though it may be to sustain this kind of approach with children, the 'craft' way which turns the composition room into a literary workshop is far more to the point than a prolonged series of exercises on the semi-colon or subordinate clauses. America, as noted already, had been using this approach to school composition for some time; its appearance in Britain had been limited to a few excellent textbooks such as O'Grady's or to the recommendations of a handful of first-rate method writers, and it had made little enough headway against the grammar-based formal essay of the secondary school.

E. G. Biaggini in *The Reading and Writing of English*, 1936 – a book intended for sixth formers – presents the pupils with prose extracts of varying quality (a piece of D. H. Lawrence contrasted with a cosmetic advertisement) for the pupils to read and evaluate by the 'practical criticism' method (Biaggini was a product of the Richards-Leavis Cambridge, and the book has a Foreword by Leavis) – the exercise leading on to a discussion of what makes good or bad writing and what the good writer will avoid.

The thirties certainly saw the exam-based textbook achieving new heights of thoroughness, some might say nastiness, but one is left with the feeling that it all has very little to do with English in the sense of using, or responding to, one's language across a range of styles or emotions. Reading through a book such as Dudley Bateman's *One Hundred and Seventy-Five English Scholarship Tests*, 1938, the whole business takes on the air of something strangely detached, an objective tester's nightmare, where a pupil's capacity to use or respond is supposedly to be estimated from the answers to such questions as: 'Write complete sentences containing (i) a second personal pronoun (ii) a Weak Verb in the Subjunctive (iii) an Adverbial Clause of Concession (iv) a Proper Noun in the Possessive Case . . .'; 'What do these initials stand for: C.L., N.S.P.C.C., A.F.A , R.D.C., Y.M.C.A. ?'; 'Name one work by each of the following (1) P. G. Wodehouse (2) Conan Doyle (3) Geoffrey Chaucer (4) Sir Walter Scott (5) Dr. Johnson'; 'Copy down these words and underline in each the syllable which has the Main Accent: scintillate, scrupulous, appanage, perquisite, exquisite'; 'Complete: "red sky at night...", "to err is...", "let the shoemaker stick..." '

The School Certificate equivalents of these are to be seen in R. W. Jepson's *English Exercises for School Certificate*, 1935 (reprinted eight times by 1944), e.g., 'Identify the figures of speech in the following: "Miss Mix scratched her head and a tin canister", "See Pan with flocks, with fruits Pomona crowned", "There are too few Solomons on the Bench" '; 'Write not more than ten lines of prose incorporating the following words in suitable contexts: mutual, divulge, palpable, debar, gratuity, salutary, amenable, acquiesce'; 'How would you classify the following works in English Literature: *Gulliver's Travels*, *The Lady of the Lake*, *The Ancient Mariner*, *Adonais*, *The Faerie Queene* . . . ?'

It is not so much that English has suffered as a principal 'testing' subject as that the testers have worked out something which has nothing whatsoever to do with English at all and foisted the monster on to the education system at large; such questions may be excellent tests of memory, of one's grasp of cliché metaphors and proverbs, of one's knowledge of fine but (for an eleven-year-old) rather useless words ('panatrope', 'appanage', 'apostate', 'prohibition'), but as tests of ability in the writing and reading of English as a medium of expression and communication they are largely useless. Worse, one knows that behind these questions lay the inevitable reduction of the prospective candidate's English lessons to a succession of learnings by heart, 'spotting', and 'practice speed tests'. It is surely time for this General Knowledge Quiz approach to English to be given the brush-off it deserves.

English and the School Certificate

When one reads through the language and literature papers of the Examining Boards from 1920 to 1960 an astonishing degree of continuity and sameness is revealed. All the Boards had established their particular patterns by 1925; from that time on the same set books, the same kinds of questions, the same general approach to the subject-matter all appear with unfailing regularity (the 1951 change from School Certificate to GCE included). An 'O' level English candidate of the early sixties would find the papers for the twenties almost unremarkable in their familiarity. He might find that the grammar questions of the twenties were a little more pedantic, the questions on the set books tending to the biographical-historical rather than to the critical, but the general pattern, content, and feel of the papers would be the same.

In 1932-3 the set books for the First Certificate in literature were as follows:

BRISTOL: a Shakespeare play and a book of prose (selected essays or *Abbot Sampson*); *She Stoops to Conquer* or *Samson Agonistes*; *Sigurd the Volsung* or *Poems of Today*; *Henry Esmond* or *A Tale of Two Cities*; Stevenson's *Travels with a Donkey*.

LONDON: a Shakespeare play; *The Golden Treasury* III or IV or *Paradise Lost* I and II; North's Plutarch or *Eothen* or Lamb's Essays; selections from the Bible or from Dryden.

DURHAM: a Shakespeare play; selections from Wordsworth or from Browning's *Men and Women*; Hazlitt's essays or *Eothen*; two of *Northanger Abbey, Villette, Quentin Durward, Barnaby Rudge*; *She Stoops to Conquer*; *News from Nowhere* (William Morris).

OXFORD: a Shakespeare play; a poetry anthology or *The Nonnes Preeste's Tale*; one of *The Pilgrim's Progress*, Lamb's Essays, *The English Admirals*.

CAMBRIDGE: a Shakespeare play; *Spectator* selections; Conrad's *The Rover*; Milton's sonnets or *Samson Agonistes*; Keats selections.

For the Higher Certificate some Boards were still setting a special period for study (Bristol and London, for example); favourite Higher Certificate set books and authors among the various Boards include: *The Faerie Queene*, Marlowe's *Faustus*, Bacon's Essays, Sidney's *Apologie for Poetrie*, Hakluyt, *The New Atlantis*, Shakespeare, Chaucer, Milton, Lamb, Carlyle, Pope, Dryden, Scott and the Romantic poets. These texts and authors changed hardly at all between 1930 and 1950 (and represent a very similar situation to that of 1900–10). The Cambridge Board, for example, set Milton (*Comus, Lycidas, Samson Agonistes* or books of *Paradise Lost*) in 1935, 1942, 1946, 1950 (selecting years at random); Bacon's Essays in 1930, 1935, 1937, 1940, 1942, 1946, 1950; Sidney's *Apologie* in 1930, 1935, 1937, 1940, 1942, 1946 and 1950.

If anything the First Certificate papers change even less, with the identical essay topics of the twenties still appearing in the fifties for some Boards. By 1920 the basic pattern of the language paper was essay and summary (or précis), with additional tests of paraphrase, letter writing, vocabulary, correction of sentences, analysis, figures of speech, etc. In the summer of 1926 the Joint Oxford and Cambridge Board set essay, précis, and such questions as: 'Write a letter', 'Paraphrase', 'Distinguish between the following pairs – judicious/judicial . . .', 'Correct the following incorrect sentences . . .', 'Explain: Crossing the Rubicon, Gordian Knot', 'Explain: alliteration, bathos . . .'. This format remains unchanged, with the exception of the later introduction of a comprehension passage (or comprehension questions on the précis passage) in each of the fourteen annual summer papers from 1927 to 1940 (inclusive) and is still unchanged in 1949, 1951 and 1952. The essay titles for 1949 are: 'Neighbours', 'A Cathedral', 'The Good Old Days' and 'Gardens', though in 1951 the candidates are offered the alternative of writing a short story or character sketch.

The London First Certificate Language paper for summer 1925 includes an essay, an exercise in reported speech, analysis (not compulsory), correcting incorrect sentences and a question on the meaning of such aphorisms as 'to bury the hatchet' or 'beat around the bush'. This pattern remains unchanged for 1930 (précis now included), 1935, 1940, 1951 (comprehension now included), 1956, 1958 and 1960. London established a separate (First Certificate) literature paper in 1920; before this language and literature had appeared together, with – by present standards – some extremely easy literature questions. For summer 1919 we find: 'Describe briefly the subject matter of the following: *The Rape of the Lock, The Compleat Angler, Maud, The Eve of St Agnes . . .*'; 'Describe the plot of the First Book of *The Faerie Queene*'; 'Select one novel of any author for appreciation and give reasons for your judgment.' (Once again we see the combination of difficult set texts – the *Faerie Queene*, for example – and easy questions which could probably be answered at second-hand with the material from some summarised history of literature.)

The London literature questions remained slightly off-key for some time; the 1925 set texts included *The Golden Treasury*, *Paradise Lost* (selected books), Tennyson selections, More's *Utopia* and selected prose of Hazlitt and Macaulay, and questions still reveal confusion with history – for example (of Jonson): 'Illustrate from the play contemporary habits and customs in striking contrast with those of our own day' or (of a study of selected Old Testament passages) with philology: 'State briefly the meaning and origin of each of the following names: Edom, Mahanaim, Jacob, Bethel, Israel, Succoth.' For 1930 the set texts and authors include Milton, *Utopia*, Macaulay and a question on Gibbon such as 'Contrast the social life of Rome in the 5th and 12 centuries.' (The Northern Board was doing the same thing; in the Higher Certificate literature papers for 1925 we find: 'Set down and discuss what you have learned from 18th century essays concerning either the Amusements or the Religion of the period.')

After 1930 the London questions come more to the point, requiring more genuine literary responses from the candidates. The set texts do not change much, however, with Macaulay, Lamb and Gibbon appearing regularly; in 1951 we find *The Golden Treasury*, *Paradise Lost*, and Carlyle's *Past and Present*, and the London 'A' paper for 1968 has in it many of these pre-1920 favourites, including *The Faerie Queene*, *Religio Medici*, Hazlitt, Scott and Tennyson – although by now there are alternative syllabuses and a much wider choice of authors both traditional and modern for the candidates.

Some of the oddest questions that come to light are: 'How do you account for the meagre output of Gray's genius?' (London Higher, 1919); 'With what measure of truth did Wordsworth say of Milton "Thy soul was like a star and dwelt apart"?' (London Higher, 1925); 'Who were the dominant literary figures in 1660, 1700, 1740 and 1780 respectively?' (Joint Matric. Higher, 1922); 'Write notes on three of the following – (a) Browning's rhymes (b) Tennyson's blank verse (c) Browning's humour (d) Tennyson's politics (e) Carlyle's etymologies (f) the Scot in Stevenson (g) Stevenson's stylistic devices' (Joint Matric. Higher, 1925).

It may be that the conclusions one can draw from such a survey are not very spectacular, but at least a picture emerges of a stable, almost rigid structure that has dominated secondary English teaching for over fifty years. All teachers know that the examination pattern has been fixed for some time, but the actual lack of change of any kind over so long a period, and involving so many pupils, is still surprising. The point is not that Tennyson's poems, Scott's novels or Bacon's essays are not suitable for school examination study (though it is impossible to get round the fact that some books most certainly *are* unsuitable at this level – *Religio Medici* or *Sartor Resartus*, say) but that the dependence upon these has remained immovably constant over far too long a period in the face of numerous possible alternatives. Why do Hardy, Wells, Conrad, Shaw, Mark Twain, Kipling, Wilde, Yeats – or for that matter George Eliot or Jane Austen – not appear more often in syllabuses after 1915?

It is useless to pretend that the School Certificate 'is not intended to dictate secondary courses'; whatever its original purpose it has long-since come to do just that, with the consequent implication (utterly false) that 'English' at secondary level means only that which constitutes Certificate English and its neat, enclosed world of précis, formal essay, grammar, Scott, Dickens, Milton, Bacon and Carlyle. If the nineteen-sixties have seen some remarkable advances by some of the Boards (including the introduction of continuous assessment, candidates taking texts into the examination with them, and the introduction of many new – often contemporary – authors) the fact remains that this particular ship has been stuck fast for far too long.

Throughout the twenties and thirties there was a constant flow of examination criticism from secondary teachers in the columns of the educational press – the summer attack on the First Certificate essay topics becoming almost an annual event. For example, in July, August and September 1925, a heated exchange between teachers and examiners can be followed in *The Times Educational Supplement*. A school master lists the essay titles set in the London Certificate that summer – 'London in Literature', 'The Thames in History', 'Mountaineering', 'The Progress of Science' and 'Why have women been so successful as novelists?' and expresses indignation at their unsuitability. He was heartily supported by another correspondent ('English specialists in secondary schools observe with growing dismay the persistent refusal of the General School Examiners to conform to the enlightened principles of English teaching which were authoritatively set out in the memorable report on the teaching of English in England') and by the *Journal of Education* which came out strongly against the examiners in an August editorial. The ritual was repeated in 1926, 1928 and 1932, the Examining Boards, however, remaining aggressively unrepentant. In 1926 one Board, having set two books of *The Golden Treasury*, asked questions exclusively on the minor or comparatively unknown poets in those books. One teacher wrote indignantly to the *Supplement* in July: 'Such stupidity in examining methods makes one despair of the future of English literature in English schools. It would seem as though examiners were doing their best to kill interest in the subject, both of teachers and pupils.'

During the thirties this kind of frank criticism continued; E. E. Reynolds (*An English Syllabus*, 1931) gives the impression that he and all conscientious English teachers are struggling under the weight of the examination requirements – 'good work is possible up to the exam year', 'Exams ruin poetry teaching', 'the best teacher may not want the examination class'. Philip (by now Sir Philip) Hartog in his article on the nature of the examination essay in *Essays on Examinations*, 1936 (published by the International Institute Examinations Enquiry) points out that with recurring topics of the traditional sort, such as 'Trees', 'Gossip' or 'The Good Old Times' candidates are simply being asked to 'Write anything about something for anybody'. The insincere stock responses of the 1890s are still required.

The Spens Report in 1938 even goes so far as to suggest that the study of set literary texts for examination purposes should cease. (Spens, remember, was concerned with grammar and technical high schools.) The Report does not denigrate literary study – on the contrary, its great value is 'universally admitted' and the Committee is anxious that English should become the 'unifying principle' in the curriculum – but is attempting to put what passes for literary study in the examination setting out of its misery.

> We have . . . grave doubts as to whether books should be used and studied at this stage in the manner that is necessary if English literature is to be an examination subject. We believe that prescribed books do more to injure the growth of a budding sentiment for literature than to encourage it, and therefore recommend *that books should no longer be prescribed in the School Certificate Examination* [their italics, p. 175].

If the external examination disappears, the teacher will be free to teach texts with 'only one purpose in view' – that of genuine appreciation.

There are, obviously, aspects of English work which can be examined (such as the ability to write in a clear, coherent way) and the Report is not opposed to external examinations as such. It does, however, add a telling comment:

> *we hold that in several important respects the influence of the examination and the process of preparation for it are inimical at present to the healthy growth in mind and body of a large number of children who pass through the Grammar School* [their italics, p. 256].

One wonders whether perhaps the Spens recommendations, sincere as they are, do not constitute an attempt to throw the baby out with the bathwater. As an alternative, could not candidates for the literature exams conceivably nominate their own texts out of a selection given to them? Could they perhaps be set better kinds of questions? Could not standards be compromised slightly in an attempt to get at the interests of intelligent young school pupils?

Could the texts be taken into the examination room to overcome the tedious emphasis on memory, where candidates are incapable of getting down to any real appreciation because they are chock full of 'useful' points which they must get down as quickly as possible (irrespective of the question) before they forget them? The Report does not explore such obvious possibilities.

While on the subject of this Report it is interesting to see how things have progressed in school English generally since 1921. This is how Spens sees it in 1938: 'we are convinced that English . . . does not yet hold that position in the studies of secondary schools to which it is entitled. For a subject which is in our view of such central importance there seems to be still too much indecision as to the main objective to be achieved . . .'[12] (it was still possible at this time under the grouping system to acquire a School Certificate without a pass in English; English was not made compulsory for a First Certificate pass until 1939).

One extremely important article on the whole examination business was that of L. C. Knights in *Scrutiny*, September 1933 ('Scrutiny of Examinations'). Knights refers to the massive numbers of candidates (in 1918, 22,873 had sat the Certificate examinations for all Boards; in 1924, 49,343; in 1931, 66,909 – see the Secondary School Examinations Council's 1932 Report), he refers to the need for marking procedures that are standardised and rapid, and to the consequent abuse done to literature by questions which fit these requirements. School literature work becomes cramming, memorising, a rejection of all that is not 'on the course'. Knights sees only one solution – abolition. 'Since the damage done to education by external "standardizing" examinations is so gross, obviously pervasive and inescapable, the time has come to press, firmly, for their abolition.'[13] He implies that the system cannot now fundamentally change, since it is its own cumbersome organisational victim – and certainly events go some way to supporting this part of his argument.

The problem of essay marking

An attack from another direction which gained momentum after 1930 was the questioning of the reliability of essay marking. In *An Examination of Examinations*, 1935, Sir Philip Hartog and E. C. Rhodes showed how different examiners could place the same examination essay anywhere between 28 per cent and 80 per cent reducing, in the opinion of the investigators, the Certificate essay to a nonsense. Other candidates (these were for the Durham Certificate) received marks ranging between 19 and 58, 37 and 71, 38 and 70 (per cent). Earlier a smaller investigation carried out by C. Roberts and H. Briscoe had been reported in the IAAM journal

AMA with similar conclusions (see the *AMA* for December 1931, and February 1932) and in 1933 G. Perrie Williams had published his attempt at a standardised marking scheme in *The Northamptonshire Composition Scale*, which worked on the basis of awarding separate marks for ideas, vocabulary, sentence structures and 'mechanics'.

Other energetic attempts to find a reliable method of marking followed, including the publication of similar detailed schemes to overcome the vagaries of individual bias. J. H. Steel and J. Talman, for example, produced a scheme in 1936 (in their *The Marking of English Composition*) which uses clusters of pluses and minuses as applied to vocabulary, content, sentence structure, sentence linking and so on, and assesses each essay with standardised criteria. Thorough as the Steel-Talman method is, the framework is still too limited to cope successfully with the enormous variety of styles which school pupils are capable of producing even within the formal confines of the traditional essay.

What also emerges from the comments of the time is the fact (and it would account for part of the confusion) that examiners were completely divided over the matter of awarding marks for originality. While some gave extra marks for the writer's imagination and inventiveness – not inconsiderable qualities with the kinds of essay titles that were going the rounds – others did not award such marks, or indeed penalised the candidate for presumption.

For a time at least it seems that the essay was in real danger of being dropped from the Language examination. The Board of Education's *Supplementary Memoranda on Examinations for Scholarships and Special Places in Secondary Schools*, 1936, states: 'No one doubts the value of instruction in composition as part of the school curriculum in English; but in view of the evidence as to the unreliability of essay questions as part of the examination, hesitation is felt in recommending the inclusion of such questions.'[14] We also find P. B. Ballard (*Teaching and Testing English*, 1939) making a similar point: 'The written essay is the traditional means of testing a pupil's progress in English. And the essay as a means of measurement has proved a broken reed.'[15]

Little wonder that research interest in the marking problem was considerable at this time – see as representative investigations the following accounts in the *British Journal of Educational Psychology*: B. M. D. Cast, 'The efficiency of different methods of marking English composition', February 1940; R. L. Morrison and P. E. Vernon, 'A new method of marking English composition', June 1941; S. Wiseman, 'The marking of English composition', November 1949; and later D. S. Finlayson, 'The reliability of the marking of essays', June 1951. All which research, though not entirely satisfactory, does in fact indicate that impression marking is as good a method as analytical marking (awarding points for specific features) particularly when two or more examiners can confer on the same piece, and that such marking is by no means as inaccurate as is commonly believed. In any case, the essay remained a central feature of the examination, with some, by no means all, Boards adopting a policy of analytical marking. Present critics of the 'O' level language papers might well say that the doubts raised by Hartog, Rhodes, and others in the thirties have even now not been satisfactorily answered.

Creative pressures: pupils' verse writing

Through the thirties the advocates of a more creative approach, particularly with regard to English in the elementary schools, continued to exert pressure on educational opinion. Finch and C. W. Kimmins in *The Teaching of English and Handwriting*, 1932, are convinced that creative work can be successful and that the outcry over declining standards is ill-founded.[16]

> The very great difficulty in the way of creative work in the schools does not lie in the inability of the children. Creative power, in measure, is possessed by probably all children; but all teachers have not recognised its nature, all teachers are not prepared to welcome its manifestations, and very few teachers have developed a technique for encouraging its expression.

Finch and Kimmins include under their list of creative activities 'Reading to deepen inner experiences' and 'Writing to express feeling and to communicate experience in a free situation'. They quote the example of the Czech artist, Cizek, in support of the freedom principle, Cizek obtaining striking and original paintings and drawings from children by allowing them complete freedom to create as they wanted. They are convinced (and they refer to Caldwell Cook's achievements in passing) that children can produce painted and written work of 'high artistic quality'. At times they come close to Susan Isaacs in recognising the 'therapeutic' value in encouraging imaginative expression:[17]

> Some teachers, who have asked children to write dreams as composition exercises, have found that the exercise is far superior as English work . . . [Clearly] there is an aspect of the child's life, ordinarily ignored in the school, but perhaps of as great value as the intellectual aspects of his life, which he wants to express but has few opportunities of expressing. The teacher of English . . . can help him to expression, and thus give him opportunities of development such as can be afforded by few.

This line of thought, and it anticipates much post-1950 thinking, was further strengthened by Ruth Griffiths's *A Study of Imagination in Early Childhood*, which appeared in 1935. From her work with young children she is convinced that fantasy is literally a means whereby the child learns, solves problems and adjusts to environmental pressures and influences. Indulging in fantasy – and *expressing* that fantasy – is not a trivial activity (as many teachers would say) but is a vitally important aspect of child education. Through free drawing and free writing children can express in fantasy symbol what they would not find easy to express otherwise, with consequent therapeutic value.

Nevertheless, far too many teachers were still very wary of 'imagination'; 'imagination and its near relative – intuition – are qualities underrated by most teachers, and perhaps by the civilization to which we belong', commented the Society for Teachers of English in 1937: 'We, as educators, train the intellect, and hope that then all will be well. But intelligence itself is not merely intellect, it is not merely the capacity to reason, but the ability to feel rightly.'[18] This is reminiscent of some of D. H. Lawrence's pronouncements on education, and once again we are moving into a long-standing and distinguished Romantic tradition, which includes Blake and Dickens among its most articulate and convincing spokesmen. How many teachers of English in the thirties who were prepared to uphold the distinctive genius of Blake considered a practical application of his Imaginative philosophy to their English work with children? How many teachers of English who have been moved by the opening chapter of *Hard Times* have considered, say, the teaching of grammatical minutiae or other 'useful' material in the light of what Dickens is really getting at? It may well be that our approach to education has been weighted on the 'factual' side (also relevant to this argument is Margaret Phillips's *The Education of the Emotions*, 1937, and more recently Ruth Mock's *Education and the Imagination*, 1970), but the point made by Finch and Kimmins above is also important; many teachers who were prepared to give creative work a try found it difficult to devise new methods to make the experiments successful over long periods of time. Where these methods were evolved, general advances soon followed, and one example of this is the appearance after 1930 of children's poetry work in free verse form (as opposed to the strict rhyming scansion with all its prosodic paraphernalia mostly used hitherto) which by its very nature put an end to the misconception that children should write poetry merely to show off their acquired knowledge of prosodic points and not as a means to actual personal expression. As with the shift in emphasis in composition (from grammar display to personal statement) this rise of free verse in schools embodied a whole new attitude to expression and reversed the form-content priority established hitherto in verse work. Since 1945 the emphasis has been almost entirely on the free verse pattern in schools, and it is clear that pupils can produce better material when they are not tied down to a rhyme scheme or metrical framework (though many junior children still seem to feel cheated in the early stages of their own writing 'if it doesn't rhyme').

In 1931 C. J. Brown included an appendix on free verse writing in his *The Writing of Prose and Verse in School* (also printing the free verse poem of an eleven-year-old). Most of Brown's poetry material in the main body of the book assumes a prosodic, scansion approach, which makes his final, encouraging, postscript on a free form all the more interesting. The Society for Teachers of English was enthusiastically advocating free form in 1937, and Norman Callan does the same in *Poetry in Practice*, 1938 (also reproducing a specimen poem by a pupil).

In the debate between the scanners and non-scanners a more fundamental belief found itself – for the first time in the century – being taken for granted generally, the belief that writing poetry is a valuable and useful exercise for all pupils, to be encouraged whenever possible as part of the writing course. This is not to say that the 'prosodic' approach with its classically derived scansion patterns did not continue, but it tended to take second place to freer forms after 1930; it is probably true to say that not until the late fifties and sixties (with books such as Margaret Langdon's *Let the Children Write*, 1961) was a sound practical basis for free verse writing made available to teachers generally, but certainly free verse exercises were being tried out by some teachers in the thirties (see also Nancy Catty's article 'Creative work in verse and prose' in the *Teacher's World*, December 1935).

In a 1932 (December) *Journal of Education* article J. L. Bradbury suggests that unless secondary pupils are allowed to try their hand at a wide range of prose and poetry styles (and not just the difficult, artificial and exclusively prose style of the essay) they will not be able to study literature with anything approaching real understanding ('A pupil learns more about rhythm and cadence from writing five lines of verse, however poor, than from scanning fifty'). Another small piece of research concerning poetry writing was reported in the *British Journal of Educational Psychology*, 1 February 1933 by Kathleen Leopold, 'The effect of creative work on aesthetic appreciation'. She had set out to determine whether training college students who practised poetry writing exhibited a better mastery over the study of poetry and poets generally than students who merely read. She concluded that writing was a great aid to general literary appreciation.

The year 1939 saw a very important publication which in effect brought children's own poetry writing of age, and this was the two-

I

hundred-page anthology of children's poems, stories and drawings, *First Fruits*, edited by Norman Morris and published by the Oxford University Press. Excluding the *Perse Playbooks*, which in any case had had a relatively small circulation, this was the first full-scale anthology of children's writing presented in its own right. There have been many such anthologies since, but it was *First Fruits* that proved beyond question the validity of this kind of publication. The poems, from children aged seven to fifteen years in ninety-eight elementary schools all over the country, are for the most part rhyming and in strict metres, and the 'doth's' and 'hath's' are still there, but the general quality of the writing is lively and original in spirit if somewhat literary in style. Whether or not the style of the material reflects the newer free verse, or the older prosody approach, is an insignificant detail compared with the fundamental importance of the book – that importance residing quite simply in the fact that children's writing was now considered (by a reputable and influential publishing company) to be worthy of publication for its own sake. The book is very much a vindication of the creative approach, as Alec Clegg's later *The Excitement of Writing* is, and in an introductory note Eveline Lowe, then Chairman of the LCC, draws attention to this point:

> I think it will be discovered that . . . children who are allowed to write freely – without fear of too much correction – or shall I say the conscious trying to satisfy an adult point of view, come to enjoy writing, and feel towards that exercise something of the satisfaction that creative effort can produce.
> Just as the making of pictures helps some children to become articulate, so writing may be the most helpful medium for others provided their spontaneity is not checked . . . and it is pleasant to believe that the days of copious red ink spread over the page of the work of a child who has made a happy effort are over. It may be worth while to add the reminder that the *enjoyment* of writing, if it can be acquired in early years, may be a priceless possession in time to come.

Achievements in the elementary schools

Even the Board of Education's 1937 *Suggestions* went some way towards justifying the creative approach, quietly dropping the 1927 strictures on 'imaginative composition' and advocating quantity as a means to quality, freedom and enjoyment as a means to genuine literary discipline. The *Suggestions* will not relinquish grammar work entirely, but come surprisingly close to such a viewpoint: 'Such grammatical work as is introduced should arise naturally from actual speech, writing and reading in the work of the class, rather than consist of formal exercises in abstract grammar. Experience tends to show that such exercises have not much value for giving command of the native tongue, which comes rather through imitation and practice';[19] 'It is only by direct contact with the spoken and written language that the teaching of Grammar can be redeemed from the unreality and sterility which have so often accompanied its teaching in the past ... *There is no need whatever for a separate Grammar lesson in the Junior School, and very little need for written grammatical exercises*'[20] (my italics). The Board's grammatical pronouncements have certainly advanced at (for them) a prodigious pace in ten years.

It is of these 1937 *Suggestions* that Charles Birchenough in his revised *History of Elementary Education* (third edition 1938) writes: 'If the difference in the education represented by the editions of 1905 and 1927 [the *Handbooks of Suggestions*] is striking, that between 1905 and 1937 is so great as to constitute a new order.' To read just the General Introduction to these new 1937 *Suggestions* is to find a breadth of outlook and concern for the real educational priorities which is very satisfactory. Sections deal, for example, with the 'Changing conceptions of education', with the 'Increasing importance attached to individual differences among children', with the 'Changed conception of discipline in recent years', and with 'The gradual widening of the Elementary School tradition'. In this Introduction are to be found such comments as: 'We realise more and more the importance of broadening the aims of education and of placing greater emphasis on the social development of children' (p. 7), or 'the aim of education should be to develop to the full the potentialities of every child at school' (p. 12). The battle in the junior schools (to establish an environment where creative method can flourish) is now seemingly won; no doubt a substantial number of teachers in 1937 still adhered to traditional formalism and the grammar-based text-book, but they appear to have become a minority (a large minority) of followers rather than leaders initiating and controlling overall elementary curriculum policy. The schools, in fact, are now ready to develop the kind of English work which distinguishes the period after 1950, and it is they who are to set the creative pace for the rest of the State system. The 1937 *Suggestions* go some considerable way in preparing the ground:[21]

> The child at the Junior School stage is by nature neither introspective nor reflective and does not take kindly to the bookish study of poetry. He wants to be up and doing, and to savour the rhythm, the language and the sentiment of the poetry he likes through active forms of expression: reading it aloud, saying it aloud, chanting it in chorus or even dramatising it; he may even be impelled by his enjoyment of it to compose verse of his own. This will do more to awaken his power of

appreciation than either the mere compulsory committing to memory of poems considered good for him, or the elaborate study of the printed word.

One must, of course, see the success of the elementary schools in terms wider than that of actual classroom method; Sir Fred Clarke, writing in 1940 (*Education and Social Change*), is convinced that 'a genuine popular philosophy of education' has at last been evolved in the elementary schools and that 'the mass of English people' has finally created a school system of its own, 'the instrument of its own clearly conceived social and cultural purposes'.[22] With its 'comprehensive' structure, liberal-humane studies, and pupil-centred attitudes, the elementary school can be said to be near achieving a long-sought ideal – 'near' because the influence of examinations is still to be reckoned with. What is also beginning to emerge in the writings of men like Sir Fred Clarke is a concern not so much with the kind of 'culture' one associates with Matthew Arnold, but with the idea of a new 'popular' culture which shall replace the old ('élitist') concept. It is true that Clarke, like Arnold, is concerned with the need to create 'social cohesion', but his cultural ideal exhibits a tendency to emphasise and rely upon the present (or even the future, compare Dewey) rather than upon the heritage and guidance of the past. Of course the 'masses' must be involved in culture, but they have a right to decide what form that 'culture' shall take (a contradiction in terms?) and their decision will be based on their experience of life as they live it. Thus, while the *general* spirit of Arnold's liberalism is still valid, the actual details of his programme with its emphasis upon the excellence of the past become increasingly inappropriate in a thirties society – or so the upholders of the 'popular' culture would say. A point has seemingly been reached where Arnold's specific hopes for the masses (the ladder up which education has been slowly climbing to its present point) are no longer entirely relevant and can be kicked away; to quote Clarke again (1940) 'The choice lies between a world which, like Aldous Huxley's *Brave New World*, has surrendered its hold upon real culture in order that it may apply techniques to the more exquisite satisfaction of animal appetites, and a world which adapts its techniques to the enrichment and wider dissemination of a *growing contemporary* culture'[23] (my italics). This tension between the ideal of a 'popular' as opposed to an 'élitist' culture has been particularly strong in the secondary schools since 1945, not least in the discussion as to what should or should not constitute literary study, and here we may turn our attention to one of the most outspoken advocates of the 'minority culture' theory, F. R. Leavis.

The New Criticism: Richards and Leavis

It is in the thirties that the 'New Criticism' begins to make itself felt in the secondary schools. The New Critical movement, associated with the names of T. S. Eliot, I. A. Richards and later with William Empson, Leavis and *Scrutiny*, had already begun its electric transformation of university English studies before 1930; the impact upon sixth-form English study (and indeed upon undergraduate study as a whole) inevitably took longer, but by the mid-thirties there are clear indications that the New Critical approach, with its emphasis on close, intelligent and sensitive reading in the 'practical criticism' situation, is being established in schools. Perhaps for the first time literary texts were put unequivocably at the centre of literary study with historical-biographical detail only just bringing up the rear or disappearing from view completely; at school level the superficial irrelevancies of 'allusion hunting', extensive biographical background, generalisation about genres and 'tendencies' and grammatical red herrings were discarded (in theory) in a single, enlightened sweep. Now the emphasis was to be upon such things as tone, style, the writer's intention, artistic structure, the use of symbol or irony, and on the general imaginative qualities of the text.

Richards's *Practical Criticism*, 1929, revealed the frightening inability of educated and ostensibly cultured individuals to read poetry and imaginative writing with any degree of accuracy. His conclusions have had widespread influence on literature teaching, including as they do the simple assertions (1) that mere 'ordinary' prose literacy is not enough when it comes to the reading of poetry (2) that pupils must be systematically taught (what they have not up to now been taught) how to read properly, and (3) that competence in such reading and in imaginative response must mean competence in living, since a richness and subtlety of emotional experience is only possible where adequate language and language-based mental concepts are available to the individual. Richards offers four kinds of 'meaning' ('Sense', 'Feeling', 'Tone', 'Intention'), each of which must be attended to if we are to begin to respond adequately to good writing, and which will form the basis of a sound 'practical criticism' analysis. The writer wishes to say something (his Sense); he has an attitude to that something (his Feeling); he has an attitude to his reader (and will adopt a certain Tone); and finally he wishes to produce a particular effect on his reader (which is his Intention).

The New Criticism represented a major advance in literary studies on both sides of the Atlantic, and is one of the principal agents of influence in English in this century. One can at least say that if School Certificate set books changed little during the thirties, forties and fifties, at least in many schools the *method* of study changed in a 'New Critical' direction, though it would be rash to assume that the change was either rapid or universal. The Ministry of Education's 1954 Pamphlet No. 26, *Language*, makes the point that I. A. Richards's work 'has been extremely influential in English schools . . . more than any other single influence, it has helped to change the spirit and method of the study of poetry in grammar schools and therefore indirectly in all schools . . . The method at its best is to be seen in Dr. Richards' own book *Practical Criticism*.'[24]

Denys Thompson's *Reading and Discrimination*, 1934, is an attempt to bring the New Criticism principles into upper form English (in effect adapting Richards's *Practical Criticism* method for the classroom), providing nearly one-hundred pages of poetry and prose extracts for pupils to study and compare, both as regards merit and different treatment of similar themes. (Biaggini's book came in the following year.) By 1935 English method writers are beginning to refer to the New Critics – P. Gurrey, for one, in *The Appreciation of Poetry*, 1935 (with his references to Leavis's *How To Teach Reading*, his quotations from Eliot, Empson and L. C. Knights, and his insistence on a new 'relevant' approach to the poem itself, which, if not uncompromisingly 'New Critical', is certainly very close to it). P. H. B. Lyon in an article in the *Journal of Education*, October 1935, writes: 'Senior boys, of course, profit enormously from the method described in Professor Richards's book *Practical Criticism*.' Roy Meldrum also, in *An English Technique*, 1935, includes books by Eliot (*The Sacred Wood*), Leavis, Empson, Richards, Ezra Pound (*How to Read*) and Denys Thompson (*Reading and Discrimination*) in his selected bibliography for secondary teachers, although in the body of the book he indicates that he has some reservations about adopting the 'practical criticism' method wholesale in upper-form study, such 'analytical literary criticism' being a new, untried and perhaps over-rated activity as far as school teaching is concerned. (We may gauge Meldrum's general attitude by noting his rather traditional remarks on the relationship of English to the classics – 'English must do what the Classics did' – which is an attitude that has worn rather thin by 1935, though to be fair to him he wrote three excellent articles on English in the senior school in *The Times Educational Supplement*, October and November 1939.)

There cannot be any question either of the considerable good which Leavis has done to upper-school literature study by emphasising both its disciplinary qualities and its humanising potential, by applying the Richards technique as a detailed and productive method of literary analysis, by redrawing the map of literary appreciation, and by giving to literature study a sense of 'specialness', which must have beneficial and satisfying effects on the young practitioner. What also distinguishes Leavis's thinking is his desire to formulate a philosophy of education which shall answer the needs of society, and into which the particular elements of 'New Critical' English shall fit. This philosophy he derives in great part from Matthew Arnold (both Richards and Leavis are convinced Arnoldians) and it includes a belief in the cultural ideal as worked out by Arnold, though with the diffcrence that Leavis clearly does not feel, sixty years after *Culture and Anarchy*, that true culture is capable of acceptance or appreciation by 'the masses'. The key passage from his 1930 essay, *Mass Civilization and Minority Culture*, is worth quoting in full simply because of the far-reaching implications it has for literature teaching; this essay places an enormous responsibility on the shoulders of English teachers, even greater than that suggested by the 1921 Report, simply because Leavis sees literature as lying at the heart of – indeed, almost constituting – culture in the widest sense of the term. We may not be prepared to follow him the whole distance (after all, art, music, architecture and a whole range of other cultural manifestations could also put a pretty strong case) but no one concerned with English teaching can fail to respond with excitement to this sort of thing:[25]

> In any period it is upon a very small minority that the discerning appreciation of art and literature depends: it is (apart from cases of the simple and familiar) only a few who are capable of unprompted, first-hand judgment. They are still a small minority, though a larger one, who are capable of endorsing such first-hand judgment by genuine personal response . . . The minority capable not only of appreciating Dante, Shakespeare, Donne, Baudelaire, Conrad (to take major instances) but of recognizing their latest successors constitute the consciousness of the race (or a branch of it) at a given time . . . Upon this minority depends our power of profiting by the finest human experience of the past; they keep alive the subtlest and most perishable parts of tradition. Upon them depend the implicit standards that order the finer living of an age . . In keeping . . . is the language, the changing idiom, upon which fine living depends . . .

To be involved in teaching English is not just to be concerned with pupils' 'reading' or 'writing' or 'spelling' but to be responsible for the health of language, and consequently for civilised thinking and living, for the growth of emotional and even moral judgment, and for the quality of life itself.

Now the 'Minority Culture' idea has not had a particularly good press in the last twenty years or so, and the gap between what Leavis is after and what, to take an example already quoted, Sir Fred Clarke (or latterly Raymond Williams in the concluding pages of *Culture and Society*) is after has become palpably wider. In study terms Leavis is saying that the best texts, the 'Great Tradition', must be explored in sensitive but disciplined detail, and that the older pupil must rise to the text or confess his inadequacy. The movement in the secondary schools, particularly in some of the comprehensive schools in recent years, has been right away from this towards a much more pupil-centred approach to reading with an emphasis on the contemporary and the 'relevant', to the point where one hears the Leavis attitudes being vigorously denounced for their inappropriateness in any school situation.

In *Mass Civilization* Leavis actually considers the notion of a new 'popular' culture – and rejects it out of hand. 'It is . . . vain to console us with the promise of a "mass culture" that shall be utterly new. It would, no doubt, be possible to argue that such a "mass culture" might be better than the culture we are losing, but it would be futile . . .' This kind of talk is not calculated to please everybody on our own egalitarian, pupil-centred, comprehensive decade. The position which the teacher of English takes up with regard to the argument will determine to a great extent the method and content of his teaching, and that position will naturally depend upon the nature of his training, the kind of school he finds himself in, the types of pupils he has to teach and his own social-class background.

Other 1930s references to the New Criticism can be seen in the 1936 *Year Book of Education* (noting the influence of I. A. Richards on school poetry study[26]), in the publication *Teaching Poetry* produced by the Society for Teachers of English in 1937 (Richards praised), in the Spens Report, 1938 (importance of Richards's critical method for schools[27]) and in Norman Callan's *Poetry in Practice*, 1938 (with its New Critical principles and comparison of prose and poetry passages in a 'practical criticism' way). Richards's *Interpretation in Teaching* appeared in 1937, a book written primarily for teachers to show the application of his theories of literary interpretation to education, with a detailed discussion on the nature of literary communication. It is an extremely difficult book, and has almost certainly had far less impact upon school English teachers than the better known (though also not always fully understood) *Practical Criticism*. Leavis was to publish his *Education and the University* in 1943, which, apart from the fashion for seventeenth-century studies which it encouraged, again gave English studies generally a powerful injection of critical adrenalin; literary study as a discipline of intelligence and sensibility is placed firmly at the centre of any genuine 'humanist' education – literature constituting the all-inclusive link between the developing specialisms, the one subject that can train, as no other discipline can, intelligence and sensibility alike. In his second Appendix ('How to Teach Reading') Leavis turns his attention to school English and notes the need for genuine and sensitive reading to be learnt in the schools: 'what has been said has obvious application at the school level, and much might be done if it were permitted, if there were teachers educated to do it, and if the examination system were not allowed to get in the way.'

English and the mass media

Another feature of the New Critical attitude as applied to school work was (and is) its concern for the admass influences which impinge upon citizens generally and upon children in particular, the tenth-rate pulp fiction, sensational journalism and shoddy mass media entertainment which teachers and pupils alike must combat with genuine standards of learnt taste and discrimination. This concern has become more marked since 1950 (consider Hoggart's *The Uses of Literacy*, 1957; *Discrimination and Popular Culture* edited by Denys Thompson, 1964; and the large number of books directed specifically at the classroom situation such as E. W. Hildick's books on newspapers, comics and films, Michael Marland's *Following the News*, 1967 (newspaper study), or Connie Alderson's *Magazines Teenagers Read*, 1968 – together with the large number of articles on the subject to be found in journals and periodicals, in the *Use of English* for example), but despite the present intense concern for such matters we find Richards in 1924 referring to 'bad art, the cinema, etc.', and to 'The extent to which second-hand experience of a crass and inchoate type is replacing ordinary life',[28] while Leavis in 1930 argues that society is being threatened by 'mass production and standardization' and by the triviality of mass media entertainment (particularly in the cinema, where cheap emotionalism assumes a hypnotic influence)[29] and a book such as his and Denys Thompson's *Culture and Environment* is, as early as 1933, already exploring the theme in detail.

The authors of *Culture and Environment* believe that the ability to read sensitively and critically will help pupils to recognise the cheap spuriousness of biased newspapers and dishonest advertising. They refer to 'pop' songs, romance magazines and bad films, insist that all this is part of the English teacher's brief (the secondary English course must include newspaper, magazine and advertisement study, together with discussion on films and radio programmes) and give some indication of the importance they attach to the problem by using such terms as 'vital culture' (without which we become sub-human) and 'quality of life' (which is being eroded) when considering what is at stake for society as a whole.

In fact such attitudes were not new even for 1933; as far back as 1907 we find Philip Hartog recommending an analysis of newspaper styles and methods of story presentation (distortion) for secondary

pupils. Roberts and Barter in 1908 talk of the 'present widespread
and utterly destructive taste for periodicals of the *Comic Cuts* type'
and Arnold Smith is referring in 1915 to the bad influence of many
newspapers with their 'mass of hastily written, slipshod verbiage'.
P. B. Ballard in 1921 discusses the 'Penny Dreadfuls' (including
tales of Sexton Blake, Bessy Bunter and Buffalo Bill) and concludes
that they are harmless (as indeed they are; what would Ballard
think of today's ghoulish or semi-pornographic offerings put out as
'entertainment' for children ?). Helen Dobson in her winning *Daily
Mail* curriculum of 1925 had also included newspaper and magazine
study for fourteen-year-olds.

The idea was not new, but it is true that it tended to assume a
more central and urgent position after 1930. In a book called
Education for Citizenship in Secondary Schools, 1936, Ernest Dyer
has a detailed article on newspaper study for pupils (good citizenship
implies the reading of good, responsible newspapers) which would
include a study of emotive journalese, news distortion, the balance
between news and merely 'magazine' features in given papers,
differing treatment of the same stories in different papers, and
advertising methods. 'It is as important to train young citizens to
read newspapers with discrimination as to read books with discrimination; and from the social point of view immeasurably more
important', Dyer concludes. The Spens Report also takes the
matter very seriously, referring to the corrupting influence which
advertising and the press can have on the impressionable secondary
pupil.

A. J. Jenkinson's survey

An extremely important book was A. J. Jenkinson's survey, *What
Do Boys and Girls Read?*, 1940. There had also been surveys of
pupils' reading tastes before, but none so detailed and comprehensive as this. In 1913 Professor J. A. Green had reported a small
survey in the *Journal of Experimental Pedagogy* of 11-plus pupils'
reading. He concluded that with the *Sunday Chronicle, News of the
World* and *Comic Cuts* heading their lists of preferences this private
reading was of an abysmally low standard. Jenkinson's survey is
much wider, with nearly three-thousand questionnaires answered
by children aged twelve to fifteen years, and it provides a basis of
pupils' actual reading tastes for English teachers to note, come to
terms with, and work from. In a very real sense this book represents
an important advance in pupil-centred studies (it has a Foreword by
Susan Isaacs) and Jenkinson's own conclusions, particularly with
regard to the books usually studied for external examinations in
secondary schools, are all the more worthy of serious consideration
for that reason. It seems extraordinary that only after something

like sixty years of secondary examining and teaching was serious research consideration given to the suitability of the texts used by direct reference to the pupils themselves, their capabilities and preferences. We have seen how teachers and examiners had (rightly) refused to compromise standards but had then gone to extremes in their demand for self-evidently 'classical' set texts of unimpeachable (by contemporary standards) quality, with a consequent over-estimation of the pupils' abilities. The candidate rose to the standard of the book, or dropped out, it was as simple as that. Susan Isaacs is not exaggerating when she remarks in her Foreword: 'The study of this book would transform the whole attitude of many teachers of English in senior and secondary schools towards the reading interests, and thus redeem much of the lives, of their pupils.'

Among the boys investigated, adventure stories are the most popular, followed by detective stories. School stories are very popular with the eleven- and twelve-year-olds, but decline in appeal between twelve and fifteen. Much-liked comics include *Comic Cuts*, *Wizard*, *Hotspur*, *Film Fun*, *Mickey Mouse Weekly* and the *Boy's Own Paper*. The boys tend to read the sensational newspapers, and many of them are visiting the cinema once every week, some more often.

As for the girls, they read more on average than boys, tending to choose more adult material (Jane Austen and the Brontës being popular) but many of them remain stuck in the romance-fantasy world of *Peg's Paper*, *Secrets* or *Flame* (whose equivalents are with us today, circulating near the two million mark). These publications are perhaps not positively harmful, and satisfy a demand for mild escapism, 'But it is likely that the social and human values underlying them are shallow, opportunist, and ill-thought-out. They are one of the agencies tending to stabilize popular feeling and insight at low levels.'[30] This simplified and immature picture of human relationships is carefully designed to appeal to the fourteen- or fifteen-year-old, who though economically an adult may still be a child emotionally.

Also interesting is the contrasting list of books which these pupils were actually studying in their schools (the information being provided by their teachers) and here a division between the senior schools (leaving age fourteen) and the grammar or high schools appears. The grammar list includes *The Faerie Queene*, *Lorna Doone*, *Eothen*, *Elia*, Goldsmith's essays, Peacock's essays, *The Golden Treasury*, Scott, Bacon and Macaulay, while the senior school list includes *King Solomon's Mines*, *Treasure Island*, the stories of H. G. Wells and modern detective stories. The senior pupils do not, of course, have School Certificate on the horizon ahead of them, but in any case their teachers seem to take a more practical line – even studying comics to get the children off onto allied, but better things, for example, and introducing quality fiction of a kind that is likely to appeal to them.

Jenkinson's conclusions are that the choice of books for secondary school and examination study must be changed to come more into line with pupils' capabilities; that the imposition of adult tastes upon children must be undertaken more gradually and sympathetically; and that the critical study of newspapers, comics and magazines must figure in the teaching of English. His claims are extremely sensible – let us at least try and estimate what children will be able to appreciate and not impose upon them books which they are incapable of understanding, let alone enjoying – and his conclusions have become even more relevant in the post-1945 period. For some reason many of the secondary modern schools were very reluctant to adopt his suggestions (as regards, for example, newspaper or magazine work, or the choice of suitable books for study) despite the fact that his survey might be considered a vital prefatory note to the 1944 Act. Writers such as David Holbrook and Michael Marland have said in the sixties very much what Jenkinson said in 1940, and their remarks have been hailed as being very 'advanced'. Since the last war the quality of magazine and comic material available has deteriorated considerably, and the pressures of commercialism have intensified tenfold, yet many schools have hardly begun to take effective steps to combat these influences upon realistic lines.

Citizenship concerns

Another feature which anticipates the post-1944 reorganisation of secondary schooling is the emphasis in the late thirties on education for 'citizenship'. *Education for Citizenship in Secondary Schools*, 1936, has already been mentioned; this book was published by the Association for Education in Citizenship and it stressed the need to give a 'real' education relevant to 'life' in a democracy (see the Foreword by Oliver Stanley) and emphasised the importance of being able to write clear, 'practical' English, see through propaganda, and converse intelligently (curiously the book also resurrects the moral fallacy, suggesting that poetry is valuable for the moral feelings it elicits, and is thus good for the young citizen). The 1936 *Year Book of Education* also included a section (Section V) on 'Training for Citizenship' (and see the 1939 *Year Book*, pp. 330 ff.), and it is made clear that the growing concern over the matter was due to a great extent to the recent rise of totalitarianism in Italy and Germany, with the consequent threat to democracy throughout Europe generally. Olive Wheeler devoted a chapter of *Creative Education and the Future*, 1936, to citizenship, referring to 'the present threat of European War', and the Spens Report states: 'Democracy is now challenged, and the duty of citizenship renders it essential that all should be taught to understand and to think to the best of their ability.'

What must not be forgotten also was that the thirties were witnessing an increasing social egalitarianism in Britain anyway, and an increasing democratic self-consciousness. It followed that if the people were going to be given a full and proper education – and they were – then the principles of good citizenship, including a sense of electoral responsibility at local and national level, became an important element in that education. Democracy is threatened where people remain ignorant of the nature of their society and the way in which it functions (it is also threatened by those who seek to exploit others for commercial as well as political purposes through the mass media, hence again the relevance of discrimination and a knowledge of 'admass' and the way it works). The Spens Report comments of the typical school in 1938 that it is not merely a 'place of learning' but a 'social unit of society' where influences are brought to bear on the children 'for the continued wellbeing of the community', and there is more than a hint of Dewey to this remark. The elementary schools of the thirties have, in fact, moved very close to embodying a number of the ideas which Dewey had put forward as early as the 1890s. These ideas include (1) a child-centred approach to education (2) the need for the child to be active and engaged in plenty of practical tasks (3) the belief that the ideal school will be an extension of the ideal home and (4) the upholding of a 'democratic' ideal – all the achievements of society being put (through the common school) at the disposal of its future members for the benefit of all. One might also add that Dewey tends to be unsympathetic to 'academic', bookish learning, and is concerned to establish a democracy which will value practical know-how and useful skills rather than the more arcane embodiments of culture.

In 1938 W. B. Little published a secondary textbook, *English for the Young Citizen*, which concentrates on the following 'practical' exercises: writing letters; reading railway timetables (problems set); reading the London Underground map; writing cheques; adding up bills; sending telegrams; booking holidays; and paying rates and taxes. In the same year C. M. and H. R. Bennett published their senior school course book, *Civic English*, which is also concerned with 'useful' information such as how to find out about local government and public services, how to use a telephone or read timetables (much of this presented in the form of comprehension exercises). Similar textbooks followed after 1944, including Margaret Laurence's *Citizenship Through English*, 1946, which advocates schemes of work on newspapers, magazines, comics, the cinema and radio for secondary pupils.

Since 1945 the virtues of such democratic knowledgeability and discrimination have been upheld against a commercial rather than against a totalitarian political enemy; in either case we see a further development of the concept of responsible education for the 'masses' gaining firm ground, together with a further widening of the scope of school English studies.

Notes

1   *Op. cit.*, p. 41.
2   *Ibid.*, Intro., pp. xiii–xiv.
3   *Ibid.*, Intro., p. xvii.
4   *Ibid.*, Intro., p. xxviii.
5   *Op. cit.*, pp. 102, 104.
6   *Op. cit.*, p. 3.
7   *Ibid.*, p. 10.
8   *Ibid.*, p. 12.
9   *Op. cit.*, p. 21.
10 *Op. cit.*, pp. 157, 175.
11 *Op. cit.*, p. 51.
12 *Op. cit.*, p. 218.
13 *Scrutiny*, II, 2, 1933, p. 158.
14 *Op. cit.*, p. 8.
15 Preface, p. viii.
16 *Op. cit.*, p. 75.
17 *Ibid.*, p. 72.

18 *Teaching Poetry*, p. 65.
19 *Op. cit.*, p. 398 (1944 reprint).
20 *Ibid.*, p. 384.
21 *Ibid.*, p. 371.
22 *Op. cit.*, p. 31.
23 *Ibid.*, p. 61.
24 *Op. cit.*, p. 145.
25 The Essay is reprinted as Appendix III of *Education and the University* 1943.
26 *Op. cit.*, p. 272.
27 *Op. cit.*, p. 225.
28 *Principles of Literary Criticism*, 1924, pp. 203, 231.
29 *Mass Civilisation and Minority Culture*.
30 *Op. cit.*, p. 219.

Chapter five 1940–70
The New English – priorities and purpose in a democratic society

Creative criteria

In 1942 a book entitled *Child Art* was published by Wilhelm Viola.
The extent to which this publication has influenced subsequent art
teaching (possibly very little; Herbert Read's *Education Through
Art*, 1943, seems to have had wider publicity) is not a matter of
concern for this study, but an outline of part of Viola's remarkable
'creative' thesis is particularly relevant at this stage, since it is in this
book that we find ourselves confronting the spirit of full-blooded
self-expressive creativity which is to develop over such a broad
front in the late fifties and sixties. Why, Viola demands, is there no
child art in the museums? Why have the qualities of genius, which
are to be found in children as well as in adults, not been recognised?
Why has no one yet fully accepted what Rousseau said about
children and their extraordinary innate abilities? The answer is that
hitherto teachers (and most adults for that matter) have not left
children free to create with originality, but have insisted on inter-
fering, falsely guiding, repressing and restricting, bringing influences to bear which are unforgivable in view of the now obvious
fact that children *can* create with startling originality, can produce
'miracles of beauty' from the subconscious ('Everything great has
originated from the subconscious'). Once free children from the
inhibiting shackles of imitation and the copying mentality and the
'vision' can materialise. 'Two generations ago nobody dreamt that
every child is a born artist ... The discovery of Child Art is
parallel with, or perhaps a consequence of, the discovery of the
child as a human being with his own personality and his own
particular laws.'[1]

Viola refers to, and is clearly greatly influenced by, the work of
Franz Cizek in Vienna; Cizek had encouraged children to paint
within a completely free environment, unrestricted as regards choice
of subject or treatment of same, and had received striking and fine
work in return (Cizek had held an exhibition of children's art work
in London in 1934, and there had been other children's exhibitions
– the Zwemmer Gallery's in 1937 or the LCC's in 1938, for example).
Viola quotes Cizek's language analogy when describing the relationship between form and content in children's paintings: 'First the
child speaks, then he learns the grammar, not the other way round';
for Cizek, as for Viola, the child can be literally 'inspired' in his
imaginative work.

Now the relevance of this to English teaching lies in its spirit
rather than in its substance. It would be very difficult to go much
further in a consideration of the child's expressive capacity (unless

to say that children's art is, has been, and always will be superior to adult art) and the advantage of going just about as far as one can without crossing the line which divides the sane from the ludicrously impracticable is that we now have a standard against which to measure degrees of 'creative' advance. It is, of course, a very short step from a consideration of children's painting such as Viola's to a consideration of their poetry writing, though it is probably true to say that terms such as 'striking originality' may be used with slightly less incongruity of a child's painting – where the primitive has its own validity – than of a poem. Viola is prepared to acknowledge that the appeal of child art lies in its expressive rather than in its representative abilities, and however acceptable 'content' without form may be on canvas, a different set of criteria come into operation where language communication is concerned. There is no need to pursue this or push on into the realms of aesthetic philosophy, but it may be that the art parallel which so many 'creative' teachers of the spoken and written word have recently promoted so enthusiastically is in fact something of a false analogy. There seem to be no doubts in Viola's mind; he believes that children produce *art*, which can stand the test of direct comparison with any valid art form anywhere.

Marjorie Hourd and the Romantic view

In 1949 Marjorie Hourd's *The Education of the Poetic Spirit* was published, which is the seminal work in the post-1945 Creative Movement in English teaching, and is all the more authentic for its detailed references to, and reliance upon, the discoveries of important psychologists such as Spearman, Isaacs, Piaget, Koffka and Kohler. She places the imaginative faculty at the centre of the educational process, takes a very firm stand on Coleridgean-Romantic imaginative theory, quotes Ruskin's panegyric on the unerring 'rightness' of imaginative perception from *Modern Painters* (Volume III. Marie Peel later uses a phrase from this passage as the title of her method book for junior work *Seeing to the Heart*) and declares that the genesis of her creative thinking stems from certain passages in Wordsworth's *Prelude*, in particular Book II, lines 233 on:

> For feeling has to him imparted power
> That through the growing faculties of sense
> Doth like an agent of the one great Mind
> Create creator and receiver both
> Working but in alliance with the works
> Which it beholds – Such unity is the first
> Poetic Spirit of our human life . . .

There are indeed times when one suspects that her view of the child is a little too near (assuming that that is what he meant) Words-

worth's 'Mighty prophet, Seer blest' notion, and like Viola she tends
to want children's work (in this case, poems) to be accepted without
reservation on an adult level, while at the same time finding them
remarkable simply because they are by children. It is significant that
she takes Ruth Griffiths to task for not distinguishing between the
imagination and mere fancy or fantasy, according to Coleridge's
Biographia definition, as applied to children's work – an indication
that she (Hourd) is prepared to attribute 'imagination' in the truly
original, creative sense to children, and underwrite the child's poetic
capacity to a new and uncompromising extent (going well beyond
Dorothy Tudor Owen's 1920 suggestions, for example). Writing later
in the *Use of English* ('Poetry and children', Winter 1952) on
originality in children's writing she quotes Shelley: 'The mind in
creation is as a fading coal, which some invisible influence . . .
awakens to transitory brightness: this power arises from within . . .
and the conscious portions of our natures are unprophetic either of
its approach or its departure.' She goes on: 'It is from these uncon-
scious sources that children, as all true poets do, gain their
inspiration.'

Given that children possess creative ability of a kind hitherto
generally unrecognised, teachers must now accept that their own
directing influence may, in ignorance of the true nature of the
creative process, be inhibiting and repressive:[2]

> It is this quality of *vision* in imagination that we need to look
> for and encourage in children's expression. This sounds very
> simple and it is; but education too frequently opens the door
> through which the inferior faculties come in. The teacher
> himself is often the meddling interloper. I do not think that we
> can teach children how to write poetry . . . But many more of
> them are poets than we think, and our job as teachers is to
> leave the way open.

Paraphrasing Coleridge on the imagination, she maintains that the
synthesising, pattern-making power of imaginative perception is as
strong in the child as in the adult, and is the most important element
in the gradual coming to terms with environment and inner feelings
which is growth and maturity. Imagination shapes experience, and
gives it significance; it follows that there must be opportunity for
free expression on the part of the child in writing, drama, and oral
work, to permit the imaginative faculty opportunity to work at its
leisure and bring this significance to the individual's experience.
Each pupil must be 'the active participant in a creative process' not
the passive recipient of the teacher's interpretations (compare
Caldwell Cook). Words become an expressive medium like paint;
the writing of a poem is, for a child as for an adult, an attempt to
'make' something in a shaping, plastic sense, and particularly

K

through symbol and metaphor children can come to terms with inner feelings which would otherwise be inexpressible, and through such symbolic expression can integrate them into an overall pattern of awareness.

From this there follows a vitally important point – and it constitutes a new criterion with which to judge children's written work – that *intensity of expression* and evidence of 'imaginative engagement' in the subject must be seen as being more important than the mere technical presentation (spelling, punctuation, paragraphing) of that subject.

By way of example she reproduces a composition by a fourteen-year-old girl which describes a tennis match (it is given in full on pages 130-1 of her book). At first glance the piece is seen to be badly written in terms of punctuation, vocabulary, spelling and general construction, and conveys an impression of hasty completion with little care for shape or development; but a closer reading (according to the author) reveals (a) intense absorption on the part of the writer (b) a convincing attention to detail (c) a vivid sense of 'atmosphere' (d) an overall unity arising out of the girl's intense absorption in the subject and her desire to describe the whole event (the characteristic imaginative pattern) (e) a freshness, liveliness and 'engagement' on the part of the writer which is ultimately everything that we should desire of the pupil in the written situation.

Now although we may not agree entirely with her over this particular piece, the fact remains that it is now much more widely accepted that in assessing pupils' written work we look for, praise, and encourage the kind of imaginative liveliness and intense personal involvement in the subject which Marjorie Hourd believes she sees here. This is certainly a long step from William Boyd's (1924) criteria, and we have clearly reached a point where mechanical competence is no longer the be-all and end-all of written expression.

One other potentially controversial conclusion can be drawn from this, and that is that IQ and the capacity for imaginative writing are not so closely linked as is normally assumed. Can good creative work be produced by pupils of below-average intelligence? – in secondary modern 'C' streams for example? Marjorie Hourd's answer is most emphatically 'yes'; imaginative capacity and intelligence *are* related 'but outside all this there remains for the person of average or lower intelligence a very rich field of expressiveness.'[3] (Though the implication is that the spelling and other features of presentation will be inferior in these cases.)

The full significance of this must be appreciated. Not all pupils are 'academically' able (capable of dealing effectively or profitably with the novels or poems traditionally involved in secondary school study or of writing what in the bad old days would be 'acceptable'

English) but all are, according to the theory, 'creatively' able. In creative expression – and the sources for that expression are the experiences of life itself, hopes, fears, loves, hates, pleasures, pains, the amalgam of daily existence – lies a common basis for our English work which will involve all pupils, the dull and the bright, equally and fully. Furthermore, one is appealing to the pupil on something more than a merely superficial exam-based level, since the appeal will be to the most personal aspects of individual experience, a 'putting the finger on' and encouragement of the imaginative shaping and expressing of, inner feelings which will literally create new areas of consciousness in a way which traditional, subject-centred study may not.

We are, in fact, moving towards a much wider definition of that very elusive word 'creativity' which is now emerging as a term applicable not only to specific classroom ways of teaching (composition, for example) but to an entire way of educational thinking (indeed it could be argued at this point that a label such as 'The New Education' or 'The New English' would be more apt). Taking an overall view of what has been happening to English teaching since 1950 we see that emphasis has shifted firmly onto the need to get all children, whatever their age, sex, IQ, school achievement, social class, home background or career prospects absorbed in the kind of work which will involve them totally as human beings (emotionally and imaginatively as well as intellectually in the factual-academic sense) in a profitable educational experience which will touch them at the deepest levels of awareness and be of permanent benefit to them. A wide range of influences, including developments of a sociological, psychological and linguistic nature, have been responsible for our arrival at this position, but at the heart of the 'new' English teaching lies a specific creative methodology of the intensive, imaginative writing kind which embodies the key values of the whole theory – so that to use 'creative' in both senses is not inappropriate.

The theory is not even new, for we merely have the 'common school' ideal as put forward for the pre-war elementary schools extended into the total range of education – junior and secondary – to include all children. Given the common secondary structure and the comprehensive school, the 'creative' key to worth-while English study will almost inevitably follow. To call this 'pupil-centred' is to state the obvious; what emerges is a new philosophy of English which can, at last, take its stand on the long-mooted but hitherto unachieved extension of the subject beyond the limitations of traditional 'subject' thinking (Sampson's theory can only become an actuality where the whole climate of English thinking changes) and which sees school English work as beginning with, depending entirely on, and ending with the experience and personality of the pupil – all else (books, skills, exercises, the familiar contents of the English showcase) being subordinate to that.

The influence of Marjorie Hourd's book has been considerable, and although as we have seen there was no shortage of 'creative' advocates before 1940, it is to her that much of the subsequent creative theory can eventually be found to lead – theory which shares both her insights and her shortcomings. One wonders why such a book, justifying creative methods at length in a scholarly and detailed way, had taken so long to appear. What is also interesting about *The Education of the Poetic Spirit* is that it takes a firm stand upon Romantic theories, and brings into the open the close link between Romanticism (theory of imagination, the artistic process, attitude to the child and so on) and creative school English teaching – a link implicit in earlier writers such as Tomkinson and Greening Lamborn, but not expressed by them with anything like the same clarity and conscious thoroughness.

Perhaps the most obvious characteristic of this Romantic bias is the insistence that children be 'left alone', be 'left free', be 'allowed' to do things, the good and the true usually following, where the classical view would include the conviction that individuals must be controlled, directed and organised to get anything worth while out of them. Those teachers who are not sympathetic to the philosophy of Romanticism both in general terms or with particular reference to the child are not likely to find much more than half of what Marjorie Hourd has to say acceptable in the long-term. Is the Romantic determination to 'trust' the child (remembering Edmond Holmes's remark in 1911 concerning the elementary teacher's mistrust of the child) an educational inspiration or naïve self-delusion? The fact remains that English teaching attitudes have shifted very strongly since 1950 in a creative direction, and this shift has been due in no small measure to her book.

A. F. Watts and the contribution of linguistic theory

In his discussion of the advances which have taken place in English teaching since the twenties, John Blackie (*Good Enough for the Children?*, 1963) suggests that there is one factor in particular that has affected teachers' attitudes, and that is the light which psychologists and linguists have thrown on the way children actually acquire spoken language in infancy. At this stage (to simplify) the process is one of constant practice on a trial and error basis, the majority of children learning the basic structure of the language before the age of five without consciously 'memorising' anything. One book which did a great deal to bring the facts of linguistic life home to teachers was A. F. Watts's *The Language and Mental Development of Children*, 1944, and, whether he realised it or not, Watts was giving substantial encouragement to certain aspects of creative thinking.

Watts outlines in careful detail the development of the child's language from the simple concrete (nouns used as labels) to the conceptual abstract, the way the various types of statement are mastered (statements indicative, exclamations, questions and imperatives), and indicates that the child can only 'internalise' each language stage as and when he is ready for it. Thus, to impose adult language structures upon the young pupil when he is incapable of absorbing them into his own instinctive usage is foolish; the structures will either be taken in at a superficial level and be reproduced mechanically and artificially when the school situation (the composition lesson, for example) requires it, or will not be taken in at all.

The importance of this point is considerable, for we have seen how earlier composition teaching was based almost wholly on the assumption that pupils must imitate and reproduce adult, formal structures from the beginning – and that 'correct' writing would only occur as a result of a successful 'learning' of those structures. It also follows that if the pupil is to be able to internalise each language stage he must receive, in addition to teacher guidance, help and stimulation, opportunity to work and experiment freely at his own linguistic level – and hence, by implication, we see the linguistic necessity for 'free writing' as well as the psychological and imaginative necessity.

Again, by analogy with the method that the infant uses to acquire spoken language, teachers must aim to improve their pupils' spoken and written English through constant practice on a trial and error basis (content will come first, and lead to form later). 'Freshness and fluency in writing what is worth reading must come first. The teacher's problem will always be to devise interesting situations . . . In short, as soon as the elementary difficulties of recording have been overcome the teacher will be wise to attend always to substance first and to technique afterwards.'[4]

The average child, of course, quickly acquires an extensive vocabulary by this trial and error method simply because words are the instruments with which he orders and masters his environment, making sense out of the chaos of impressions around him by applying specific labels to specific objects in order to understand them. New words which are necessary to him in this ordering process will be remembered precisely because they are so useful to him. We may go further here, and say that while the infant is mostly concerned to understand his physical environment (with concrete nouns) the child of school age is almost equally concerned to find precise, for him, labels which will make sense of inner feelings and emotions (using abstract terms) or at least to understand them through analogy or symbol. Growth and maturity mean successful adjustment to the world around; that adjustment will be achieved where the 'inner' life is harmoniously related to the external world, where sense impressions and experiences received from the outer world can be ordered, related to the already known and thus given significance. At the same time the achievement of inner patterns of significance is to a great extent dependent upon expression – in writing, for example – where vague, unrealised inner feelings are 'placed' (and thus comprehended) by the creation of external (written, word-based) pattern. It therefore follows that the process of 'labelling to understand' is a continuous one throughout life, and that to write with imaginative absorption in a free situation is to help give order to the inner life; without such opportunity for expression the personality of the pupil cannot grow or develop as it should, so that 'free' writing can be said to be one of the most important of *learning* activities. It also follows that words which are found to be necessary to complete this pattern-making will be remembered, probably permanently, where lists of words merely given out in the hope that they will be used at some time by the child will not. Language can almost be seen as a by-product, a by-product of the child's absorption in, and desire to have an understanding of, new and interesting situations; thus effective language teaching (at school) will seek to draw the pupil into absorbing and novel experiences so that he is automatically looking for the new words with which to explore and understand them.

The grammar debate continued

In the meantime the familiar grammar-format textbooks (some still advocating the imitation of 'model' passages, or giving outlines to be expanded after the fashion of the twenties – along with the inevitable parsing and analysis) continued to appear. These clearly satisfied a need at school level, but are conventional in terms of the peculiar grammar tradition characteristic of this country – see as examples, *The Active English Course* by G. S. Humphreys and J. C. Roberts, 1939; *Creative English* by S. C. Glassey, 1941; *English Practice for Secondary Schools* by A. S. Robertson, 1946; *Modern English* by John Russell, 1948; *English Composition* by G. H. Holroyd, 1949; *English Exercises for Grammar Schools* by A. R. Moon and G. H. McKay, 1950; or *Enjoying English* by W. G. Croker, 1951.

Pamela Gradon, writing the 'Teaching of Grammar' chapter in the English Association's 1946 symposium, *The Teaching of English in Schools* (edited by V. de Sola Pinto), tries hard to keep a balanced view and be fair to both sides in the grammar-no grammar war. She is aware that grammar teaching needs to be defended, and examines carefully the motives for teaching it; she rejects the foreign language fallacy (knowing formal grammar does help in the learning of other languages, but this is not an argument for teaching it), rejects the notion that grammar teaches 'logical' thinking, and agrees that it will only help children to improve their written skill over a very limited area, but ends rather lamely where she started, advocating definite formal grammar teaching both before and after the age of eleven – presumably echoing the Association's general view. Despite her effort to bring grammar up to date, her rejection of some of the false arguments which have given support to grammar teaching in the past, her cursory nod at the importance of spontaneous written work, and her desire to see an easing off in the teaching of slower children, her article is firmly traditional and another good example of the 'I know it has few advantages, but . . .' position.

In 1947 W. J. Macaulay published the results of his investigation into grammar teaching in Scottish schools ('The difficulty of grammar', *British Journal of Educational Psychology*, November 1947), concluding that the conceptual nature of the subject is such that it cannot be grasped with any real understanding by pupils under the age of fifteen or sixteen (hence the parrot nature of much of the learning and the lack of transfer into the written situation). He suggests that the teaching of formal grammar in the junior school (and the Scottish primary and secondary schools have tended to emphasise its importance) is time completely wasted, and that only in the best classes of the senior secondary schools can it be introduced with any degree of success. He rejects the idea that grammar knowledge is necessary for correct expression; 'I think our figures show conclusively that the assumptions on which our courses in grammar for primary and junior secondary schools are founded, are unwarranted by the facts and indeed false.' (Macaulay's conclusions are confirmed by F. Cawley in his investigation of secondary modern pupils, 'The difficulty of English grammar for pupils of secondary school age', *British Journal of Educational Psychology*, June 1958.)

Similar conclusions were drawn by Dr Elizabeth Baranyai of the Psychological Research Station in Budapest, in her survey of Hungarian children (aged nine to ten years) and their learning of formal grammar (see the *Use of English*, Autumn 1949). The children had received regular instruction in the grammar of their language, but when simple tests calculated to test their retention and *understanding* of the subject were given to them it was clear that they had grasped less than two-thirds of the material at best. She concludes that beyond recognising nouns and verbs (and then only when they are presented in the context of actual sentences) children aged nine to eleven years are unable to understand what is involved in grammar work, and on average do not have sufficiently developed mental equipment to deal with the kind of conceptual thinking needed to understand it.

The challenge of the secondary moderns

At first the appearance – on paper at least – of the secondary modern schools gave rise to a good deal of talk concerning the need for new English courses, but with very little seeming to be done. In fact, the methods advocated for the new schools in the years immediately following 1944 were largely traditional, being watered down versions of the grammar school diet with a sprinkling of the 'citizenship' idea, and although a large number of new English textbooks appeared claiming to offer a new approach to the subject many of them actually exhibited the worst of traditional attitudes, assuming (among other things) that sentence-based exercises in grammar must automatically enjoy a new lease of life in the new secondary organisation.

Margaret Laurence (*Citizenship Through English*) for all her efforts to create new methods is tied unmistakably to the world of the formal essay, prosody, Scott, Browning and Longfellow. The English Association's 1946 Symposium is equally traditional (with the exception of a first-rate chapter on poetry by L. A. G. Strong), as was another method book purporting to aim at the new school situation, *The Experience of Poetry in School*, 1953, edited by Victoria Brown, which admittedly encourages the idea that children should write their own free verse poetry (see the section by J. Widdows), but otherwise has the unmistakable grammar school flavour (don't become obsessed with prosody and figures of speech, but do as much as you possibly can).

The enormous possibilities of the new secondary situation were certainly recognised by some people, and anxiety was expressed lest the opportunities should be lost in English teaching. A leading article in *The Times Educational Supplement*, July 1944, put the matter in a nutshell:

> it is highly probable that for many years the grammar school
> will have a greater prestige than the modern school . . . and the
> great danger to education might well be that the modern school
> will attempt to challenge comparison with the grammar school
> in curriculum. English . . . might well suffer more than any
> other subject from an attempt at imitation, and a magnificent
> opportunity might be thrown away. For grammar school
> English to be imposed upon the modern school would be a
> most retrograde step, particularly as its present value in the
> grammar school is doubtful, dominated as it is by the school
> certificate examination.

(The writer goes on to suggest that what is needed in the modern schools is a flexible syllabus with plenty of personal writing and drama work, a wide choice of books and a non-grammar, non-examination approach to English generally.)

The weight of conservative custom was, however, heavily against the likelihood of an upsurge of new secondary English thinking overnight, even with the sound basis of non-Certificate work which had obviously been laid in some of the senior schools in the thirties. Sir Philip Hartog, looking back to his first (1907) book in *Words in Action*, 1947, notes the depressing lack of change in general classroom practice over that period, and how, despite the creative efforts of many teachers and the originality of many method writers, English has remained in a none-too-lively rut. Is the English pupil of 1947 required to write on better essay topics than the pupil of 1907? Generally speaking, no. Has the artificial imitation of model styles given way to more genuine expression? Generally speaking, no. Has grammar been demoted to its proper subordinate place? No. Does the English pupil of 1947 write better English than his 1907 predecessor? Probably not. Have the ideas on how to get good writing which he put forward in his first book become obsolete through advances in the interim? No.

Perhaps Sir Philip is being unduly pessimistic (although his views merit the most serious consideration) and there is enough truth in his remarks to make all teachers of English in schools, past and present, feel a little uncomfortable. On the other hand, we are unquestionably justified now (in 1971) in saying that considerable advances have been made in several areas of the subject since Sir Philip's remarks in 1947, and that these advances have been due in no small degree to the eventual rethinking of English teaching made necessary by the existence of the secondary modern schools and the provision of secondary school courses for all children. This is not to say that the secondary English tradition maintained by the grammar and public schools since the beginning of the century has been altered solely in a one-way direction from the practices in the best modern and later comprehensive schools; the changes have originated in both camps to the mutual advantage of both, but the point is an important one, since when a genuinely new approach to English was established in the best modern schools, its influence spread into all secondary teaching, and, for better or worse, has produced an approach to English of the 'whole-pupil' creative kind quite different from the Certificate-orientated tradition.

The fact is that neither the School Certificate examinations nor the kinds of English courses for so long associated with them, are particularly relevant to 60 per cent (more or less) of secondary pupils. As long as the 'non-academic' children were kept apart in elementary schools life could go on much as before, but from the time that all children found themselves in self-contained secondary schools or, even more important, when all children from any given area were to be found in the *same* school, taught by one English department and comprising the full possible range of academic ability, the need to work out new approaches to English teaching became unavoidable. The facts of life, educationally speaking, have changed – hence the increasingly rapid advance of 'creative' attitudes in the widest sense as mentioned above as an obvious (the obvious ?) solution to the new situation, and the considerable modifications which have been made to the traditionally persistent and not always wholesome ideas concerning the nature of 'English', its content and purpose. So a process which we will see beginning in some of the modern schools in the fifties (there the unacademic children were, and what kind of English work could one do with them ?) has, in many of the comprehensives, effected remarkable changes in English method thinking – though it would be wrong to assume that these changes have occurred everywhere.

Thus we again see, as with the elementary schools in the twenties and thirties, social and political pressures, first for secondary education for all, then for comprehensive secondary education, having oblique but decisive effects on English with the inevitable tendency to reject or at least drastically modify the methods associated with the grammar schools (now confronted for the first time by opponents their own size – or bigger – the elementary schools, however pupil-centred or 'relevant' their courses, never having been able to take them on alone).

At the same time, to keep the record straight, it must be pointed out that the grammar schools have had some very progressive English thinkers of their own since 1945, and that method writers such as Harry Blamires, J. Patrick Creber, Frank Whitehead or J. H. Walsh (all writing with the grammar school or grammar stream in mind) have brought originality and liveliness into Certificate-based course work. In 1951 (*English in Education*) Blamires was tempering his advocacy of plenty of grammar work with remarks such as: 'Free expression and creative activity must be encouraged in English composition just as they are nowadays in Art' or (on the impossibility of 'teaching' composition to anybody) 'You can only give them opportunity for constant practice, and strive by every means in your power so to stimulate their minds and imaginations that they actually make use of the opportunity offered.'[5]

The answer for the moderns (1) A. E. Smith

Probably the first method book to face up to the new demands made on English by the post-1944 modern school was A. E. Smith's *English in the Modern School*, 1954. Smith is convinced that ten years after the Education Act the modern nettle has not yet been grasped, and he goes on to offer a wide range of excellent practical ideas for oral and written work which are suitable for such classes. He lays emphasis on speech exercises of a genuinely conversational kind; recommends the study of comics, newspapers and magazines; recommends teaching pupils how to use books for reference purposes; emphasises 'real' writing of the short story kind; recommends the use of films and records by the teacher; and believes that literature work will be more successful if it is weighted towards modern fiction. His book lists represent an important breaking of new ground: Scott, Dickens, and Stevenson are included, but so also are books by Evelyn Waugh, Thurber, Orwell, Nevil Shute, T. H. White, Jack London, Arthur Grimble, and A. J. Cronin. He also believes that formal grammar work is quite unsuitable for modern pupils:[6]

> The plain fact is that no one ever wrote a whit the better for having an outdated English Grammar open by his side, and it should be realised that the grammarians' efforts to reconcile ever-changing usage with their set formulae must inevitably leave them well in the rear of current practice. With children in the Modern School we shall be well advised to spend our time . . . educating their ears to recognise and to demand accepted forms and usage . . .

Smith, in fact, is approaching modern work from scratch, and is not simply modifying or diluting already existing material to suit modern requirements. This, of course, can only be done by someone who has actual experience of the new classroom situation (which Smith clearly has) and who is prepared to adapt to its demands, and thus far his approach cannot be faulted. Where his book has limitations is in its failure to take full stock of the enormous changes which are taking place in secondary education, and in not really facing up to the full implications of secondary education for all. Granted that his approach to secondary modern English is practical, unhackneyed, and the most imaginative to date, the fact remains that he begins and ends with the traditional set of English counters – 'good writing', 'good reading', 'good listening' – which, though always of central importance, have tended to assume a distinctly old-fashioned air in the welter of argument and discussion which has overtaken the subject since, and which are now taken for granted as by-products in the pursuit of wider aims (the point will become startlingly clear if a reading of Smith's *English in the Modern School* is immediately followed by a reading of, say, Fred Inglis's *The Englishness of English Teaching*, 1969, though the cautious and the conservative may still prefer the former).

The answer for the moderns (2) David Holbrook

It is with David Holbrook's *English for Maturity*, 1961, and *English for the Rejected*, 1964, that secondary modern English method really moves firmly and convincingly into the postwar creative advance (the latter book being, among other things, the first published attempt to provide English material suitable for use with 'C' and 'D' stream or ESN borderline children – although Holbrook had earlier published articles in the *Use of English* in 1953, 1954, 1957 and 1959). It is no coincidence that Holbrook's introductory remarks to *English for Maturity* on the secondary modern schools are almost identical to George Sampson's remarks in *English for the English* on the elementary schools. Holbrook is really initiating the second major battle in the same war; the junior schools have been won, now the campaign must be carried into the newly-created secondary sector where the bulk of the nation's eleven- to fifteen-year-olds are desperately in need of assistance. Nor is it a coincidence that Holbrook's Introduction is preceded by a short quotation from one of Arnold's letters on the need to spread 'civilisation'. The modern schools, he asserts at the outset, fulfil an educational role as important as that of the grammar schools or the universities; the English teachers in them 'are helping train the sensibility of three-quarters of the nation: and they are helping create its capacities for living . . .' The social-class prejudices, complacency and defeatist attitudes of so many parents, administrators and teachers have effectively smothered the important educational responsibilities which Holbrook is attempting to redefine with an insistence which cannot be pushed aside. 'Vocation, class, status have nothing to do with the need for every individual to be equipped to meet the large and small crises of every life . . . snobbery [and that for Holbrook includes the attitude that modern pupils are failed duds] is out of the question when we come face to face with love or death, to seek the satisfactions derived from life, and to try to maintain some sense of order in our lives.'[7]

The fact is, he goes on, that secondary modern English teachers have tremendous advantages over their grammar colleagues, freed as they are from the need to pursue tired, exam-based 'classics' in a system which, however liberal its original intentions, has come to a pitch of 'factual' obsession where all civilising or humanising has ceased. Of course modern pupils with their limited abilities cannot cope with grammar courses, but why not turn the argument on its head and say that the grammar tradition has gone astray in its inability to sustain an education which shall depend as much on the eliciting of (imaginative) expression as on the imparting of facts? The modern schools, unhampered by a century of academic protocol, can turn to a genuinely creative education based not on the gifted minority but on the 75 per cent of 'average' pupils, which form of education can become the ideal for all schools. What is needed is 'a new education'; 'Let us invent our own methods of work, and start again from scratch', having in mind the fact that 'The nourishment and exercise of the imagination is the root of true literacy in all, from low stream children to the genius.' Like Sampson, Holbrook is convinced (*English for the Rejected*) that the failure up to now to find a new education at the 11-plus level fitted to the needs of the majority of the nation's children is a failure on the part of society to understand what a civilised, humane (and imaginatively creative) life should be. The traditional insistence that IQ shall be the ultimate standard by which to judge children is appallingly limited; what, Holbrook asks, has amount of intelligence got to do with one's need for friendship, success, identity, love, a sense of purpose or achievement? – and it is these universal experiences which creative English with its encouragement of imaginative work and personal expression can best elaborate and refine. (This same point is made later by Albert Rowe, co-author of the 'creative' course book *English through Experience*: 'No one has yet proved that the children we label average and below-average in intelligence are also in this category as regards their senses and feelings. Are they not as capable of responding to the natural world as the others? Of course. Do they only feel average and below-average hatred, anger, sorrow, joy, lust, love? . . . Well, of course not.'[8])

Although the social-class problem lies behind much of what Holbrook is saying (the modern schools are for 'the masses', so that to evolve worth-while modern English is to evolve 'English for the masses') he does not, apart from the necessary references to Jackson and Marsden's *Education and the Working Class*, make a meal of the business; his intense concern for the 'failures', the 'problem' children, the 'dregs' – particularly those from slum neighbourhoods – requires no further commentary.

As well as being wholly committed to creativity, Holbrook is also a Leavisite to the extent of upholding the unique central role of English in the continued maintenance and promotion of civilised thinking and living, and this view goes inevitably with his outspoken criticism of the 'pop' and commercial world, and with his bitter attacks on the debasement of language by mass media entertainment and advertising. He believes that English studies can be the key to personal growth and maturity in an immature society, and he is a good representative of the post-1945 tendency to see English, not as a subject or a series of skills to be learnt, but as a means of creating awareness, sensibility, emotional balance and personality (through response to literature and through spoken and written expression). It is not merely good writing or accurate reading that the teacher is after, but personality growth and development in the pupil, and it follows that the English teacher's starting point must be the pupil, not what he, the teacher, considers English ought to be, or what it has been in the past, but what the pupil will make it in the effort (begun afresh each time) to marry what English can offer with what the pupil needs.

It is true that, like Holbrook, A. E. Smith has also approached the secondary modern situation almost wholly on its own terms, but where Holbrook goes much further than Smith is in coming to English from an entirely new direction – not by cataloguing and reviewing the traditional body of school English content and then rejecting what he no longer considers to be desirable or useful, but by taking the non-academic school pupil and the twentieth-century environment he finds himself in (with its family relations, styles of living, class structure, jobs, entertainments, sex, newspapers, music, politics, religion, architecture, ideals, recreation) and then working out English material which will enable the pupil to understand, judge, participate in, accept or reject the various elements which go to make up the complex experiences of 'life'. And this is not merely the citizenship ideal of the thirties but a deeper concern for the pupil as a future member of an adult society in terms of imagination, sensitivity, taste, capacity for experience, emotional maturity and ability to lead a useful, fulfilling and whole life in the face of the inhuman, reductive forces which beset us in the age of technology and urban suffocation. We cannot, in fact, ignore either the nature of the pupil or the nature of his environment any longer, and any education which is worth while must take account of the fact that our industrial century is working increasingly to dehumanise and devitalise the individual, and will work to combat these forces (English studies, see Leavis, being the best weapon we have). The teacher must help his pupils to combat the corrupting, enervating misuse of language by the mass media, which saps that language of its vitality and reduces thought to cliché (and like Richard Hoggart, Holbrook is convinced that despite the deadening influence of the mass media the working-class still retains an instinctive vigour and vitality which the educator can use).

Now this is the real breakthrough that Holbrook represents; not a modification of the existing English teaching tradition but the formulation of an entirely new concept of 'English' based on the pupil's needs in a particular society (our society) – that need, it goes without saying, being best answered by creative teaching methods. At the end of Holbrook's English teaching scheme lies not so much a taxonomy of practical English skills and accomplishments, but a catalogue of personal attributes and character traits desirable for every individual – not just good spelling, but awareness of the complexity of human emotions, not just good writing, but an ability to respond adequately to beauty or the spiritual realities of existence.

Brief reflection will show that this is a very old ideal. If we return to Jacks's *The Education of the Whole Man*, 1931, we will find hopes expressed *à propos* of the elementary school that at last 'the people' have arrived at a point where they can make their own judgments about education, and will begin to demand an education for themselves of the 'whole man' type *based on their experience of life, work, and the social reality around them* (not what 'authority' feels they ought to need, but what they do need). 'First of all,' Jacks writes, 'we should consider what kind of life we would like to lead, now we approach the age of automatic machines, less drudgery in work and greater leisure.'[9] And Holbrook has written (the *Use of English*, 1959): 'The central problem of our age is to develop a use of living, with its own vitality and wisdom, for all . . .'

We might also add that one thing which distinguishes Holbrook's method writing is the use of a style which, by its sprightliness and down to earth manner, compels the reader's attention. English method books have generally been characterised by quiet good sense or gently persuasive dullness, and it is to Holbrook's credit that he has made the medium positively entertaining, though he can be extremely irritating in the sweeping nature of some of his most outspoken comments as well as being exciting.

Like Marjorie Hourd, he is convinced that the most important moment in the writing programme is when the child's pen is on the paper in a situation of free but intense expression, and also like her he insists that teachers look at the content of the writing (and particularly at the figurative, symbolic use of language, which for him is evidence of that crucial ordering of inner experiences which is itself growth and insight) not merely at its mechanical or formal competence. He does not believe that grammar knowledge helps expression (*'nobody ever learnt to write well from lessons in formal grammar or "practical" text-book exercises . . .'*, *The Secret Places*, his italics), insisting that it is through the *use* of language that skill comes ('the way to develop one's mastery over English is to live within a rich context of its lively use, by reading, listening, and talking', *English for Maturity*). He also takes a strong Freudian 'therapeutic' line (referring on several occasions in several books to Melanie Klein's *Our Adult World and its Roots in Infancy*) and believes that in using language to name or label inner feelings, the child is exorcising potentially confusing forces – although he has latterly become too concerned with such features, suggesting in *Children's Writing*, 1967, for example, that all children must be given the opportunity to tackle 'the backlog of psychic problems' inherited from infancy. There is no denying the satisfaction that can attend the expression and 'writing out' of certain experiences, but the class teacher is embarking on very dangerous ground where he assumes that interpretations in depth psychology are part of his everyday teaching brief.

Finally it need hardly be said that Holbrook is convinced that the less bright children can produce imaginative work of the highest quality, and in *Children's Writing* he has reproduced a wide range of material to prove the assertion.

Creativity and democracy: culture or anarchy?

It must now be becoming obvious, and particularly after considering Holbrook, that there is a very close link between recent 'creativity' and social class concerns. We may express this generally in terms something to the effect that 'creative' English is 'the people's English', that through creative methods 'the masses' have at last found an educational framework which can support them adequately – the common culture being in fact a 'creative' culture. 'This is the democratic ideal,' writes A. G. Hughes in 1951, 'the liberation of the creative spirit in every individual.'[10] Are we justified then in saying that the hopes for a truly liberal and humane education put forward by Arnold in the last century are on the verge of realisation ? David Holbrook would presumably say 'yes', but other educationists would answer with an emphatic negative on the grounds that Arnold's culture – the only culture worthy of the name – has been completely lost sight of in a morass of pupil-centred, Romantic, undisciplined self-expressive anarchy. The grammar school *aficianados* (and their views should be given full consideration) would obviously not see the idea of the common, creative culture as being the answer to all our problems. Professor G. H. Bantock, for example, believes that the cultural ideals of Arnold which seemed to be gaining such excellent ground in the schools in the twenties have in fact been sabotaged by an upsurge of working-class influence which has successfully diverted the stream in a self-expressive, line-of-least-resistance, essentially anti-cultural direction. Thus Arnold, Leavis, and the idea of culture as a body of excellence existing in its own right for the individual to measure himself against have been forced aside by a standardless insistence on every man's – or pupil's – right to be his own (creative) judge and arbiter of personal achievement. In *Freedom and Authority in Education*, 1952, Bantock describes the 'Progressive' revolution in education (the characteristics of that revolution being, according to him, an emphasis on means rather than ends, on impulse rather than on intellect, on expression rather than on absorption) and goes on:[11]

> Yet all revolutions . . . are the products of a need. The coming to power of new classes has demanded a recognition of their

plight and of their cultural disinheritance; or at least, of their disinheritance from that particular type of self-conscious culture which, in the past, has been the prerogative of the richer, upper and 'educated' classes.

> the nineteenth century myth of the noble savage has been replaced by the myth of the noble scion of the masses who is to provide us with those expressions of genuineness, spontaneity, dynamism, creativity, originality . . . which, conceived in the sort of way in which they are normally conceived, the superficial taste of our age finds so desirable . . .

The root of the problem, Bantock believes – and here he is on Leavis's minority culture ground – is that the vast majority of the population can find no place in the traditional educational system (in the sense of 'real', grammar-public education) simply because 'their mental abilities are inadequate to the discipline exacted'. The result is that the majority (always right) set up their own ideology which then swamps everything else. The democratic spirit of the thirties elementary school with its self-expressive concerns has spread at a rate and in a way that now 'threatens' the entire system, and Bantock sees Dewey's sinister influence in the background. Dewey, it need hardly be repeated, was concerned precisely with this 'democratic' ideal and with the need to modify existing 'academic' attitudes to education; as well as absorbing facts children must have scope 'to make, to do, to create, to produce, whether in the form of utility or of art'; 'The imagination is the medium in which the child lives . . . Shall we ignore this native setting and tendency, dealing, not with the living child at all, but with the dead image we have erected, or shall we give it play and satisfaction?' (*The School and Society*).[12]

Only time will reveal the true worth (or not) of Bantock's argument; in the meantime it would be extremely unwise to assume that 'creative' English teaching has established itself simply because the majority of children cannot be taught in any other way. Evidence overwhelmingly indicates that they *can* be taught in other ways, and that those ways since 1900 have frequently been pedantic, dull, and largely wasteful in their failure to engage the children fully in the study material, and in considering the wider and important issues which Bantock and Holbrook raise, we must not lose sight of the desire of every teacher of English worth his or her salt to make the English lesson absorbing, lively, and profitable so that the children are fully and willingly involved in their reading, writing and oral work to the limit of their capacities. The enormous problem facing the teacher of English today is that he must not allow the difficulties of secondary reorganisation to deflect him, or lose his nerve in the face of Bantock's pessimism, but must continue to work for the only

L

kind of education that matters – an education which marries pupil-centred concerns and a true sense of standards in a system which steers a mean between pupil-centred standardlessness and the upholding of standards which only a small minority of pupils can hope to approach.

English or social studies?

Perhaps the real danger arises where the 'Dewey' system is exaggerated in the hands of politically-committed English teachers who also see themselves as part-time sociologists. If Dewey is concerned with the practical side of life and with the children's 'social awareness' – their knowledge of society, its structure and workings – he is also adamant in insisting on the importance of imaginative experience. There has tended to be, in recent years, an excessive concern among some progressive English theorists for the former without the redeeming influence of the latter in an attempt (seemingly) to absorb English work into an unholy alliance with the social sciences. An example of this is the course book, *Reflections*, by Clements, Dixon and Stratta (for fourteen- to eighteen-year-olds, 1963) with its trendy comprehension passages on old age, the colour problem, urban planning, factory conditions, the mass media, the causes of crime, Hiroshima (no details omitted), or world poverty, and with an embarrassingly obvious sympathy for all those hackneyed 'nobility of labour', 'stop exploiting the working people', 'working-class communities are *good* communities' egalitarian catch-phrases. The book has had an astonishingly successful sales record, and has had no lack of imitators, but good though it may be to try and make secondary pupils, and especially disadvantaged pupils, aware of the social realities (abuses?) around them, an approach as obviously circumscribed and *prosaic* as this (essay suggestions: 'Working mothers – advantages and disadvantages', 'Find statistics on the size of families (with children) in Great Britain . . .', 'What is the point of having Unions in various trades and professions?') is too narrow to have anything more than a marginal influence in the long-term.

The trend embodied in a book such as this is worth noting, however, since it represents one way in which the creative 'whole-child' approach can develop (the working-class pupil with his innate good sense, sound judgment and natural capacity for sympathy can be trained in a social awareness and discrimination which will effectively prevent the attempts of the bosses to make a monkey out of him). The book is prefaced by MacNeice's 'Prayer before Birth',

I am not yet born; O fill me
With strength against those who would freeze my

humanity, would dragoon me into a lethal automaton,
would make me a cog in a machine . . .

with implications (the dehumanisers becoming distinctly and
exclusively middle class if not positively Tory) which might surprise
the poet.

Other course books in the *Reflections* style include Gordon
Lawrence's *Take a Look*, 1965; John Daniel's *Approaches*, 1965
(which includes a strange mixture of Zola, Barstow, Ruskin, Simone
de Beauvoir, Martin Luther King, Margaret Meade and others, con-
tributing to such topics as authority and revolt or old age and death –
though to give Daniel credit, his book is aimed at students in further
education and is subtitled 'An Anthology for English and Social
Studies'); A. Cattell and H. Gardiner's *Outlook 14/16*, 1968; and
R. S. Fowler and A. J. Dick's *English 15/16*, 1970 (including such
'relevant' topics as drugs, V.D., childbirth, illegitimacy, colour
prejudice and divorce).

Creative English and the grammar schools

In fact, despite the remarkable new look in method publishing it
would be quite wrong to assume that creativity has swept the board
since the mid-fifties as far as the textbook market is concerned.
Textbooks of an uncompromisingly traditional nature have continued to appear, although the stream has been abating somewhat
since 1965. Grammar-based books of the phrase-clause-sentence-
paragraph-formal essay approach are clearly still in widespread use
(see the bibliography for a representative list) although one wonders
why reputable publishers should feel the need to keep re-issuing
material fifty or sixty years old under new authorship instead of
simply revising and reprinting. Recent method books intended for
grammar school English teachers have generally deprecated the
continuing unimaginative style of language textbooks, but have
assumed, with GCE pressures, that some kind of formal grammar is
going to have to be taught through the schools, the traditional textbook package being as good an aid as any. We must also take note
of such pronouncements as those of the IAAM's 1952 Memorandum,
The Teaching of English, where it is still insisted that grammar study
promotes clear thinking, and that pupils will write better for being
able to clause analyse sentences. Grammar school method writers
seem increasingly to find themselves caught between two lines of
fire; thus W. H. Mason (*For Teachers of English*, 1964) will be found
insisting that some grammar teaching is essential (such as material
relating to types of clauses, simple analysis, the parts of speech)
although he has earlier remarked: 'The formal teaching of grammar
makes negligible difference to the child's ability to write well.' What

is even more disturbing is the fact that formal grammar as a separate timetabled subject is still being taught in a very few junior schools and by the use of pre-1940 textbooks into the bargain.

Despite the strictures of Holbrook and others on the irredeemable nature of the grammar school English course, is it possible to reconcile the demands of GCE with a less formal, more creative kind of teaching? The answer is almost certainly 'yes', though some teachers have been reluctant enough to try a new approach. By encouraging pupils to write and discuss in a personal, imaginative way, emphasising writing as a 'craft', it is possible to bring them to a point where they can meet their examination requirements and yet gain in many other ways at the same time. The pre-GCE years need not be strictly regimented along a 'succession of skills' rut (nor has it been in some grammar schools); indeed aiming only at the exam skills (neatly compartmentalised précis, comprehension, 'vocabulary' etc., each practised in isolation) is not only extremely limiting and dull, but dangerous as being more likely to produce failure by the hit or miss nature of the situation, and in any case is hardly likely to bring home to the candidates, successful or not, the sense that written communication is worth while for its own sake – a situation which is not helped by the nature of the language examination itself, which may not always be closely concerned with the things that really matter.

J. Patrick Creber in his *Sense and Sensitivity*, 1965, has outlined a first-rate scheme of work for grammar pupils along 'craft', creative lines, proving how easy it is to convert the pre-GCE years to this kind of work – not in a 'self-expression at all costs' manner, but aiming at a disciplined, accurate and imaginative use of language calculated to involve the personality and resourcefulness of the pupil to the full in a variety of realistic situations. Slightly more conservative but still lively with its material on story writing is J. H. Walsh's *Teaching English*, 1965, and Simon Stuart (*Say*, 1969) also offers creative methods of dealing with GCE classes, and his priority is also to get pupils writing, not in an impersonal, formal essay manner, but from a personal viewpoint in situations where they are forced to confront themselves and their own feelings; once get pupils to face their own fears, hopes, opinions and convictions and real writing can begin. (One fault of Stuart's book is its somewhat excessive preoccupation with depth psychology and Freudian transference.)

Since 1949 the journal the *Use of English* (which began as *English in Schools* in 1939), edited by Denys Thompson (now by Frank Whitehead), has consistently advocated more creative English courses in all schools, and the journal, with its strong commitment to imaginative self-expression by children on the one hand and to the critical methods of Richards and Leavis on the other, represents a line of thinking which secondary schools, including grammar schools, have been moving gradually towards in the last fifteen years (*Use of English* local groups were united to become the National Association for the Teaching of English – NATE – in 1963).

Some official views: SSEC, Newsom and Plowden Reports

But problems remain. The 1964 Report of the Secondary School Examinations Council on the 'O' level language examinations (the Council's eighth report) paints a very gloomy picture. 'Among the schools consulted we found almost unanimous agreement that the standard of competence in English among sixth formers had declined in recent years'[13] – and this not because of creative 'permissiveness', quite the contrary; this decline, the Report goes on, is probably due to the fact that (1) 'traditional methods of studying the English language in secondary schools have not been wholly effective' (although those methods have doggedly persisted); for example, Latin-based grammar is still taught, and the examinations 'have naturally followed the same pattern and so have tended to prolong a misdirected method of teaching' (2) reading and writing in any case are less important now as a means of communication (3) the competition for university places has caused pupils to study only their specialisms and neglect their English. In the summer of 1963 over 350,000 candidates sat 'O' level Language, but the Council is not satisfied with the nature of the examination: (i) it encourages the cramming of separate 'skills' which have only an indirect connection with good writing (ii) the reliability of marking is not so irreproachable that further research could not be undertaken to find out ways of improving it (iii) the examination encourages a very questionable essay style, unnatural, insincere and artificial, with 'still too high a proportion of titles such as "Islands", "Waiting Rooms", "Shop Windows", or "All That Glisters is not Gold" ' (iv) the grammar questions are equally unsuitable and undesirable: 'we share the view that they are of doubtful utility . . . and that in their present form they do great harm.'

The Committee members hesitate to denounce the external examination system completely since they believe that the coming Certificate of Secondary Education will change the situation dramatically, but they indicate that some far-reaching changes should be effected in the existing 'O' level system.

The Ministry of Education's 1954 pamphlet, *Language*, is also somewhat despondent. There have been advances in the subject since 1920 – in sixth-form literature study (with the influence of 'practical criticism') and in the overall approach to writing – but are school leavers better on average in 1954 in the use of language than their predecessors in the 1920s and 1930s? Formal grammar is still given far too much emphasis; old-fashioned essays are still much in evidence; the tedious minutiae of prosody are still relentlessly pursued; and poems are still approached in an 'allusion-hunting' manner.

The Newsom Report (1963) notes that many secondary modern pupils never reach the point where 'real' English begins, and that in far too many secondary schools (still) inappropriate and unimaginative English courses continue, though there has been no lack of general pressure for change or encouragement from method writers: 'Some teachers, including many who have never been trained for teaching English, give them [the pupils] a watered down version of what they remember from their own grammar school experiences. Much use is made of textbooks providing endless exercises in comprehension, composition and the like . . . Poetry is "done": drama may occur on Friday afternoons and towards Christmas . . .'[14] Speech work is neglected, or ignored; library deficiencies are marked; and newspaper and other mass-media study is the exception rather than the rule. Despite the fact that a whole new way of English thinking is now being worked out in the non-grammar secondary sector, there is no escaping the unwillingness – or inability – of many teachers to forget the past and make a new (pupil-centred, modern-centred) start.

'Newsom', in fact, takes a strongly creative line: 'The best way to study writing is to practise it. Children only learn writing by writing'; 'The English lesson . . . is most likely to offer those opportunities which allow adolescents to write out of themselves what they are not always prepared or able to talk about . . .'; 'Teachers whose sole standard is correctness can dry up the flow of language and shackle creative and imaginative writing before it is under way.'[15] Throughout the whole discussion of English work 'grammar' is not mentioned once.

The Plowden Report (1967) is, however, much more satisfied with the situation in the primary schools, which is to be expected in view of their recent history and development since 1935. 'Perhaps the most dramatic of all the revolutions in English teaching is in the amount and quality of children's writing'; 'In a growing number of junior schools, there is free, fluent and copious writing on a great variety of subject matter . . . Sometimes it is called "creative writing" . . . To this kind of writing . . . we give an unqualified welcome'[16] (two free verse poems by children are reprinted on page 220 of the Report's first volume). Plowden also comes out strongly against the practice of taking classes systematically through course books of English exercises; money would be better spent on building up school and class libraries than on textbooks of this kind; children 'learn to write by writing and not by exercises in filling in missing words.'

Of all the Board, Ministry or Department Reports since 1900

Newsom and Plowden have been the most up to date with current developments and thinking in English teaching, indeed Plowden's comments on certain aspects of English work are just about as 'advanced' (assuming the validity of such a concept as applied to something as complicated as English) as anything published by the same date with junior classes specifically in mind. This, of course, is entirely consistent with a report which comments enthusiastically on open plan organisation, criticises streaming, and heartily welcomes the disappearance of the 11-plus. The influence of the two Reports on actual school practice we will not attempt to gauge.

Children's poetry writing

The period 1960-70 might well be called the 'decade of pupils' anthologies'. In 1959 Marjorie Hourd and Gertrude Cooper published *Coming Into Their Own*, an anthology of 132 poems by junior children (more rhymed than in free verse). In 1960 Boris Ford produced *Young Writers, Young Readers*, a collection of children's prose, poetry and drawings (six to eighteen years), the quality of which is sometimes exceptional (some of the material had appeared in the *Journal of Education* in 1955, 1956 and 1957). In 1960 also the Dolphin Company published *Life Through Young Eyes*, another collection of children's art and writing, and in 1962 came Michael Baldwin's *Poems by Children 1950-61* (121 poems by children aged seven to eighteen years). Alec (now Sir Alec) Clegg's *The Excitement of Writing*, followed in 1964, and was the first anthology of 'official' status, being produced under the aegis of the West Riding LEA. Again, the poetry and prose (from both junior and secondary schools in the county) is often outstandingly good, and the collection is a very convincing justification of the creative free-writing approach in showing what some children are capable of (and should certainly be read by every teacher as an antidote to the traditional under-estimation of children's written capabilities). *Sprouts on Helicon*, edited by Judith Earnshaw, appeared in 1965 (sixth-form poems, with an Introduction by Herbert Read) and in the same year came *The Keen Edge*, edited by Jack Beckett (100 poems by children, mostly in free verse form), and *The Eye of Innocence* edited by Robert Druce (with some rather provocative remarks about pupils' capacity for poetic achievement).

There could be no more serious an acknowledgment of the importance and integrity of children's writing than the appearance of these anthologies; they are both a product of, and a powerful encouragement to, the creative movement in school English, and will stand out as a distinct and significant phenomenon in the history of the subject in this century. Now that the idea of children's anthologies has become an accepted part of the educational scene it is probable that fewer will be published in the future, though the action has in many cases moved into hundreds of school classrooms where children are producing school or class anthologies for internal publication – which is the practical result that one would hope for. One interesting development in this quarter has been the use of children's own writing as the principal ingredient in composition course books; in *Fields of Experience* by J. H. Walsh and F. Tomlinson, 1968, the approach to the writing topics is made through passages of twelve- to fifteen-year-olds' writing used as examples and stimuli.

Along with the appearance of these anthologies has gone a new lease of life for poetry method books, the best of which over this period include James Reeves's *Teaching Poetry*, 1958; Michael Baldwin's *Poetry Without Tears*, 1959; Margaret Langdon's *Let the Children Write*, 1961; Eric Bolton's *Verse Writing in Schools*, 1966; *Presenting Poetry*, edited by Thomas Blackburn, 1966; and Brian Powell's *English Through Poetry Writing*, 1968. From these the teacher can gather an abundance of good ideas and practical suggestions for use at all school levels – some of those suggestions being: children must write poetry as a regular classroom activity in a multitude of forms and patterns (such as free verse, couplets, haiku, ballad form or cryptogram) in response to diverse stimuli (including music, pictures and interesting objects); teachers must concentrate on the enjoyment which is to be had from poetry work and must find time simply to read poetry aloud to children; poems should be used for choral speech purposes, teacher and class 'working' orally with the poem; figures of speech hunting or metrical concerns should be reduced to a minimum – some writers would say to the point of disappearing completely; children must be given as wide a range of poems as possible, chronologically, thematically and (in translation, of course) nationally; teachers must make full use of records and tapes in the poetry lessons; and, finally, these writers are convinced that the educational value of poetry writing for children in terms of imaginative development, perceptual accuracy, sensitivity, vocabulary increase and for a sense of worth-while achievement is considerable.

Let it be said now that much of the poetry writing which is done in schools is little more than the old lesson in adverbs and adjectives, metaphor, 'descriptive' work and finding the 'right language', done as it should be done with reference to personal and convincing situations and with a definite end-product which has an integrity of its own – the free form or simple arrangement of compact imagery in unstructured lines helping the pupil and looking better on the page as a 'poetic' pattern. It is true that a few children are capable of producing astonishing effects (astonishing by children's standards, striking by universal standards) and in manipulating language for imaginative, expressive purposes they are surely coming to the heart of 'English', but the majority will probably produce poetry that is notable (if at all) simply because it is written by children. Any teacher who regularly encourages his or her pupils to write poetry knows that in the majority of cases the child's poem leans very heavily on the vocabulary, phraseology and atmosphere of the original stimulus, indeed the sceptic is justified in not taking a good deal of children's anthologised, printed or school-duplicated poetry very seriously for this reason. It is also a fact that adults often see 'striking phrases' where the child has merely written listlessly or unthinkingly and is quite unaware of the significance of what he has said – though the Romantic theorist would say at this point that this is entirely irrelevant, the end-product being what matters.

As an exercise in the use of language, poetry writing by children has no equal, and for sheer absorption and involvement for the pupils it cannot be bettered; the reservations come when the poems produced are judged as poems *per se*. Certain educationists are ambiguous on this point. Marjorie Hourd tends to put children's writing on a par with adult productions, and to use such Romantic (and sometimes emotive) terminology as 'inspiration' or even 'genius' when discussing them. Robert Druce, though rejecting the 'inspiration' approach, seems to be doing the same thing in *The Eye of Innocence*, suggesting that children write *poetry* – uncompromising poetry; he certainly does not distinguish between the term as applied to, say, MacNeice, Hopkins or Auden, and 'poetry' as applied to the school pupil, and his wholly serious 'new critical' evaluation of some of the children's poems in the book serves to confirm this. The fact remains that though I can evaluate a pupil's poem 'unseen', my assessment will be imperfect without knowing the pupil's age and having some idea of his or her general English ability – which is another way of saying that children's writing requires special treatment when it is judged and assessed, and that therefore it cannot stand the test of unseen comparison with adult work which stands or falls on its merits irrespective of the writer's age, education, social class, or any other extra-literary criteria. The observation is obvious to the point of banality, but needs to be made in the face of some teachers' apparent determination to push the child-centred approach to extremes.

It is also very dangerous to assume that teachers need now only leave their children 'free' and an endless flow of originality will automatically follow; every experienced teacher knows that for every hour of 'giving out' the pupil needs something like three hours of 'putting in' – of reading, discussing, listening and observing. Of course, here we come back to the differences between the Romantic as opposed to the Classical view of the child, and there is no getting away from the fact that writers such as Marjorie Hourd,

William Walsh (*The Use of Imagination*, 1959), Sybil Marshall (*An Experiment in Education*, 1963) or Marie Peel (*Seeing to the Heart*, 1967) – all outstanding and influential writers on English teaching, and all deeply committed to creativity and imaginative self-expression principles – invariably take their stand upon the Romantic-Coleridgean definition of the imagination, adopt a Wordsworthian line when discussing the growth of the child's sensibility, and take little account of other poetic forms (such as the Metaphysical of the seventeenth century or the 'wit' of the eighteenth) which, among other things, are likely to be at odds with the Romantic philosophy and in practical terms are too difficult for imitation by a child, demanding as they do intelligence as well as passion, adult knowledge-ability as well as 'feeling'. William Walsh, for example, is putting forward theories which are Romantic to the finger tips, and acknowledged to be so – the nineteenth century suppressed the child, the twentieth century has recognised and 'freed' him, only a few nineteenth-century writers did the child justice (Coleridge, Wordsworth, Dickens) and so on.

But is the Romantic faith in the child justified? and may not a view of the child's capacity for creativity which sees no further than Romantic hypotheses be short-sighted and unrealistic? Michael Baldwin makes a number of thoughtful remarks in the Introduction to his (pupils') anthology *Poems by Children 1950–61*:[17]

> in our current treatment of child art we are the guilty victims of a number of historical fallacies . . . One of these fallacies is that we live in an age of imaginative liberation for the young . . . The voice of the modern child, we are told, is the true voice; it is the voice of the child eternal . . . Unfortunately there is no evidence to support the idea that the young always could have been like this if only their elders and betters would let them . . . It is true that we have forged new keys to unlock new doors, but I fancy that most of the rooms were empty until we walked into them . . . We may appear to ourselves to do better for our children, but this is probably the result of living in an age which has reorientated itself towards the primitive in art and the psychotic in imagination. We have seen youth and age divided not by a ladder but by a barrier, and we have knocked the obstacle down. But there was a time when the ladder was truer, and it may become our image again . . . For the moment it is a sobering thought that the ease with which children become adult today may be merely because the adults are culturally so like their children.

For the child writer, as for the Romantic poet, it is the *intensity* of the work rather than its form that is the primary criterion, and as John Bayley points out (*The Romantic Survival*, 1957[18]) the adolescent imagination must be 'irresponsible' (i.e. not capable of evaluation on adult terms) precisely because 'it is not called upon to judge what it experiences by any other standard than its own intensity.' A 'liberation' which merely leaves the young writer as his own standard will see him more confined and restricted than before.

It is tempting to see a possible if somewhat fanciful parallel between the development of English (and art) teaching in this century and the development of the literary and cultural movements in Britain in the eighteenth and nineteenth centuries. The Romantic Movement in literature swept away the 'unimaginative', 'mechanical' literary approach of the eighteenth century with its emphasis on the 'imitation' of classical genres and its distrust of the personal or idiosyncratic; in the same way children now write freely, personally and imaginatively where before they copied, imitated or performed mechanical 'genre' exercises. Such a development in teaching is immeasurably satisfactory, though we should not forget the dangers inherent in the Romantic-individual approach, and which the latter part of the nineteenth century has shown to be a hair's breadth from the genuine creative process – personal expression degenerating into the repetitive emptiness of bogus and trivial 'aestheticism', self-expression for self-expression's sake.

As for the assessment of children's writing, perhaps Boris Ford's is the most sensible attitude (as given in his Introduction to *Young Writers, Young Readers*): 'This anthology, though not claiming to be Literature in the adult sense . . .' is nevertheless well worth reading (which it is). Against this we must be very cautious of such terms as 'staggering sophistication' (of junior pupils' writing – Sybil Marshall, *An Experiment in Education*, p. 165) or of such remarks as 'it is remarkable that our literature contains so little that is written by children and young people' (Jack Beckett, *The Keen Edge*, p. 7) or 'Older Juniors will pour out fine poems week after week' (Sylvia Huggler, 'Poems by Children' in *Presenting Poetry*, p. 35).

Creative writing: a definition

The key method books in the post-1950 creative English movement include Dora Pym's *Free Writing*, 1956, which describes the use of various sense stimuli to encourage writing (showing junior pupils various striking objects or pictures and telling them to 'Write whatever comes into your head'); William Walsh's *The Use of Imagination*, 1959; Holbrook's *English for Maturity*, 1961 (and subsequently *English for the Rejected*, 1964, *The Secret Places*, 1964, *Children's Writing*, 1967) and Margaret Langdon's *Let the Children Write*, 1961, an account of free verse writing as it developed spontaneously in her work with a Junior class, leading on to the use of sense stimuli situations. Frank Whitehead's *The Disappearing Dais*,

1966, reviews the creative possibilities in secondary work (while at the same time rejecting all that is misguided or pretentious in some of the current creative excesses) and Marie Peel (*Seeing to the Heart*, 1967), Barry Maybury (*Creative Writing for Juniors*, 1967 – here working through separate sense stimuli of touch, sight and taste to such stimulus situations as blowing bubbles, setting fire to paper, listening to music, or pouring water) and S. M. Lane and M. Kemp (*An Approach to Creative Writing in the Primary School*, 1967) offer junior material.

From these (and other) authors the basic characteristics of post-1950 creativity as applied to the writing situation can be summarised as follows: 1. 'Imitation' now gives way to 'creation'. The pupil's writing is accepted as having an integrity of its own; he is encouraged to produce in his own way what he can best do. The finished product is assessed as much for its liveliness and imagination as for correctness of spelling and punctuation. A personal, individual viewpoint is encouraged. The teacher corrects as helper in the creative process rather than as an examiner. 2. The pupil's own activity and initiative is stressed in discussing and choosing topics, or in deciding methods of treatment. 3. The pupil's writing must be 'personal' in the sense that he must draw upon his own resources (memories, feelings, experiences, vocabulary) in the writing. 4. Children can only learn to write by writing and will not learn through the completion of sets of textbook exercises or dummy runs. They must be encouraged to write as often as possible on as many types of subjects as possible. They will not approach writing via prolonged practice in the construction of sentences, then paragraphs, then whole compositions, but will go in at the deep end. 5. Pupils cannot write 'cold'. They must be given starting points, and ideally these will be stimuli (discussion, pictures, objects, reading, music, drama) that are sufficiently vivid to engage their interest to the extent that they *want* to say something. At this point they are left to deal with the subject as and how they like. 6. Pupils' imaginations must be stimulated, and imaginative writing exercises be used as often as possible. Since the way to the imagination lies through the senses, stimuli of a visual-tactile-auditory nature will be used. 7. The act of writing in 'real' situations comes first; the skills of grammar, spelling and punctuation afterwards. To reverse this order is to defeat one's purposes. It is believed that with constant writing of the right, engaged kind, and with corrections relevant to each piece of work, pupils will outgrow many faults. 8. By encouraging the child to express through ordered language inner feelings and emotions (which may be disordered or incompletely realised) we involve him in a genuinely 'educative' process, helping him to come to terms with his inner and outer world, with a possible therapeutic effect for disturbed children. Thus English and the use of written language becomes a means of developing personality. 9. Writing is seen as being a creative activity with words becoming a creative medium like paint or clay. The pupil is encouraged to *make* things with words and to enjoy this building process. 10. The whole subject 'English' is seen as a unity (not as an assemblage of separate pieces – 'spelling', 'grammar', 'punctuation', 'reading', 'writing', 'talking' etc.) based at root on the pupil's ability (a) to *use* his language, (b) to *respond* to that language over the whole range of possible language forms and styles, that use/response involving the full range of the pupil's imaginative, emotional and intellectual capacity. 11. Where the pupil's writing is personal he will work at his own linguistic level and will be able to internalise the various language stages as and when he becomes ready for them. 12. By stressing the 'craft', 'making' approach to writing, children gain insight into the craftsmanship of the books and poems they read (and it goes without saying that the writing programme must be supported by the widest possible range of reading material to be used with and by the children if creative written work is to be successful).

As for grammatical work, different teachers take different views, but by and large creative English will not include grammar teaching as such. Pupils will be instructed on an individual basis in the principles of spelling, punctuation, style and correct syntax as those points arise out of their own work and become relevant to them, but the swing is very much away from grammar teaching, particularly in the junior schools, and separate grammar exercises given in their own right are seen as being more or less useless, there being virtually no transfer to the written situation. It is not uncommon now for children to be told once in a while to concentrate on completing their stories or descriptions, letting the spelling and grammar take care of themselves, with a view to encouraging a sense of achievement in a finished item rather than handing in a half-completed, correct (more or less) piece of work – a procedure which would have profoundly shocked teachers in former times, but which may well have more beneficial effects in the long run.

It is also clear that no teacher is going to be able to teach creatively unless he or she has some insight into the creative process from first-hand experience, and it is extremely important that teachers themselves write, paint, act or play a musical instrument (or at least participate in the creative experience by reading imaginative literature, seeing good theatre or listening to music). The teacher who himself tries to use words as a medium of expression will know what the difficulties and satisfactions of personal writing are, and will be better able to steer his pupils into similar experiences at their own level. This is perhaps neglected in the teacher training courses, where insight into proper creative expression might well be emphasised more – along with the equally indispensable study of a main subject in depth. It does not follow that the poet- or painter-teacher will automatically be a better teacher; but it is hard to see how the creative method of teaching written English can be promoted effectively by anyone who has never experienced personal 'creative' satisfaction – and whose own response to language, for example, is unschooled and dulled through lack of use. (One might also add that the method is equally unsatisfactory in the hands of someone who sees sublimity in the most easily-achieved, obvious banalities.)

The success of Frank Whitehead's in-service course of creative writing for serving teachers at the Sheffield Institute, 1966–7 (described in his book *Creative Experiment*, 1970) suggests that this is a very profitable field for further experiment, and that the experience of such work can have a profound influence on one's view of English teaching. The course was successful in two ways, Whitehead writes in his Foreword:

> In the first place we all felt we had gained immensely in our insight into what it is we ask our pupils to do when we persuade them to write personally, imaginatively, creatively. In the second place the quality of our writing was so much beyond our expectations that we believed, rightly or wrongly, that some of it would be of interest to a wider audience. The creative powers of children and adolescents have rightly been celebrated in a number of books and anthologies published during the past twenty years; it is surely encouraging to be able to demonstrate that unpractised adults can reveal potentialities which are similar and no less striking.

David Holbrook, in *The Exploring Word*, 1967, has produced a creative training programme for the colleges and departments of education which takes the same line. Instead of continuing to perpetrate the worst excesses of academic 'Eng. Lit.' in Main English and B.Ed courses, the colleges (he insists) should aim at encouraging personal, imaginative schemes of work from students which will give them experience of the creative process and be of far greater benefit to them as future teachers of English (a fair point, spoilt in the book by his refusal to give any of the colleges any credit whatsoever for intelligent thinking).

A new grammar? Further linguistic considerations

The dismissal of grammar work is of course still very controversial. The lack of any substantial connection between grammar knowledge and written ability has been confirmed in a small piece of research by Nora Robinson in 1959, and she concluded (after studying second- and fourth-form pupils in four grammar schools) that there is a very low degree of relationship between knowledge of grammar and composition ability – in fact, she found that the lowest of her correlations was between grammar knowledge and grammar accuracy in writing. ('The relation between knowledge of English grammar and ability in English composition', abstract of a thesis, the *British Journal of Educational Psychology*, June 1960.)

We are at present witnessing the establishment of a new 'structural' or 'transformational' grammar, which, following recent theories in the field of structural linguistics, has made the traditional grammar largely obsolete, and new-style 'grammars' have actually been published with schools in mind (Mittins, Fries, Whitehall) though they are not yet in widespread use in this country. This new grammar has been hailed by several educationists as being the answer to all our grammar problems in schools; P. Gurrey (*Teaching English Grammar*, 1961) maintains that the old grammar is now doomed (and parsing and analysis in the old way with it) and that the 'new' grammar, taking its (descriptive) stand on English as it is actually used in speech, will supersede it as a valuable aid to pupils in their learning of English (in fact, Gurrey's new grammar is not, in 1961, quite as radical as that of Fries or Whitehall). The National Association for the Teaching of English also made a somewhat over-enthusiastic bid to use transformational grammar in schools, and there is certainly a strong case for teaching older secondary pupils the basic elements of structural linguistics. The danger remains that such teaching could easily become a mechanical drudgery, pointless and quite irrelevant, since it remains to be seen whether a knowledge of such grammar can actually improve spoken and written expression. By its very descriptive nature, it seems very unlikely that it would, though it would undoubtedly give pupils insight into the processes of thought and logical structure in a way that (though often claimed) the old grammar patently did not. One spin-off from the current linguistic programme which has given the creative approach to writing a strong boost is the suggestion that 'correctness' is a relative thing and that the child may have a standard of correctness which is quite different from the adult's, which is an obvious way of saying that we should standardise children against each other and not against mature, adult writing. In any case, the whole emphasis in structural linguistics is upon language as something which exists in use (not as a separate thing-in-itself) with the further implication that children should spend as much time as possible *using* language rather than studying it.

Perhaps some of the most useful research on English and the new linguistics has come from the Communication and Research Centre at London University, where an attempt has been made to relate recent linguistic discoveries to the school situation generally (a set of booklets has been published, see for example 'The Subject Matter of English' by R. Hasan and S. Lushington, 1968, or 'Current Attitudes to Written English' by P. Doughty, 1968). The research questions the concept of 'good' English as a fixed entity; modern linguistics has shown that the 'goodness' of a piece of writing can only be judged according to its context (intention, prospective reader, subject-matter) which suggests that teaching effective English expression is not so simple as it has tended to appear. The style of the formal essay as required of pupils for so many years (and constituting the criterion of excellence in written expression) must now be seen as being merely one out of a hundred possible modes of good expression, and we will be on firmer ground if we replace the notion of 'good' English with the notion of 'appropriate' English – appropriate to any given situation – and seek to make our pupils linguistically adaptable over as wide a range of communicative situations as possible. It is also emphasised that imposing 'good' adult structures on pupils irrespective of their readiness for those structures and without regard to their level of conceptual-linguistic development is misguided, and may lead to a situation where the pupil masters the structures superficially, and reproduces them mechanically, but never makes them a permanent part of himself (A. F. Watts's point). A good deal of a pupil's 'knowledge' (as shown in a short examination answer or in an essay) may be no more than a successful manipulation of the language appropriate to that subject or topic with no deeper grasp or real understanding underneath.

The new linguistics approach to English teaching is certainly 'creative' in laying stress upon the need to practise children in a wide range of styles and written situations, rather than regarding an adequate rendering of 'A walk in the country' as the desirable climax to a course in writing. M. A. K. Halliday writes: 'The replacing of the monolithic concept of "good English", a mythical register assumed to be superior for all purposes and in all contexts, by the notion of an English rendered effective precisely by its ability to assume various styles in response to different needs, has been one of the major sources of advance in English teaching theory and practice' ('Linguistics and the Teaching of English' in *Talking and Writing*, edited by James Britton, 1967). What we must now accept is the fact that rather than using one language we use and have to learn a range of 'languages' or language registers appropriate to the situations we find ourselves involved in, and what is even more important, we need to acquire the necessary linguistic tools to deal adequately with our personal and emotional experiences and relationships. Where the necessary linguistic tools are missing (as they will be in the adolescent pupil, for example) there can be no full understanding of, or ability to participate adequately in, those experiences. Pupils must be provided with the language which will allow them to understand and deal sensitively with love, grief, tenderness, sympathy, loyalty, indignation, anger, love of place and all the other complex emotional experiences of life. So many older pupils are completely at a loss when asked to discuss or evaluate a poem; they lack the language set and emotional concepts necessary for the task, and it is the responsibility of the English teacher to provide them, methodically and deliberately, with this kind of language (I. A. Richards's point in *Practical Criticism* – the qualities needed to respond adequately to imaginative writing being precisely those needed to respond to life's most worthwhile experiences).

The new look in textbooks

As already noted, the creative movement, sceptical of the value of textbook exercises (other than comprehension exercises), has tended to reject the textbook as a teaching aid and has been somewhat caustic on the subject into the bargain. Take, for example, the comments of the anonymous writer in *English in Education*, edited by Brian Jackson and Denys Thompson, 1962 (chapter 6); textbook writers, the argument goes (themselves often hard put to it to write good English), produce the stereotyped goods not for the benefit of children but for other teachers. And what do teachers want? Plenty of questions with right/wrong answers that make quiet lessons with easy marking at the end (all based on the false assumption that the various exercises are ends in themselves); plenty of familiar material (unchanged from their own school days); and plenty of solid factual matter that can be passed back and forth from teacher to pupil in satisfying chunks. Holbrook (*The Secret Places*, chapter 10) believes that the dreary and monotonous textbook drill 'is preserved simply by the appalling conditions in schools – the large classes, overworked and undertrained teachers', by the meanness of LEA's in book expenditure, and by the timidity of heads and departmental heads. It is almost as if there were a conspiracy to uphold the textbook routine as being wholly beneficial to children's growth in English usage when, in fact, it does them little or no good, and may even do harm by restricting their use of language. Frank Whitehead believes that the 'textbook fallacy' arises out of the fact that many teachers of English still cling to a 'faculty' misconception concerning the subject; 'We are still inclined to think of a child's linguistic abilities as an aggregate of separate limbs or muscles each of which needs to be duly "drilled" and "exercised" in the interest of the development of the whole' (*English Versus Examinations*, edited by Brian Jackson, 1965; these views he had put forward earlier in the *Use of English*, Summer 1952). The fact is that 'in all too many secondary classrooms ...

M

what we shall find, masquerading under the guise of teaching, is no more than a prolonged, repetitive practising of examination tasks which are artificial, limited, and trivial.'[19]

This, of course, applies to the traditional textbook. What has happened since 1960 is that textbooks in an entirely new style have begun to appear, these being collections of source material in an anthology sense (to promote and stimulate discussion and writing by children) rather than being course books of graded skills. They rely increasingly on the use of photographs (Michael Marland, for example, has produced in *Pictures for Writing*, 1966, a book based almost entirely on photographs as stimuli for pupils' writing, and see also T. R. Wood and C. R. Edwards's *Look Here*, 1969) and often adopt a 'thematic' approach, that is to say a series of topics (the seasons, home and families, holidays, space travel, animals, the supernatural) are represented by relevant prose and poetry extracts drawn from a wide range of authors, with suggested writing assignments added. In fact, such textbooks become collections of prose and poetry as much for the teacher's use as for the children's; the teacher who wishes the class to write on a particular topic will read passages from the textbook to set the scene, establish mood and suggest vocabulary.

This 'thematic' or 'topic' approach embodies the new thinking in English in two ways: first the format assumes the unity of the subject, bringing prose, poetry, reading, comprehension, talking and writing together – given the topic, the things that one can do with it are almost unlimited, and all are valid 'English' activities; second such a theme-centred approach is only another way of putting the pupil firmly at the centre, and making him the starting point for all the work. Themes are chosen in the first place because they are 'relevant' and of immediate concern to the pupil, and then suitable poems and prose extracts are chosen to fit the theme. The themes at secondary level (see above) may take the form of 'social' concerns – old age, modern youth and so on, and the 'thematic' framework has been incorporated into some CSE schemes. Good examples of this type of book include: *Reflections* by S. Clements, J. Dixon and L. Stratta, 1963; *English Through Experience* by A. Rowe and P. Emmens, 1963; *Topics in English* by Geoffrey Summerfield, 1965 (this a teacher's book); *Impact One and Two* by R. H. Poole and P. J. Shepherd, 1967; *Themes* by E. M. Hunnisett, 1967; *The Oxford English Source Books* by Nancy Martin, 1968; and *Aspects of English* by D. S. Higgins, 1970. Already there is a somewhat standardised pattern emerging as publishers vie with each other to get their own versions on the market, but at least we are witnessing a dramatic change in the form of school English textbooks, and this after something like sixty years of grammar-based conformity. The most recent trend at the time of writing seems to be away from books altogether towards a free format using packs of material (separate sheets of photographs, poems, extracts, stories, drawings, newspaper cuttings or maps) for 'thematic' English use by classes (see, for example, Peter Abbs's *English Broadsheets*, 1969). These packs may also include optional extras such as records, tapes, or, in book form, supplementary anthologies of poetry or prose.

The standard book of comprehension exercises has also continued through from the thirties and forties, and is still rightly regarded as being an essential part of English work in the great majority of schools. Good versions include: *Fifty Comprehension Tests* by W. S. Mackie, 1950; *English Composition* by A. F. Scott, 1951; the Oxford Comprehension Course, *Understanding and Enjoyment*, by N. C. Martin, D. and A. Griffiths, 1952; *English One to Five* by Raymond O'Malley and Denys Thompson, 1955; *English for Secondary Schools* by H. R. Thomas, 1961; *English Enterprise* by R. Campbell and R. Greenwood, 1963; or *Complete English* by E. G. Thorpe, 1963.

Current attitudes to literature: the relevance of 'the relevant'

The creative movement in its approach to literature study has also produced some far-reaching changes in recent English practice. The inevitable pupil-centred basis is taken for granted, and texts are used in order to try and extend the experience and imaginative capacity of the pupil, encouraging him to 'place' and come to terms with emotional experiences and 'find himself' in the reading. The suitability of novels, plays, stories or poems is judged by their capacity to touch the pupil personally and arouse responses in him; the texts will be used to trigger off (as stimuli) writing or talking, and if they succeed in doing this they have largely fulfilled their purpose (hence the popularity of the short story which lends itself easily to classroom study and imitation – see the large number of recent anthologies for schools, including *People and Diamonds* edited by Holbrook, 1962; *Modern Short Stories* edited by Jim Hunter, 1964; *People Like Us* edited by A. Rowe, 1965; *Facing Facts* edited by H. Moody, 1966; *Slings and Arrows* edited by T. Belton, 1966; *Twentieth Century Story and Statement* edited by M. Meredith, 1967; or *Life in Action* edited by R. Egford and A. Weeks-Pearson, 1969). The literature must be 'relevant', that is, it should preferably be contemporary, and should contain scenes, situations and characters which the pupil can recognise as being part of his own world, and if it deals with the kinds of 'problems' which adolescents are likely to experience (and a discussion of literature study naturally applies more to the secondary than to the junior school) then so much the better. Rather than testing the pupil against the text, the text is tested for its suitability, relevance, entertainment capacity, against the pupil, and will be rejected if it fails to fulfil the functions required of it. A criterion for selection might well be, does the novel or poem help the pupil 'to live'? rather than asking whether the work is an important part of the 'Great Tradition' deserving study as a landmark in the cultural heritage. In theory this approach actually widens the possible field of literature suitable for study well beyond the old-style Certificate canon of the twenties and thirties, though in practice the extension of interests has been limited almost exclusively to the twentieth century with an increasing disregard for literature before 1900.

In the past the *raison d'être* for literature study in schools has been more taken for granted than precisely defined; the examination system has ensured that speculation on the possibility of different approaches to literature has remained speculation, and as we have seen, texts remained firmly rooted for a very long time. Between 1900 and 1920 method writers usually referred passionately but rather vaguely to such things as 'truth, beauty and goodness' when discussing the purpose of school literature study, and although there was no shortage of opinion maintaining, first, that literature should be studied and second that it should be studied as literature and not as grammar, even the best writers on the subject tended to remain non-committal when the matter of purpose and benefits came up. After Richards and Leavis a much more positive kind of thinking emerges, based on the cultural-civilisation ideals of the 'best' which has been written, handed on to the future, and involving individuals in a personal challenge (literary inadequacies being inadequacies of an imaginative and personal kind) in their difficult but incalculably valuable attempt to respond adequately and intelligently to the structured visions of the best literature. This development did not, however, alter the uncompromisingly text-centred approach to secondary school literature study; in fact, it tended to intensify such an approach, making literature even more a discipline of sensitivity and maturity than a matter of vaguely emotive good intentions. 'Pupil-centred' literature study, if it existed anywhere at the secondary level before the 1950s, was to be found in the thirties senior schools where teachers were seemingly content to allow enjoyment to be the main criterion in their choice of pupils' texts, and where Rider Haggard, Conan Doyle, and H. G. Wells were more likely to be circulating than Carlyle or Ruskin.

The change of scene since 1950 has been a dramatic one, and the reasons for this change have already been outlined. With the movement into the centre of the educational picture of the mixed ability, modern school (or equivalent) class there has come a drastic revision of our ideas of school literature. If literature study is now pupil-centred, that pupil is a non-grammar, average or below average child in an old-style 'C' stream class, not concerned with GCE, not much of a reader, and probably from a home where books are never opened. The answer to the question 'What kind of reading can we possibly do with him or her?' has been, rightly or wrongly, 'provide him/her with "relevant" twentieth-century prose and poetry, presented perhaps under topic or thematic headings ("Homes", "Marriage", "War") which will add an additional framework of interest, and show that reading can be an entertaining activity.'

Whether or not all teachers have come to agree with this, a large number of publishing houses certainly have. A recent selection of educational blurbs relating to secondary literature anthologies includes: 'All the stories should prove thought-provoking as they pin-point the challenges and dilemmas which face young people who are growing up in the modern world' (Blackie); '. . . poems and stories, chosen for their relationships to the everyday living experience of many young people aged 14 to 18' (OUP); 'A book designed to encourage a critical awareness of the problems and controversial issues that will confront the school leaver' (Harrap); 'A wide range of different types of writing on various themes through which students may "approach" and consider problems and attitudes in present-day living' (Faber).

It is certainly high time that we paid serious attention to our pupils' likes and dislikes and to their actual capacity for literary experience, and this 'relevance' approach is excellent as far as it goes. Faced with a pupil who never reads we are justified in using pretty well anything if it will get him reading, and English teachers have made excellent efforts in the last few years to meet the challenge of the non-reader (whose need, after all, is perhaps greater than anyone else's); in any case modern writing has an indispensable place in any school reading scheme, including not only 'realistic' descriptions of modern life, but also science fiction, crime and detection, ghost stories, westerns, romance stories, spy or war stories (the Longmans school series is very well planned in this respect; see for example the science fiction volume, edited by S. H. Burton, 1967). In the past our text-centred tradition has been too inflexible, and has at times proved itself to be ridiculous in its pious attempts to bring adolescents to terms with books that few adults can properly appreciate, but the fact remains that if teachers insist on seeing the 'relevance' approach as being the be-all and end-all of literary work, then we are out of the curriculum fat into the curriculum fire. It was suggested in the Introduction that fallacies arise in English teaching where matters good in themselves but of only partial importance are elevated into central positions to dominate the subject. There is a very real danger that we are at present in the process of concocting a 'relevance' fallacy at the expense of real literature work. The trouble with the 'modern' and the 'relevant' is that it dates so quickly; today's best seller may well be a meagre

M*

has-been in two years' time when its essential triviality has had time to emerge, and what children surely need today more than anything else (their society being what it is) is a sense of permanence and continuity, of the valuable which remains valuable whatever the vicissitudes of popular taste or journalistic fashion. Literature study is under fire anyway at the present time, with arguments derived somewhat haphazardly from the social sciences asserting that the 'literary' experience is not much better than a social evening at the local, each being matters of personal taste and equally important as social behaviour patterns. More seriously there is a move towards a demand for the exclusively modern and 'relevant' among university English students, and we must be very careful when we come down enthusiastically on the side of 'relevant' school literature work to ensure that our motives are ours, evolved in the light of what we want for our children and (most important) what they are *capable* of, and are not derived from a society at large which will tolerate literature – and our teaching of it – only as long as it falls in with its totally inadequate concepts of human individuality and individual experience. The CSE examination has tended to favour the 'modern' approach; some CSE syllabuses cannot be faulted in their wide range of books for study, but a few have gone very far towards an exclusively contemporary approach, and it would be a retrograde step if the (much needed) modification of the GCE examination by a merger with the CSE should result in a secondary literature examination devoted nine-tenths to post-1950 writing, one-tenth to pre-1950.

If the sole criterion for choice of texts is to be whether or not they 'pin-point the challenges and dilemmas which face young people who are growing up in the modern world' what is going to happen to *Pickwick*, *The Ancient Mariner*, *A Midsummer Night's Dream*, *The Rape of the Lock*, *Under the Greenwood Tree*, *She Stoops to Conquer*, Chaucer's *Prologue*, Tennyson's *Idylls*, Keats's *Ode to Autumn* – or for that matter to Poe's *Tales of Mystery and Imagination*, *The War of the Worlds*, the *Odyssey*, Conrad's *Typhoon*, Garner's *Elidor*, *Reynard the Fox*, *The Land of Green Ginger*, *The Lost World*, *The Hunting of the Snark*, or *The Lord of the Rings*? The answer must be that they will fail to make the grade and will presumably be abandoned as old-fashioned, middle-class grammar school museum pieces, when it may very well be that their complete 'irrelevance' is the one feature which will make them work most effectively upon the imagination and emotions of the adolescent reader.

It is unlikely that all those who would disagree with this would go so far as to justify the superiority of contemporary 'realistic' literature for sociological reasons, but such arguments have been advanced. For example, in the Introduction to his anthology of modern prose extracts (*Prose of this Century*, 1966) Derek Stanford writes: 'If we pick up a book of eighteenth-century prose, we shall often be surprised how uniform it seems: the same tone, the same construction can be heard again and again. Turn to a shelf of twentieth-century books, and a greater diversity of accent is apparent. We have only to read some dozen present-day good novels to become convinced that the characters are *speaking* and the authors are *writing* quite differently in each.' There are no 'racial bars' in modern writing, he goes on (see Naipaul's pidgin-dialect), there are no 'class taboos' (see Wells's cockney), all proof of our 'democratic', 'individual' age. Now apart from the fact that this reveals a total inability to understand eighteenth-century literature (the point is made not to be offensive, but to suggest that some secondary teachers are less acquainted with what literature really means and is all about than they should be) there is here a complete confusion between literary criteria and social-class criteria in judging writing. Here again is a narrowing of purpose which is anything but in the interests of the pupils since it encourages an attitude to literature which is false, illiberal, foolish and self-defeating. If 'middle-class' literature is out, and the prosaic 'relevance' of Barstow and Braine are in, we have effected a very dubious exchange, to say the least.

Another feature of much present literature teaching is the tendency to take bits of books in anthologised form and use these as part of the topic study in hand – the selection of the 'right' kinds of books (Barstow, Braine, MacInnes, Orwell, Storey, Sillitoe) is thus narrowed further by the choice of the 'right' passages in them, and this can present some very stereotyped samples (see as typical anthologies, G. C. Urwin, *A Taste for Living*, 1967; Penelope Manners, *Novels of Today*, 1967; E. Cope and N. Stephenson, *Never Till Now*, 1968). The tendency then is to stress purely the 'content' aspects of the writing without paying attention to stylistic or imaginative features. Reading becomes reading for fact, when any literary experience which is worth anything must include some consideration of style, aptness of description, sense of atmosphere, imagery, symbol, unity and imaginative insights – the qualities that distinguish literature from good reporting. It is, obviously, quite wrong to confine 'literature' to novels, stories, poems and plays; travel books, biography, autobiography, memoirs, journals, letters and diaries have been under-represented in reading syllabuses in the past, but it is not a particularly good idea to weight pupils' reading too heavily towards non-fiction writing; thus an exclusive diet of such writers as Paul Brickhill, Thor Heyerdahl, Joy Adamson, Cousteau, Grimble or J. H. Williamson (*Elephant Bill*) – to mention some popular CSE authors – will restrict the scope of the course to an entertaining but low-gear level. The fact is that we do not know exactly how literature affects and influences us or know what is happening when we read it; much of the response, as with music, say (and the argument is equally applicable to children), is indefinable and inexpressible working at depth in the individuals' emotional system. While we are busy simplifying the business for our pupils with the intention of helping them as much as we can we may well be rendering quite impossible the other 75 per cent of literary experience which we have tidied out of existence. To put it in practical terms we will probably be doing our pupils more good by putting a poetry anthology such as Holbrook's *Iron, Honey, Gold* into their hands (with its range of carefully chosen poems covering several centuries, though not the tired 'classics' usually associated with this kind of approach) than giving them the exclusively modern 'relevance' of Ted Hughes's *Here Today* or Baldwin's *Billy the Kid*, important though the last two may be as starting points for confirmed non-readers of poetry, and good though they are as anthologies in their own right.

It is also a fact that a small minority of CSE syllabuses are involving their candidates in the study of meretricious trivia, the third-ratedness of which is chiefly arraignable for its underestimation of the non-academic pupil's capabilities. Let us by all means consider some or all of the following as having written suitable material to read with pupils between twelve and sixteen years of age: Aldiss, Allingham, Asimov, Balchin, Ballard, Banks, Barstow, Beaty, Braine, Bradbury, Canaway, Cather, Chapman, Christie, Christopher, Corbett, Cousteau, Durrell, Fleming, Hersey, Heyerdahl, Hines, Hoyle, Innes, Jacobsen, Le Carré, Linklater, London, Maclean, Mason, Masters, Monsarrat, Moorehead, Naughton, Salinger, Sansom, Shaefer, Shute, Sillitoe, Simenon, Steinbeck, Storey, Sutcliff, Tey, Thurber, Treece, Waterhouse, Weyman, Williamson, Wister, Wodehouse and Wyndham; but within this selection there exists an enormous range of style and quality, and the most careful selection is going to be needed to sort the short-term dispensable from the long-term valuable. This is no easy task, and teachers are burdened enough as it is, but an avid pursuit of the modern for its own sake can easily lead to unprofitable time-spinning. The fact that the same modern authors are continually reappearing edited or anthologised for school purposes seems to suggest that a stereotyped pattern of choice could already be setting in. An ominous sign is the basic similarity of so many of the short story anthologies with their by now predictable reliance on Dylan Thomas, Saroyan, Muriel Spark, Katherine Mansfield, Hemingway, Lawrence, Sansom, Frank O'Connor, Doris Lessing and Scott Fitzgerald. It may be that we have not looked far enough afield for prose texts material and could pay more attention to (translated) non-British writing for example.

The 'relevance' case has been put very convincingly by Louise Rosenblatt in *Literature as Exploration*, 1970 (first published in

America in 1968), so convincingly in fact that the weaknesses in her argument tend to be overlooked. In her Preface she distinguishes between the 'sociological' approach to texts (using them as social documents merely) and what she calls the 'aesthetic' approach (a kind of art-for-art's-sake narrowness) and maintains that the teacher must steer a course between the two. She then devotes the greater part of her book to the advantages of the former, dealing with the art-form side (symbol, style, imagery, writing as an art form) in less than twenty-eight pages. When she declares that the student (high school) 'must be able to absorb from the literature of the past and of the present what is sound and relevant to his own needs in this age'[20] she is in fact referring to the factual fodder of social and social-psychological material. Literature becomes a springboard for discussion about the student's own behaviour, a kind of literary therapy where the patient's complexes are what matter: 'After reading *Hamlet* the . . . student . . . often turns to theorizing about the rational and irrational elements in human behavior' (true, but that has nothing to do with *Hamlet*). She further maintains that it is a pity that teachers of literature are not also well informed as psychologists and sociologists; because they are not, their discussion of characters in books must remain 'superficial'; 'The problem is that the average teacher or college instructor in literature is not necessarily equipped to handle these topics in a scientific spirit. Hence the discussion of characters and motivation tends to follow the superficial lines of ordinary everyday conversations about people . . . To provide a critical framework, the instructor needs some knowledge of the dominant conceptions in psychology.' Thus teachers of literature fail their pupils by not getting what they really need across to them.

Now this, to borrow from Jane Austen, hardly merits the compliment of a rational answer. We know perfectly well that works of literary art are not written to be probed 'scientifically' (the professional psychologist rightly scoffs at the notion) and as for a knowledge of the 'dominant conceptions in psychology' we are presumably to ignore Arnold's criticism because he hadn't read Freud, or Bradley's because he hadn't read Eysenck, or Johnson's because he hadn't read any of them.

We get to the heart of Louise Rosenblatt's argument when she admits that her attitude is largely based on that of her own pupils, who want 'information' and 'relevant experience' in their reading that can help them in their lives. Now the pupils have an excellent case, despite the fact that they have been misled into thinking that literary study is something which it isn't; of course literature can help them to live in indirect and indefinable ways, but to elevate this by-product into a system is to make nonsense of literary studies. One cannot help feeling that Louise Rosenblatt finds herself to be in rather a fix; she obviously wants to do the best she can for her pupils, on the other hand she clearly has (despite the foregoing) a genuine feeling for literature, and while at one moment she is saying that to give in to the pupils' demand for 'relevance' may lead the teacher 'to do injustice to the text' – an injustice which is wholly justified – she later admits that 'the clarification of the reader's personal understanding of the novel or poem or play carries with it a responsibility to the text itself.'[21]

The confusion in her argument in fact reveals the impossibility of having it both ways – of having a form of literature study worthy of the name which is also totally pupil-centred. She is also a victim of the behavioural science school, and one does not know whether to extend sympathy or hilarity to such comments on the English teacher as: 'Without such knowledge [of the behavioural sciences] he will probably be very effectively undoing in the English classroom whatever the teachers of social studies may have succeeded in accomplishing.'[22] Perhaps the 'relevance' fallacy is really a 'social studies' fallacy.

A book which is on much sounder ground is Sydney Bolt's and Roger Gard's *Teaching Fiction in Schools*, 1970. The authors believe that children are not being taught the vital technique of reading imaginative literature as such, but are being fed with 'reportage' and factual prose when they are actually capable of imaginative 'critical' assessments of writing from a very early age. Even small children listening to fairy tales are responding not only to the story but to the *way* the story is working, its shape, deliberate repetitions, irony, its insistence that some things be taken for granted as unremarkable while others be noted as unusual, comic or sinister. The authors suggest that the question teachers should ask of the child's response to reading is not 'Has he got it?' (understood the facts) but 'How is he to take it?' (what kind of response is demanded at each advance in the tale). All fiction demands of the child an imaginative involvement which requires that he accept certain things, ignore certain things, and assess certain things – and children understand this instinctively. Writers, including children's writers, are concerned as much with plot pattern, symbol or irony as with facts; their appeal is as much to the imagination as to the intellect, to the intuitive as to the rational. Bolt and Gard conclude: 'If its unique educational value is to be realised, fiction must be read critically . . . this means that it must not be read as fact.'[23]

It is ironic that the creative approach, which owes its very existence to a faith in the imaginative capacity of the child, has taken a direction in secondary school literature work which is both pupil-centred (providing relevant material to increase the pupil's 'awareness' and develop him as an individual) and anti-imaginative in the sense that 'relevance' comes to assume social-external not personal-intuitive attributes. Is it so very difficult to provide adolescent pupils with a suitable range of literature both ancient and modern, or to try and get them responding imaginatively to the imaginative? We cannot retreat automatically into the defence that 'they don't want it' – we don't know until we try, and if Fred Inglis's survey of secondary pupils in *The Englishness of English Teaching* is a reasonably accurate estimate, then it is clear that non-grammar pupils are not hostile to the literature of previous centuries but would actually like more of it than they are getting. If the discipline problems are such that a school feels that anything approaching imaginative literature study is impossible then by all means go for a series of topics on sexual relationships, marriage, illegitimacy, drugs, or abortion, but let us not delude ourselves that this is the best and only way to encourage reading, writing or discussing, or indeed that what the pupils think they want is what they really need.

Just how are we to react, confronted by fractious and difficult pupils who have a hearty distrust of books, to comments such as: 'Part of the initiation into literature should be a glimpse of the glory of language, a fostered sense and feeling that language is a form of beauty with its roots in the imagination' (George Sampson, 1921); 'Through suitable modern poetry . . . the pupil should be led back to the classical examples of English verse; and the teacher should not neglect those great pieces of English literature which have stood the test of time' (the 1931 Primary School Report); 'All the pupils, including those of very limited attainments, need the civilising experience of contact with great literature, and can respond to its universality, although they will depend heavily on the skill of the teacher as an interpreter' (The Newsom Report, 1964)? The answer is that we must do the best we can, always bearing in mind the fact that some seemingly attractive solutions to the teaching problems that confront us may be little better than a premature sell-out to the very utilitarian, anti-imaginative forces we are fighting.

Texts and examinations: wider horizons?

As far as poetry is concerned children (and particularly junior school children) are certainly being introduced to a much wider range of verse writing today, if only in small doses and with an emphasis on contemporary poets. Taking three typical anthologies – *Every Man Will Shout* (R. Mansfield and I. Armstrong, 1964), *Happenings* (Maurice Wollman and David Grugeon, 1964 – interestingly a 'middle school' anthology which has as a middle school method counterpart, D. Mattam's *The Vital Approach*, 1963) and Penguin's *Voices* (Geoffrey Summerfield, 1968–70) – we find poems by Yevtushenko, Robert Lowell, Ted Hughes, Robert Frost, MacNeice, Dylan Thomas, Lawrence, Ogden Nash, Wilfred Owen, Conrad

Aiken, Prevert, Graves, Arthur Waley, E. E. Cummings, James Reeves, Kirkup, Larkin, Roethke and Emily Dickinson. This range is all the more exciting in view of the conservatism manifested in anthologies before the Second World War. A broadening of attitude is also evident in the adoption of new, contemporary set books by the Certificate Examining Boards, where, for example, prose by Priestley, L. P. Hartley, Lawrence, William Golding, Graham Greene, Van Der Post and Ivy Compton-Burnett, the poetry of Eliot, Graves, Owen, Hughes, Gunn, Dylan Thomas and Auden, and drama by Willis Hall, Pinter, Wesker, Whiting, Bolt and Osborne have become established as examination regulars.

Whether all the educational publishers have managed to keep up is another matter. In a 1968 *Use of English* article Emmeline Garnett lists the number of available (in print) editions of popular school literature texts. At the top comes *Treasure Island* (with 29 editions available), followed by *Kidnapped* (21), *Gulliver's Travels* (19), *A Tale of Two Cities* (18), *Jane Eyre* (17), *David Copperfield* (17), *Lorna Doone* (16), *Little Women* (15), *Great Expectations* (14), *Robinson Crusoe* (13), *The Pilgrim's Progress* (12), *Pride and Prejudice* (12), *Coral Island* (11), and *Ivanhoe* (9). Granted that there is an overseas market for these books and that well-meaning but out of touch relatives tend to be conservative when it comes to present giving, the figures are still incredible; publishing houses are not charitable concerns, and there is clearly a demand (in sets of thirty for the stock cupboard?) for these editions. When Fred Inglis, in his survey of secondary pupils (*The Englishness of English Teaching*), asked for lists of what the pupils considered were important poems he received (overwhelmingly) the following: 'Snake' (Lawrence), 'Daffodils' (Wordsworth), 'The Highwayman' (Austin), 'The Revenge' (Tennyson), 'The Inchcape Rock' (Southey), 'Elegy' (Gray), 'Hiawatha' (Longfellow), and 'Break, break, break' (Tennyson).[24]

To be fair to the General Certificate Examining Boards, who could be said to be partly responsible for this state of affairs, there can be no doubt that they have taken steps to adapt to the changing pattern of English teaching since 1965. As one example, the Cambridge 'O' Language paper for summer 1968 has a good selection of writing (rather than 'essay') topics, such as: 1. 'How will you spend your evenings when your GCE examinations are over?' 2. ' "Protest Marches": Would you ever take part in one?' 3. 'Railways in Britain'. 4. 'Souvenir Hunting' or 'Bringing Back Presents'. 5. 'Write a short story of your own invention beginning with the words, "My uncle was always borrowing money" and ending with "He died very rich aged ninety-six".' 6. 'A pen-friend from Africa or India has asked you to describe the house you live in . . . write a reply'. 7. 'The last day of your holiday at a seaside resort'. 8. 'Preparing for a party'. 9. 'What thoughts and feelings are inspired by the accompanying picture' or 'Write a story suggested by the picture' (café, motorcycle boys, two girls). The choice is now much wider, the ideas and situations are more relevant to the experiences of the candidates, and they receive much more help with regard to suggestions as to how the topic might be tackled.

This sort of thing is very recent; if we follow the Joint Oxford and Cambridge Board's 'O' Language papers, we find for 1961: précis, comprehension, correction of sentences, punctuation and an essay on 'Advertisements' or 'The Use of Leisure' or 'A Walk at Night' or 'Teenagers'. For 1963 there is précis, comprehension, correction of sentences, a vocabulary exercise, and an essay on 'Doctors', or 'Doing it Yourself' or 'Antique Shops' or 'Greed'. But the 1965 (summer) paper has précis and comprehension only, with traditional essay subjects ('Record Breaking', 'Hair', 'Your Family', 'Home is the Girl's Prison and the Woman's Workhouse. Discuss') and also an additional composition section which is much more up to date, including: 1. 'Describe in some detail an initiative test for members of your own form, including all the instructions necessary for taking it.' 2. 'A house is close to a field where battery chickens are reared. Write, as the householder, a letter to the owner of the chickens complaining about the enterprise.' 3. 'Consider what problems would arise in case of fire at your school, and describe the kind of fire-drill which might overcome them.' The Oxford Board also altered its regulations in 1965 to introduce a two-paper language examination based on composition (both 'factual' and 'free' – paper 1) and on comprehension (including a passage of imaginative writing – paper 2), and there have been other experiments in examination by continuous assessment (by the JMB for example).

In 1966 NATE (*English Examined: A Survey of 'O' Level Language Papers*) found that essay subjects were still generally unsuitable, dull or old-fashioned, and that where Boards did include 'imaginative' topics they were often simply juvenile and of a 'Lost in the Caves' or 'A Perilous Journey' kind. They also found that the worst kinds of grammar questions were still being set, and that the passages set for comprehension were often dull and sometimes badly written. The survey makes L. C. Knights's point that the vast administrative problems facing the Boards make streamlining, standardising, and stereotyped questions inevitable, and the investigators add the following comments and recommendations: (1) the essay demands a very questionable kind of 'correctness', and a much wider range of writing topics must be introduced, (2) isolated grammar questions must cease to appear, (3) the unnecessary and false division between 'language' and 'literature' must end, (4) literature set books are still unsuitable in many cases, and passes are obtained through reliance on rote memorising without any genuine reading; the range of books must be extended and these books should be taken into the examination room by the candidates, (5) an oral test must be an integral part of any English examination, and (6) some scheme of internal assessment should be brought in to supplement or replace the present scheme as soon as possible. The survey comments, somewhat grimly, 'There are few signs as yet that Boards have thought out properly the nature of the skills they seek to test', but a hearty welcome is given to the tentative reforms made very recently by some Boards (Oxford, the JMB and the SUJB for example) as a result, the survey believes, of CSE pressures.

Frances Stevens's survey of the 'A' level literature examination (*English and Examinations*, 1970) is also very critical. She concludes from the study of actual JMB examination papers and scripts for 1964 that questions can still be impossibly obscure, or demand quite irrelevant material; that candidates seem to be obsessed with a need to hunt down figures of speech and other allusions (which indicates the kind of teaching they are getting); and that all too often candidates write carefully prepared essays, reproducing a complicated system of 'points' (on plot, characters or style) without giving any impression of personal contact or involvement with the text. She makes the point that as long as the emphasis in literature examinations is on *memory*, the candidate will never be able to sit down and do the question justice, because the need to go through the correct recall sequences will effectively prevent the possibilities of a proper critical response to the text in the light of the questions.

It is impossible to guess at the extent of the influence which the establishment of the CSE and the style of CSE English papers have had on GCE thinking. If recent 'O' language papers are taking a more realistic and lively approach to writing, they are certainly coming into line with the kind of written tasks recommended by the Secondary School Examinations Council in their 1963 Bulletin, *The CSE: some suggestions for teachers and examiners*. The Council, for example, outlines a possible paper that might be set (Appendix 5 of the Bulletin):

Question 1, Write a composition of from 250–300 words on ONE of the following. You may use the notes and suggestions or you may disregard them if you wish. (a) My Career. (Describe the career you have chosen; say what job you will do when you begin; how this fits in with the industry or profession as a whole; the qualifications needed by a beginner; the prospects of promotion; what do you find attractive in this career.) (b) A Family Holiday. (c) Racial Trouble. (d) Continue for about 200 words one of the following descriptions: (i) 'It was built for a great many people, and as usual they were all there . . .' [etc.] Question 3, Write a composition of about 200–300 words on ONE of the following: (a) Retell in your own words one of the parables of the New Testament and apply it to people of the present day. (b) Which game or physical activity would you like to see introduced at your school? (Describe your school and the games played.)

It is not merely that the less academic pupils will have to have help, but that this kind of combination of helpful suggestions with sensibly chosen topics is desirable for all candidates – and can only cause good candidates to do even better. In the same Bulletin the SSEC suggests that Examining Boards in the past have not always defined exactly what it is that they want to examine as far as English is concerned, and what skills they want the candidates to display. The Council offers the following as a basis for CSE thinking:[25]

> English, well-taught, should train a 16-year-old secondary school pupil to use the language confidently, appropriately and accurately, according to the circumstances in which it is used. He should be able to speak his own mind, to write what he has thought, and to have a care for the correctness of written and spoken English. He should be able to understand what he reads and hears, to master the ideas and restate them in his own way. He should have some understanding of the different uses of language, of the language which relates, describes, evokes, persuades and is the instrument of the creative imagination.

Examiners should look as much for lively and personal expression as for accuracy, though it is assumed that at least one section of any paper will be marked strictly on an accuracy basis.

At the time of writing it is impossible to say what the likely outcome of the Schools Council's Investigation of the Secondary Examinations situation is likely to be. There are strong pressures to combine GCE and CSE (and preserve what is best in both) and also to eliminate the false division between language and literature in the examination situation. At present CSE remains an academic second-best in the minds of many people; the fact is that in its approach to certain aspects of English it has a great deal to commend it, and can teach the GCE system a thing or two. As for the CSE 'crammers' which have appeared on the textbook market recently ('This book will, it is hoped, be particularly useful for classes taking the examination') the least said the better.

Conclusion

Is creativity then a way of thinking and a way of teaching English which is without reproach, and have we, in finally achieving what seems to be a genuinely pupil-centred philosophy of English, at last raised the subject to a level which will see the next seventy years out efficiently and effectively? The answer can only be that it seems unlikely. There is no reason to suppose that we have stopped manufacturing fallacies, and since English is peculiarly susceptible to a Red Queen kind of locomotion, we are going to have to move on to retain the ground we have achieved to this point. We know that social changes mean educational – and therefore English teaching – changes; we know that by the year 2040 such predictable (let alone utterly unpredictable) items as the structure of society generally, its culture (or lack of it), its class system (if any), its career patterns, its educational features (length of school life, the examination system, treatment of gifted/handicapped children, new subjects, nature of Higher Education, training and role of teachers) as well as the general discoveries in the fields of psychology, linguistics and the social sciences will all have undergone considerable development and change to the point where many of the English teaching theories of today will seem quaint at best, ludicrously antediluvian at worst. It is not so much that we have moved, in the last seventy years, from a clutch of fallacies to enlightenment as that we have moved from one English fallacy to another – but then, given the nature of time, a fallacy is merely the name we give, with all the confident patronage of hindsight, to something we no longer consider to be strictly appropriate or relevant to the main business of English teaching, whatever we happen to think that is at any given moment (after all, the first, *The Times Educational Supplement*, reviewer of Sampson's *English for the English* believed that 'This somewhat windy plea for the teaching of more humanities in the elementary schools, and for an improvement in our educational system generally, perpetuates a good many fallacies'). We have clearly reached a point where there is substantial agreement among teachers that the best – the only – way to approach English is by establishing a 'philosophy' or total view first (of the pupil's needs, of the nature of 'English', and of the nature of the long-term goals we are after) and then shaping the separate subject elements to fit that overall pattern, rather than working at those separate elements in the hope that their application to the pupil will achieve something. That philosophy or total view has been extended and expanded in the years since 1945 to an astonishing degree, and it seems certain that the confines of 'English' as a school subject, so narrow and short-sighted in the past, will continue to be pushed outwards in the next seventy years.

The weakness of the 'overall' theory, of course, is that if we get the philosophy wrong then it is likely that everything will be wrong, and it would be idle to pretend that at present all teachers are happy with the creative approach and its pupil-centred assumptions. The tide is now running very strongly in a pupil-centred, self-expressive,

anti-examination, anti-grammar, common culture, 'relevant' literature direction, but this is a British rather than an international
phenomenon, and we are determined far more than we realise by
the irrational and sometimes accidental developments of the subject
in the past. The American representatives at the 1966 Dartmouth
(USA) seminar on English teaching made the point that current
British attitudes to English studies are determined, whether
teachers realise it or not, by a sense of release from, or rebellion
against, a long-established authoritarian regime only now showing
signs of relaxation (see Herbert Muller's report of the American
view of the seminar, *The Uses of English*, 1967). Surprisingly, since
'USA' and 'progressive' in its non-pejorative sense are usually linked,
some of the American delegates actually expressed dismay at the
British soft-pedalling of 'rules', 'skills' and 'discipline' in reading and
written work. John Dixon (writing the British account of the
seminar, *Growth Through English*, 1967) notes that 'the prevailing
American concern seems to be with the danger . . . of a chaotic
approach to operational English associated with a "child-centred"
curriculum in which the major concern was social adjustment and
not a child's growth in intellectual, imaginative and linguistic
power.'[26] (A concern, one might add, which is not exclusively
American.) There is further irony here in that 'democratic' Americans
are expressing concern at the nature of 'the people's' (creative)
English in British junior and secondary schools as it has developed
in the increasingly liberal (political and cultural) atmosphere since
the 1930s. British agreement with the Dartmouth American view
might well express itself in the words of Sir George Pickering, *The
Challenge to Education*, 1967, as follows: 'Britain is obsessed with
the function of education as an instrument for levelling society and
for eradicating the privileges of wealth and ancestry' and as education
is sacrified on the altar of egalitarianism so English is sacrificed on
the altar of pupil-centred creativity with its mixture of self-expression and *Reflections*-like 'social awareness'.

Be that as it may, the fact remains that the advances which have
taken place in English teaching in this country since 1945 are
tremendously exciting, and we have at least gone some way to make
up for the stagnation which has distinguished the subject in the past.
Out of the present intense soul-searching will at least come a body
of theory for future decades which will be distinguished by its
positive rather than by its conservatively negative qualities, and
there can, after all, be a quality of illumination in splendid wrong-
mindedness which is not to be found in a cautious re-treading of the
safe and the familiar. Whatever the reasons, there is no doubt that
English has at last got its heart in the right place, and all talk of
'standards', classroom procedures, or specific teaching practices
apart, there is no disputing the fact that English teaching priorities

are now (theoretically) more thoughtful, humane, far-sighted, imaginative and worth while than they have ever been before.

It is not creative methods so much as their abuse that can bring disrepute on the present movement. Where those methods are not properly understood, all sorts of unfortunate situations can arise, and some teachers may be tempted to retreat behind the vision of the liberated 'child-wonder', good for twenty years of spontaneous original expression, and abdicate what should be their teaching responsibilities. There is also evidence which suggests that where the 'new' English is not properly understood the skills of spelling, punctuation, sentence structure and style generally are not only being put second to actual writing, but are being ignored almost to the point of disappearing completely. It is true that a creative experience of writing is much more likely to make the pupil spelling- or expression-conscious, but creative writing *by itself* can do nothing for spelling, which is going to have to be tackled in a traditional, formal way. To leave children to circle endlessly in a colourful abundance of their own unchecked spontaneity is to leave them stewing in their own unformed linguistic juices to nobody's advantage.

The removal of the 11-plus examination with its attendant cut-and-dried syllabus and formal textbooks has left many teachers uncertain of their goals and without a sense of progression or purpose in their work with children, so that each piece of work exists merely in and for itself (it is here that the Plowden Report is weak; an enthusiastic support of creative English without giving specific and sound overall aims – beyond the 'growth' of the child – is not very helpful in the long-term). All teachers must seek to explore the current philosophy of English and then evolve practical methods which will embody their own considered and thought-out version of that philosophy with due regard for pupils' needs and for standards. In the absence of an external examination it becomes extremely difficult to find standards of comparison to test the achievement of one's children by, and we are perhaps too easily satisfied with some of the poems and stories which our average to able pupils can turn out efficiently and regularly, though perhaps not always with the full application and positive effort that those productions may seem to involve.

There remains, nevertheless, an important difference between the quality of the machine and the quality of our handling, or mishandling, of it, and we have in many of the new English techniques the most potent instruments for the achievement of real education if we will only apply them properly. But we must not let the opportunities seep away in half-hearted or incorrect application, nor lose sight of what really matters in a fog of Romantic or egalitarian exaggeration. Almost certainly the old demands on children were greater; they may have been the wrong demands (complex analysis at eleven, the whole history of literature at sixteen) but at least expectations were high. We have yet to reconcile the good post-1950 methods with the standards of expectation of the first and second decades of the century.

Notes

1 *Op. cit.*, p. 7 (1944 edn).
2 *Op. cit.*, pp. 82–3.
3 *Ibid.*, p. 162.
4 *Op. cit.*, p. 122 (1957 reprint).
5 *Op. cit.*, p. 37.
6 *Op. cit.*, p. 130.
7 *English for Maturity*, p. 7.
8 Essay in *The Practice of English Teaching*, edited by G. Owens and M. Marland, 1970, p. 60.
9 *Op. cit.*, p. 8.
10 *Education and the Democratic Ideal*, p. 5.
11 *Op. cit.*, pp. 15, 44 (1970 edn).
12 *Op. cit.* (1915 edn), pp. 26, 61.

13 *Op. cit.*, p. 2.
14 *Op. cit.*, p. 152.
15 *Ibid.*, pp. 157, 159.
16 *Op. cit.*, p. 219.
17 *Op. cit.*, p. 17.
18 *Op. cit.*, p. 133.
19 *The Disappearing Dais*, p. 236.
20 *Op. cit.*, p. 22.
21 *Ibid.*, pp. 51, 114.
22 *Ibid.*, p. 133.
23 *Op. cit.*, p. 27.
24 *Op. cit.*, pp. 155–6, 168.
25 *Op. cit.*, p. 34.
26 *Op. cit.*, p. 72.

Bibliography

A. *Chronological list of elementary/junior and secondary school English textbooks, grammars, readers and poetry anthologies, arranged under subsections*

1 TEXTBOOKS AND GRAMMARS

CORNFORD, L. C., *English Composition*, London, 1900.

GWILLAM, W. J., *Grammar Combined with Composition*, Manchester, 1901.

LONGMAN & CO., *Junior School Composition*, London, 1901.

FOWLER, J. H., *A First Course in Essay-Writing*, London, 1902.

LOW, W. H. AND BRIGGS, J., *Matriculation English Course*, London, 1902.

WILLIAMSON, W., *Junior English Examination Papers*, London, 1902.

　A Class Book of Easy Dictation and Spelling, London, 1902.

NESFIELD, J. C., *Senior Course of English Composition*, London, 1903.

MAXWELL, C. H., *Composition for Schools and Colleges*, London, 1904.

CAMPBELL, D., *First History of English Literature*, Edinburgh, 1905.

HYDE, MARY F., *Practical English Grammar*, London, 1905.

ROBERTSON, J. LOGIE, *Outlines of English Literature*, Edinburgh, 1905.

HASTINGS, EDITH, *Exercises for Parsing in Colour*, London, 1906.

MARSH, LEWIS, *Combined Course of Literary Reading and Composition*, London, 1907.

NELSON & CO., *Picture Essays*, London, 1907.

NESFIELD, J. C., *Aids to the Study of Composition*, London, 1907.

EDMUNDS, E. W. AND SPOONER, F., *Readings in English Literature*, London, 1908.

RAHTZ, F. J., *Junior English*, London, 1908.

WILLIAMS, A. M., *English Grammar and Composition*, London, 1909.

BEARD, W. S., *A First Course in English*, London, 1910.

JONES, FRANK, *A First English Course*, London, 1910.

MARSH, LEWIS, *Picture Composition*, London, 1910.

MURISON, W., *English Composition*, Cambridge, 1910.

ASMAN, H. N., *Selections from English Literature*, London, 1911.

ROONEY, C., *English Composition from Models*, London, 1911.

TREBLE, H. A., *Exercises in English*, London, 1911.

FEASEY, J. EATON, *Teaching Composition*, London, 1912.

KITCHENER, E. E., *English Composition for Junior Forms*, London, 1912.

MORGAN, R. B., *A New English Grammar for Junior Forms*, London, 1912.

MUSHET, J., *Exercises in English*, Edinburgh, 1912.

O'GRADY, H., *Matter, Form and Style*, London, 1912.

ROSE, J. D., *Elementary English Grammar Through Composition*, London, 1912.

WEST, A., *Elements of English Grammar*, Cambridge, 1893, revised 1912.

NOTMAN, N., *Exercises in English Grammar*, London, 1913.

KENNY, E. J., *Composition from English Models*, London, 1913.

OGILVIE, G. AND ALBERT, E., *A Practical Course in Secondary English*, London, 1913.

PICKLES, F., *Composition Through Reading*, London, 1913.

TREBLE, H. A., *English Prose Passages for Repetition*, Oxford, 1913.
BALLEY, E. J., *A Course of Practical English*, London, 1914.
BEWSHER, F. W., *Exercises in English*, London, 1914.
EADES, JOHN, *New English Course*, Leeds, 1914.
NESFIELD, J. C., *Matriculation English Course*, London, 1914.
TAPPAN, E. M., *A Brief History of English Literature*, London, 1914.
YOUNG, W. T., *A Primer of English Literature*, Cambridge, 1914.
GERRISH, C. M. AND CUNNINGHAM, M., *Practical English Composition*, London, 1915.
GREEN, G. H., *Composition for Junior Forms*, London, 1915.
KENDALL, GUY, *Essay Writing*, London, 1915.
PRITCHARD, F. H., *English Extracts and Exercises*, London, 1917.
CHALMERS, J. C., *The Primary School Grammar*, Glasgow, 1918.
NORMAN, J. S., *English Grammar*, London, 1918.
MAIS, S. P. B., *English Course for Schools*, London, 1919.
ABBOTT, E. C., *English Composition*, London, 1920.
HAMMOND, C. E. L., *English Composition*, Oxford, 1921.
MARRIOTT, J. W., *A Year's Work in English*, London, 1921.
REANEY, P. H., *Practice in English*, London, 1921.
MORGAN, R. B. AND TREBLE, H. A., *A Senior English Grammar*, London, 1922.
ADDIS, W. J., *Précis and Paraphrase*, London, 1923.
FORTEY, ISABEL, *Practice in English*, London, 1924.
PICKLES, F., *Reading, Narration, Composition and Drawing*, London, 1924.
POCOCK, GUY, *Exercises in English*, London, 1924.
CRUSE, AMY, *A New Course of Composition*, Oxford, 1925.
FRY, ISABEL, *A Key to Language*, London, 1925.
WESTON, W. J., *English Grammar and Composition*, London, 1925.
WILSON, R., *Spoken and Written English*, London, 1925.
EVANS BROS, *Direct Method of Teaching English*, London, 1926.
HENDERSON, B. L. K., *The English Way*, London, 1926.
POTTER, F. F. AND BAMFORD, T., *Scholarship English*, London, 1926.
SAMPSON, GEORGE, *Cambridge Lessons in English*, Cambridge, 1926.
TWENTYMAN, G. A., *Elementary English Grammar and Composition*, London, 1926.
WILSON, R., *Reading and Thinking*, London, 1926.
BOYD, C. C., *Grammar for Great and Small*, London, 1927.
EDMUNDS, E. W., *A Senior Course of English Composition*, London, 1927.
LAY, E. J. S. AND BRAY, E., *Composition for Upper Classes*, London, 1927.
PRIDEAUX, P. H., *A Course of Grammatical Training*, London, 1927.
MARRIOTT, J. W., *Matriculation English*, London, 1928.
OLIPHANT, L., *A Matriculation English Course*, London, 1928.
ROBINSON, F. W., *Test Papers in English Literature*, London, 1928.
GRANVILLE, C. AND SIMPSON, A., *A Four Years' English Course*, London, 1929.
STEPHENSON, J. D., *Foundations of English Grammar and Composition*, London, 1929.
TIPPING, L., *English Composition for Beginners*, London, 1929.
COLES, A. J., *Thought in English Prose*, London, 1930.
BROWN, C. J., *The Writing of Prose and Verse in Schools*, London, 1931.
KENNY, E. J., *An English Course for Juniors*, London, 1931.
MOON, A. R. AND MCKAY, G. H., *A New English Course*, London, 1931.

POLKINGHORNE, R. K., *Easy Steps in English Composition*, London, 1931.
PRESCOT, H. K., *Literature in the Classroom*, London, 1931.
ROBINSON, F. W., *Test Papers in English*, London, 1931.
WEBB, A. M., *English Grammar and Composition*, London, 1931.
HOTHERSALL, H., *English Composition*, London, 1932.
KERR, W., *The English Apprentice*, London, 1932.
POTTER, F. F., *Common Sense English Course*, London, 1932.
SWEANEY, ALICE, *Everyday English for Juniors*, Oxford, 1932.
DILTZ, B. C., *Models and Projects for English Composition*, London, 1933.
HUNTLEY, A., *English Composition*, London, 1933.
SWANN, R., *Simple Tests in English*, London, 1933.
TIPPING, L., *Matriculation English Grammar*, London, 1933.
WESTAWAY, F., *The Teaching of English Grammar*, London, 1933.
BAYLISS, A. E. M., *School Certificate English*, London, 1934.
DAVIES, T. V., *A Junior English Class Book*, London, 1934.
THOMPSON, DENYS, *Reading and Discrimination*, London, 1934.
HEAP, W. L., *The Teaching of English Composition*, London, 1935.
JEPSON, R. W., *English Exercises for School Certificate*, London, 1935.
PINK, M. ALDERTON, *An English Course for Schools*, London, 1935.
WALMSLEY, A. M., *A Modern English Course for Schools*, London, 1935.
BIAGGINI, E. G., *The Reading and Writing of English*, London, 1936.
BROWNE, J., *English Grammar and Composition*, London, 1936.
CAMPBELL, W., *English for Junior Scholarships*, Oxford, 1936.
DAVIES, A. F. AND L. A., *A Modern English Grammar*, London, 1936.
GLASSEY, S. C., *A Progressive Course in English Composition*, London, 1936.
JEPSON, R. W., *English Grammar for Today*, London, 1936.
WOOD, F. T., *School Certificate Exercises in English*, London, 1937.
BATEMAN, D., *One Hundred and Seventy-Five English Scholarship Tests*, London, 1938.
BENNETT, C. M. AND H. R., *Civic English*, London, 1938.
LITTLE, W. B., *English for the Young Citizen*, London, 1938.
MORRISON, L. A., *An English Work Book*, Edinburgh, 1938.
SUSSAMS, T. W., *Everyday English for Seniors*, London, 1938.
ALLEN, E. E. AND MASON, A. T., *An English Grammar of Function*, London, 1939.
HUMPHREYS, G. S. AND ROBERTS, J., *The Active English Course*, London, 1939.
MARSHLAIN, T. P., *English Rules and Exercises*, London, 1939.
VENABLES, F. I. AND WHIMSTER, D. C., *English for Schools*, London, 1939.
WALL, W. D., *Exercises in Comprehension*, London, 1940.
GLASSEY, S. C., *Creative English*, London, 1941.
ROBERTSON, A. S., *English Practice for Secondary Schools*, London, 1946.
RIDOUT, RONALD, *English Today*, London, 1947.
MOSBY, F. AND THOMAS, J., *Sense, Feeling and Thought*, Oxford, 1948.
RUSSELL, J., *Modern English*, Glasgow, 1948.
HOLROYD, G. H., *English Composition*, London, 1949.
O'MALLEY, R. AND THOMPSON, DENYS, *English for the Living*, London, 1949.
MACKIE, W. S., *Fifty Comprehension Tests*, London, 1950.
MOON, A. R. AND MCKAY, G. H., *English Exercises for Grammar Schools*, London, 1950.
CROKER, W. G., *Enjoying English*, London, 1951.

SCOTT, A. F., *English Composition*, Cambridge, 1951.
BARKER, D. W., *Exercises in Good English*, London, 1952.
DAVIDSON, W. AND ALCOCK, J. C., *English Grammar and Analysis*, London, 1952.
ECKERSLEY, C. E. AND MACAULAY, M., *Brighter Grammar*, London, 1952.
MARTIN, N. C. AND D. AND GRIFFITHS, A., *Understanding and Enjoyment*, Oxford, 1952.
BRIGHT, J. A., *Junior English Composition and Grammar*, London, 1954.
BURTON, S. H., *A Comprehensive English Course*, London, 1954.
GENTLE, G. G., *Progressive Exercises in English*, London, 1955.
CLELAND, W. P., *English for Primary Schools*, London, 1956.
LAWLEY, A. H. AND M., *English for Schools*, London, 1956.
NICHOLSON, K. F. AND BRIGHT, J. A., *English Language for School Certificate*, London, 1956.
CANDLIN, E. F., *A General Certificate English Course*, London, 1957.
WALSH, J. H., *Graded Exercises in English*, London, 1958.
WOOD, F. T., *A Course in English Composition*, London, 1958.
HOWE, D. H. AND BAMBRIDGE, G. DE P., *Practical English*, Oxford, 1959.
CUNNINGHAM, W. T., *English Alive*, London, 1960.
MOUNTAIN, A. B. AND BARNES, W., *Effective English*, Huddersfield, 1961.
THOMAS, H. R., *English for Secondary Schools*, Oxford, 1961.
YGLESIAS, J. R. C. AND HUGHES, C. F., *Pleasure in English*, London, 1961.
GOLDING, G. F. AND MAYO, R. A., *An Examination Course in English*, London, 1962.
CAMPBELL, R. AND GREENWOOD, R., *English Enterprise*, London, 1963.
CLEMENTS, S., DIXON, J. AND STRATTA, R., *Reflections*, Oxford, 1963.
ROWE, A. W. AND EMMENS, P., *English Through Experience*, London, 1963.
THORPE, E. G., *Complete English*, London, 1963.
HOLDEN, C. L., *A Comprehensive Course in English Composition*, London, 1964.
DANIEL, J., *Approaches*, London, 1965.
LAWRENCE, G., *Take a Look*, London, 1965.
MARLAND, M., *Pictures for Writing*, London, 1966.
HOSSACK, A., *A Fourth Year GCE English*. London, 1967.
HUNNISETT, E. M., *Themes*, London, 1967.
POOLE, R. H. AND SHEPHERD, P. J., *Impact One and Two*, London, 1967.
THOMPSON, DENYS AND MARLAND, M., *English for the Individual*, London, 1967.
CATTELL, A. AND GARDINER, H., *Outlook 14/16*, London, 1968.
CHAPMAN, L. R. H., *English Composition Lessons*, London, 1968.
ETHERTON, A. R. B., *Graded English for Secondary Schools*, London, 1968.
JUPP, T. C. AND MILNE, J., *Guided Course in English Composition*, London, 1968.
LAMB, G. F., *Composition and Comprehension for CSE*, London, 1968.
MARTIN, NANCY, *The Oxford English Source Books*, Oxford, 1968.
WALSH, J. H. AND TOMLINSON, F., *Fields of Experience*, London, 1968.
WOOD, T. R. AND EDWARDS, C. R., *Look Here*, London, 1969.
WYNNE, J. A. AND STAGG, S. A., *English Workshop*, London, 1969.
FOWLER, R. S. AND DICK, A. J., *English 15/16*, London, 1970.
HIGGINS, D. S., *Aspects of English*, London, 1970.

2 READERS

The Temple Readers, 1–7 (Dent), London, 1901.
Chambers' Fluent Readers, 1–6, London, 1902.
Macmillan's Story Readers, London, 1903.
Macmillan's New Globe Readers, 1–5, London, 1905.
The Excelsior Readers, 1–6 (Oliver and Boyd), Edinburgh, 1907.
Chambers' Effective Readers, 1–6, London, 1909.
Macmillan's Junior Class Reader, London, 1931.
The New Foundation Readers, 1–4 (ULP), London, 1937.

3 POETRY ANTHOLOGIES

HENLEY, W. E. (ed.), *Lyra Heroica*, London, 1891.
PETERSON, W. (ed.), *Junior School Poetry Book*, London, 1902.
WINBOLT, S. E. (ed.), *English Poetry for the Young*, London, 1904.
WOODWARD, W. H. (ed.), *A Book of English Poetry*, Cambridge, 1904.
PERTWEE, E. (ed.), *English History in Verse*, London, 1906.
SMITH, J. C. (ed.), *A Book of Verse for Boys and Girls*, Oxford, 1908.
THOMSON, L. (ed.), *Poetry for Junior Schools*, London, 1909.
GRAVES, A. (ed.), *Poems for Infants and Juniors*, London, 1910.
MORISON, R. AND WOODBURN, W. (eds.), *Progressive Poetry for Juniors*, London, 1911.
SALT, L. G. (ed.), *English Patriotic Poetry*, Cambridge, 1911.
MACMILLAN & CO'S *Children's Anthology of Verse*, London, 1913.
MAXWELL, S. (ed.), *Poetry for Boys*, London, 1914.
THE ENGLISH ASSOCIATION, *Poems of Today*, London, 1915.
GRAHAME, K. (ed.), *The Cambridge Book of Poetry for Children*, Cambridge, 1916.
FLETCHER, R. (ed.), *The Children's Poetry Book*, London, 1920.
WALTERS, L. D.'O (ed.), *An Anthology of Recent Poetry*, London, 1920.
INGPEN, R. (ed.), *Choice of the Best Poems for the Young*, London, 1922.
WILSON, R. (ed.), *Junior Modern Poetry*, London, 1922.
DE LA MARE, W. H. (ed.), *Come Hither*, London, 1923.
MEYNELL, ALICE (ed.), *The School of Poetry*, London, 1923.
JAGGER, J. H. (ed.), *A Book of English Poems*, London, 1924.
STRANG, H. (ed.), *One Hundred Poems for Girls*, Oxford, 1925.
BAIN, A. W. (ed.), *A Poetry Book for Boys and Girls*, Cambridge, 1927.
SIMPSON, A. LE M. (ed.), *Young Pegasus*, London, 1930.
POCOCK, G. (ed.), *A Poetry Book for Boys and Girls*, London, 1933.
MEGROZ, I. AND R. (eds.), *Modern Poems for Children*, Wisbech, 1935.
WILKINSON, W. AND N. (eds.), *The Dragon Book of Verse*, Oxford, 1935.
STONE, J. A. (ed.), *Take Your Choice*, London, 1949.
SMYTH, W. M. (ed.), *Poems of Spirit and Action*, London, 1957.
HOLBROOK, D. (ed.), *Iron, Honey, Gold*, Cambridge, 1961.
BALDWIN, M. (ed.), *Billy the Kid*, London, 1963.
HANRATTY, J. (ed.), *The Wheel of Poetry*, London, 1963.
HASSALL, C. (ed.), *Poems for Children*, London, 1963.
HUGHES, TED (ed.), *Here Today*, London, 1963.
MANSFIELD, R. AND ARMSTRONG, I. (eds.), *Every Man Will Shout*, Oxford, 1964.

WOLLMAN, M. AND GRUGEON, D. (eds.), *Happenings*, London, 1964.
SUMMERFIELD, G. (ed.), *Voices*, Harmondsworth, 1968.
JONES, RHODRI (ed.), *Themes*, London, 1969.

4   RECENT PROSE ANTHOLOGIES

HOLBROOK, D. (ed.), *People and Diamonds*, Cambridge, 1962.
HUNTER, J. (ed.), *Modern Short Stories*, London, 1964.
KENNETT, J. (ed.), *Modern Reading for Modern Times*, London, 1965.
ROWE, A. W. (ed.), *People Like Us*, London, 1965.
BELTON, T. (ed.), *Slings and Arrows*, London, 1966.
MOODY, H. L. B. (ed.), *Facing Facts*, London, 1966.
STANFORD, D. (ed.), *Prose of this Century*, London, 1966.
ADCOCK, J. (ed.), *English Through Literature*, London, 1967.
MANNERS, PENELOPE (ed.), *Novels of Today*, London, 1967.
MEREDITH, M. (ed.), *Twentieth Century Story and Statement*, London, 1967.
URWIN, G. G. (ed.), *A Taste for Living*, London, 1967.

B. *Board, Ministry and Department of Education Reports and Publications*

BOARD OF EDUCATION, The 1900 Schedules for Elementary Schools in the B.
   of E.'s *Report for 1899–1900*, HMSO, 1900.
The 1904 *Code of Regulations for Elementary Schools* ('The Red Code'),
   NUT, 1904.
The 1904 *Code of Regulations for Secondary Schools*, NUT, 1904.
The 1905 *Code of Regulations for Elementary Schools*, NUT, 1905.
The 1906 *Code of Regulations for Secondary Schools*, NUT, 1906.
The 1907 *Code of Regulations for Elementary Schools*, NUT, 1907.
The 1908 *Code of Regulations for Elementary Schools*, NUT, 1908.
Handbook of Suggestions for Teachers, HMSO, 1905.
Circular 753, *The Teaching of English in Secondary Schools*, HMSO, 1910.
Handbook of Suggestions for Teachers, HMSO, 1914.
The Teaching of English in England (The Report of the Departmental
   Committee appointed to inquire into the position of English in the
   Educational System), HMSO, 1921.
*The Differentiation of the Curriculum for Boys and Girls respectively in
   Secondary Schools*, HMSO, 1923.
Handbook of Suggestions for Teachers, HMSO, 1923.
Some Suggestions for the Teaching of English in Secondary Schools,
   HMSO, 1924.
The Education of the Adolescent (The Hadow Report), HMSO, 1926.
Handbook of Suggestions for Teachers, HMSO, 1927.
*Report of the Consultative Committee on Books in Public Elementary
   Schools*, HMSO, 1928.
Report on the Primary School, HMSO, 1931.
Handbook of Suggestions for Teachers, HMSO, 1937.
Report on Secondary Education (The Spens Report), HMSO, 1938.

N

Curriculum and Examinations in Secondary Schools (The Norwood
Report), HMSO, 1943.
MINISTRY OF EDUCATION, *Education 1900–1950*, the Report of the Ministry for
1950, HMSO, 1950.
Pamphlet No. 26, *Language*, HMSO, 1954.
Half Our Future (The Newsom Report), HMSO, 1963.
DEPARTMENT OF EDUCATION, *Children and Their Primary Schools* (The
Plowden Report), HMSO, 1967.

C. *Publications of other official bodies*

The Year Book of Education for 1932, 1933, 1936, and 1939.
THE SECONDARY SCHOOL EXAMINATIONS COUNCIL, *Report of the Investigators . . .
into . . . the approved First Examinations in English, July 1918*, HMSO, 1919.
*Report of the Investigators . . . into . . . the Second Examinations in English,
July 1920*, HMSO, 1921.
The CSE: some suggestions for teachers and examiners, HMSO, 1963.
The Examining of English Language, HMSO, 1964.
THE ENGLISH ASSOCIATION, Leaflet 8, *Types of English Curricula in Girls'
Secondary Schools*, Oxford, 1909.
Leaflet 12, *Summary of Examinations in English affecting Schools*,
Oxford, 1909.
Leaflet 14, *The Early Stages in the Teaching of English* (Miss Gill),
Oxford, 1910.
Pamphlet 26, *The Teaching of English at the Universities* (S. Leathes),
Oxford, 1913.
Pamphlet 37, *English Papers in Examinations for Pupils of School Age*,
Oxford, 1917.
Pamphlet 43, *The Teaching of English in Schools* (J. Morley), Oxford, 1919.
THE IAAM, *Memorandum on the Teaching of English*, Cambridge, 1923.
The Teaching of English, Cambridge, 1952.
THE ASSOCIATION OF ASSISTANT MISTRESSES, *Memorandum on the Teaching of
English*, London, 1932.
Memorandum on the Teaching of English, London, 1956.
THE JOINT COMMITTEE ON GRAMMATICAL TERMINOLOGY, Final Report (*On the
Terminology of Grammar*), London, 1911.
LONDON UNIVERSITY COMMUNICATION RESEARCH PAPERS, *The Subject Matter of
English* (R. Hasan, S. Lushington), London, 1968.
Current Attitudes to Written English (P. Doughty), London, 1968.
THE NATIONAL ASSOCIATION FOR THE TEACHING OF ENGLISH, *English Examined:
A Survey of the 'O' Language Papers 1964–65*, London, 1967.

D. *'Method' books and books concerned with the teaching of English,
arranged alphabetically by author*

BAKER, E., *Education for Citizenship in Secondary Schools*, Oxford, 1936.
BALDWIN, MICHAEL, *Poetry Without Tears*, London, 1959.

BALLARD, P. B., *Teaching the Mother Tongue*, London, 1921.
  Teaching and Testing English, London, 1939.
BATCHELDER, W. J., *Notes on the Teaching of English*, London, 1913.
BATE, R. S., *The Teaching of English Literature in Secondary Schools*, London, 1913.
BLACKBURN, T. (ed.), *Presenting Poetry*, London, 1966.
BLACKIE, J., *Good Enough for the Children?*, London, 1963.
  English Teaching for Non-Specialists, London, 1969.
BLAMIRES, HARRY, *English in Education*, London, 1951.
BOLT, SYDNEY AND GARD, ROGER, *Teaching Fiction in Schools*, London, 1970.
BOLTON, ERIC, *Verse Writing in Schools*, Oxford, 1966.
BOWEN, H. COURTHOPE, *English Literature Teaching in Schools*, London, 1891.
BRACKEN, GRACE, *The Teaching of English in Secondary Schools for Girls*, London, 1924.
BRITTON, JAMES (ed.), *Talking and Writing*, London, 1967.
BROWN, VICTORIA (ed.), *The Experience of Poetry in School*, Oxford, 1953.
BROWNE, E. G., *Lectures on the Teaching of English*, Liverpool, 1924.
CALLAN, N., *Poetry in Practice*, London, 1938.
CAMPAGNAC, E. T., *Lectures on the Teaching of Composition*, London, 1912.
CARPENTER, G. R., BAKER, F. T., AND SCOTT, F. N., *The Teaching of English*, New York/London, 1903.
CHUBB, P., *The Teaching of English*, New York/London, 1902.
COLLINS, J. CHURTON, *The Study of English Literature*, London, 1891.
COOK, H. CALDWELL, *The Play Way*, London, 1917.
COVERNTON, E., *The Teaching of English Composition*, London, 1909.
CREBER, J. W. P., *Sense and Sensitivity*, London, 1965.
CRUMP, G. H., *English for Schools*, London, 1929.
CUTFORTH, J. A., *English in the Primary School*, Oxford, 1951.
DAVIDSON, E. F., *Modern English Teaching*, London, 1930.
DE SOLA PINTO, V. (ed.), *The Teaching of English in Schools*, London, 1946.
DIXON, J., *Growth Through English*, London, 1967.
ELTON, G. Y., *Teaching English*, London, 1929.
FINCH, R., *How to Teach English Composition*, London, 1919.
  The Approach to English Literature, London, 1923.
FINCH, R. AND KIMMINS, C. W., *The Teaching of English and Handwriting*, London, 1932.
FINLAY-JOHNSON, HARRIET, *The Dramatic Method of Teaching*, London, 1911.
FOWLER, J. H., *The Art of Teaching English*, London, 1932.
GAGG, J. C., *Teaching Written English*, London, 1955.
GURREY, P., *The Appreciation of Poetry*, Oxford, 1935.
  The Teaching of Written English, London, 1954.
  Teaching English Grammar, London, 1961.
HADDOW, A., *On the Teaching of Poetry*, London, 1925.
HARTOG, PHILIP, *The Writing of English*, Oxford, 1907.
  Words in Action, London, 1947.
HAYWARD, F. H., *The Lesson in Appreciation*, London, 1915.
HOLBROOK, DAVID, *English for Maturity*, Cambridge, 1961.
  English for the Rejected, Cambridge, 1964.
  The Secret Places, London, 1964.
  Children's Writing, Cambridge, 1967.

The Exploring Word, Cambridge, 1967.

HOURD, MARJORIE, *The Education of the Poetic Spirit*, London, 1949.

INGLIS, FRED, *The Englishness of English Teaching*, London, 1969.

JACKSON, B. AND THOMPSON, DENYS, *English in Education*, London, 1962.

JAGGER, J. H., *Modern English*, London, 1925.

Poetry in School, London, 1928.

LAMBORN, E. A. GREENING, *The Rudiments of Criticism*, Oxford, 1916.

Expression in Speech and Writing, Oxford, 1922.

LANE, S. M. AND KEMP, M., *An Approach to Creative Writing in the Primary School*, London, 1967.

LANGDON, MARGARET, *Let the Children Write*, London, 1961.

LAURENCE, MARGARET, *Citizenship Through English*, London, 1946.

LEWIS, R. T., *Composition Through Story Writing*, London, 1927.

MACPHERSON, W., *Principles and Method in the Study of English Literature*, Cambridge, 1908.

MARSHALL, SYBIL, *An Experiment in Education*, Cambridge, 1963.

MASON, W. H., *For Teachers of English*, Oxford, 1964.

MATTAM, D., *The Vital Approach*, Oxford, 1963.

MAYBURY, BARRY, *Creative Writing for Juniors*, London, 1967.

MELDRUM, ROY, *An English Technique*, London, 1935.

MULLER, H., *The Uses of English*, New York/London, 1967.

OWEN, DOROTHY TUDOR, *The Child Vision*, Manchester, 1920.

OWENS, G. AND MARLAND, M. (eds.), *The Practice of English Teaching*, London, 1970.

PALMER, H. E., *The Teaching of English*, London, 1930.

PEEL, MARIE, *Seeing to the Heart*, London, 1967.

PITMAN'S NEW EDUCATOR'S LIBRARY, *The Teaching of English*, London, 1922.

POTTER, F. F., *English in the Junior School*, London, 1930.

POWELL, BRIAN, *English Through Poetry Writing*, London, 1968.

PRITCHARD, F. H., *Training in Literary Appreciation*, London, 1922.

English and the New Prospect, London, 1930.

PYM, DORA, *Free Writing*, London, 1956.

RATCLIFF, A. J. J., *The Teaching of English in Upper Forms*, London, 1926.

REEVES, JAMES, *Teaching Poetry*, London, 1958.

REYNOLDS, E. E., *An English Syllabus*, Cambridge, 1931.

ROBERTS, A. E. AND BARTER, A., *The Teaching of English*, London, 1908.

ROBERTS, A. E. AND PRATT, A., *English Verse Composition*, London, 1916.

ROSENBLATT, LOUISE, *Literature as Exploration*, London, 1970.

SAMPSON, GEORGE, *English for the English*, Cambridge, 1921.

SMITH, A., *Aims and Methods in the Teaching of English*, London, 1915.

SMITH, A. E., *English in the Modern School*, London, 1954.

SOCIETY FOR THE TEACHERS OF ENGLISH, *Teaching Poetry*, Oxford, 1937.

STUART, SIMON, *Say*, London, 1969.

SUMMERFIELD, G., *Topics in English*, London, 1965.

THOMPSON, DENYS (ed.), *Directions in the Teaching of English*, Cambridge, 1969.

TOMKINSON, W. S., *The Teaching of English*, Oxford, 1921.

TREBLE, H. A., *The Teaching of English in Primary Schools*, Oxford, 1927.

WALSH, J. H., *Teaching English*, London, 1965.

WELTON, JAMES, *Principles and Methods of Teaching*, London, 1906.

WHITEHEAD, FRANK, *The Disappearing Dais*, London, 1966.
Creative Experiment, London, 1970.

E. *Anthologies of children's own writing*

ANON., *Life Through Young Eyes*, Oxford, 1960.
BALDWIN, MICHAEL (ed.), *Poems by Children 1950–61*, London, 1962.
BECKETT, JACK (ed.), *The Keen Edge*, London, 1965.
CLEGG, A. (ed.), *The Excitement of Writing*, London, 1964.
COOK, H. CALDWELL (ed.), *Perse Play Books*, I–VI, Cambridge, 1912–17.
DRUCE, ROBERT (ed.), *The Eye of Innocence*, Leicester, 1965.
EARNSHAW, JUDITH (ed.), *Sprouts on Helicon*, London, 1965.
FORD, BORIS (ed.), *Young Writers, Young Readers*, London, 1960.
HOURD, M. AND COOPER, G. (eds.), *Coming Into Their Own*, London, 1959.
MORRIS, NORMAN (ed.), *First Fruits*, Oxford, 1939.

F. *Journals and Periodicals*

Journal of Experimental Pedagogy
BRIDGE, G. F., 'Text books', Vol. II, No. vi, 1914.
GREEN, J. A., 'The teaching of English I', Vol. I, No. iii, 1912.
'The Teaching of English II', Vol. II, No. i, 1913.

Journal of Education
ZIMMERN, ALICE, 'Literature as a central subject', September 1900.
WILKINS, A. S., 'The place of literature in education', June 1901.
BARNETT, P. A., 'English literature and English schools', March 1902.
WILLCOCKS, M. P., 'Literature as a school subject', February 1903.
PRINGLE, G. C., 'The teaching of literature in schools', April 1903.
WHITE, E. M., 'A neglected aspect of composition', February 1906.
BURRELL, A., 'English', January 1907.
ROBINSON, STEWART A., 'The teaching of English in schools', April 1907.
HODGSON, GERALDINE, 'The function of literature', May 1907.
DAWSON, E., 'A model literature lesson', August 1908.
COXHEAD, G. E. S., 'English composition', July 1914.
FLETCHER, R., 'English in the lower forms', June 1916.
TANT, ETHEL, 'An experiment in the teaching of English', September 1917.
USHERWOOD, J. F., 'Article on the 1921 Report', July 1922.
ARNOLD, J H., 'The teaching of English', July 1928.
COLQUHOUN, B. S., 'The teaching of English in girls' prep schools', July 1929.
BRADBURY, J. L., 'Unadventurous English', December 1932.
WALMSLEY, A. M., 'The English Essay', February 1934.
LYON, P. H. B., 'Literature teaching', October 1935.

The Times Educational Supplement
Miscellaneous reviews, editorials and letters.

British Journal of Educational Psychology

BURNS, D. G., 'Newspaper reading in the secondary modern school', Vol. XXV, Pt. 1, February 1935.

CARSLEY, J. D., 'The interests of children (10–11 yrs) in books', Vol. XXVII, Pt. 1, February 1957.

CAST, B. M. D., 'The efficiency of different methods of marking English composition I', Vol. IX, Pt. 3, November 1939 (Part II followed in Vol. X, Pt. 1, February 1940).

CAWLEY, FRANK, 'The difficulty of English grammar for pupils of secondary school age' (Abstract of an M.Ed. thesis), Vol. XXVIII, Pt. 2, June 1958.

FINLAYSON, D. S., 'The reliability of the marking of essays', Vol. XXI, Pt. 2, June 1951.

LEOPOLD, KATHLEEN, 'The effect of creative work on aesthetic appreciation', Vol. III, Pt. 1, February 1933.

MACAULAY, W. J., 'The difficulty of grammar', Vol. XVII, Pt. 3, November 1947.

MORRISON, R. L. AND VERNON, P. E., 'A new method of marking English composition', Vol. XI, Pt. 2, June 1941.

ROBINSON, NORA, 'The relation between knowledge of English grammar and ability in English composition' (Abstract of an M.Ed. thesis), Vol. XXX, Pt. 2, June 1960.

WHITEHEAD, FRANK, 'The attitudes of grammar school pupils towards some novels commonly read in school', Vol. XXVI, Pt. 2, June 1956.

Educational Research

PAFFARD, M. K., 'The teaching of English literature in secondary schools', Vol. V, No. 1, November 1962.

The Teacher's World

CATTY, NANCY, 'Creative work in verse and prose', December 1935.

Scrutiny

KNIGHTS, L. C., 'Scrutiny of examinations', Vol. II, No. 2, September 1933.

The Use of English (formerly *English in Schools*, 1939–49)

Article on Dr Elizabeth Baranyai's research into grammar teaching, Autumn 1949.

GARNETT, EMMELINE, 'Your fifty favourite books', Spring 1968.

HOLBROOK, D., 'Greyfriars behind the gashouse', Autumn 1959.

HOURD, M., 'Poetry and children', Winter 1952.

MITTINS, W. H., 'The set book stakes', Spring 1966.

WHITEHEAD, FRANK, 'English through exercises', Summer 1952.

G. *General*

ADAMS, JOHN (ed.), *The New Teaching*, London, 1918.

ALDERSON, CONNIE, *Magazines Teenagers Read*, Oxford, 1968.

BALLARD, P. B., *The Changing School*, London, 1925.

BANTOCK, G. H., *Freedom and Authority in Education*, London, 1952.

BEACOCK, D. A., *Play Way English for Today*, London, 1943.

BENSON, A. C. (ed.), *Cambridge Essays in Education*, Cambridge, 1917.

BIRCHENOUGH, CHARLES, *A History of Elementary Education*, London, 1914.

BOYD, WILLIAM, *Measuring Devices in Composition, Spelling and Arithmetic*, London, 1924.

CLARKE, FRED, *Education and Social Change*, London, 1940.

CONNELL, W. F., *The Educational Thought and Influence of Matthew Arnold*, London, 1950.

DAVIS, VALENTINE, *The Matter and Method of Modern Teaching*, London, 1928.

DENT, H. C., *1870–1970: Century of Growth in English Education*, London, 1970.

DEWEY, JOHN, *The School and Society*, Chicago, 1899.

Essays on Examinations (International Institute Enquiry), London, 1936.

FLEMING, C. M., *Research and the Basic Curriculum*, London, 1946.

GEORGE, A., *The Montessori Method*, London, 1912.

GRIFFITHS, RUTH, *A Study of Imagination in Early Childhood*, London, 1935.

HALL, STANLEY, *Adolescence*, London, 1908.

HARTOG, P. AND RHODES, E. C., *An Examination of Examinations*, London, 1935.

HILDICK, E. W., *A Close Look at Magazines and Comics*, London, 1966.

HOLMES, EDMOND, *What Is and What Might Be*, London, 1911.

HOGGART, R., *The Uses of Literacy*, London, 1957.

HUGHES, A. G., *Education and the Democratic Ideal*, London, 1951.

ISAACS, SUSAN, *Intellectual Growth in Young Children*, London, 1930.

JACKS, L. P., *The Education of the Whole Man*, London, 1931.

JENKINSON, A. J., *What Do Boys and Girls Read?*, London, 1940.

KENWRICK, JOYCE, *Junior School Projects*, London, 1935.

LEAVIS, F. R., *Mass Civilization and Minority Culture*, Cambridge, 1930.

Education and the University, London, 1943.

LEAVIS, F. R. AND THOMPSON, DENYS, *Culture and Environment*, London, 1933.

LOWNDES, G. A. N., *The Silent Social Revolution*, Oxford, 1937.

LYNCH, A. J., *Individual Work and the Dalton Plan*, London, 1924.

MACMILLAN, MARGARET, *Education Through the Imagination*, London, 1904.

MOCK, RUTH, *Education and the Imagination*, London, 1970.

MONTGOMERY, R. J., *Examinations: An account of their evolution as administrative devices in England*, London, 1965.

MORRIS, JOYCE, *Standards and Progress in Reading*, (NFER) Slough, 1966.

NUNN, PERCY, *Education: Its Data and First Principles*, London, 1920.

PALMER, D. J., *The Rise of English Studies*, Hull, 1965.

PETERSON, A. D. C., *A Hundred Years of Education*, London, 1952.

PHILLIPS, MARGARET, *The Education of the Emotions*, London, 1937.

POTTER, STEPHEN, *The Muse in Chains*, London, 1937.

QUILLER-COUCH, ARTHUR, *On the Art of Reading*, Cambridge, 1920.

RICH, R. W., *The Training of Teachers in England and Wales during the 19th Century*, London, 1933.

RICHARDS, I. A., *Practical Criticism*, London, 1929.

Interpretation in Teaching, London, 1937.

STEEL, J. H. AND TALMAN, J., *The Marking of English Composition*, London, 1936.

STEVENS, FRANCES, *English and Examinations*, London, 1970.

TILLYARD, E. M. W., *The Muse Unchained*, London, 1958.
VIOLA, WILHELM, *Child Art*, London, 1942.
WALSH, WILLIAM, *The Use of Imagination*, London, 1959.
WATTS, A. F., *The Language and Mental Development of Children*, London, 1944.
WHEELER, OLIVE, *Creative Education and the Future*, London, 1936.
WILLIAMS, RAYMOND, *Culture and Society*, London, 1958.

Index

Abbs, Peter, 171
Adams, John, 60, 64, 74
'Admass', 129, 133
Aims and Methods in the Teaching of English, 18, 42
Albert, E., 61
Alderson, Connie, 129
Allen, E., 110
AMA, 118
Andrew, S. O., 97
An Examination of Examinations, 117
Armstrong, I., 179
Arnold, J. H., 20, 99
Arnold, Matthew, 27, 40, 72, 73, 77, 83, 88, 124, 127, 148, 152
Asman, H. N., 59
Assistant Mistresses' Association 106, 107

Baker, F. T., 62
Baldwin, Michael, 159, 160, 162, 176
Baldwin, Stanley, 94
Ballads of the Brave, 17
Ballard, P. B., 14, 24, 25, 41, 69, 82, 88, 96, 118, 130
Bamford, T., 95
Bantock, G. H., 152-3
Baranyai, Elizabeth, 143
Barnett, P. A., 14
Barter, A., 7, 20, 23, 41, 43, 62, 130
Barton, J. E., 69, 70
Batchelder, W. J., 14, 41, 43, 44
Bate, R. S., 36, 59, 62
Bateman, Dudley, 111
Bayley, John, 162
Beacock, D. A., 53
Beckett, Jack, 159, 163
Belton, T., 171
Bennett, C. M., 133
Bewsher, F. W., 37
Biaggini, E. G., 111, 126
Birchenough, C., 123
Birmingham University, 3
Blackburn, Thomas, 160
Blackie, John, 140
Blamires, Harry, 146

Board of Education: *Books in Public Elementary Schools*, 33, 89, 100; *Circular 753*, 8, 13, 33, 34; Elementary School Regulations, 28; 1887 English Schedules, 76; 1900 English Schedules, 4-5; 1926 English syllabus, 100; 1905 *Handbook of Suggestions*, 12, 31; 1914 *Handbook of Suggestions*, 63-4, 79; 1923 *Handbook of Suggestions*, 100; 1927 *Handbook of Suggestions*, 100-1, 103, 123; 1937 *Handbook of Suggestions*, 122-4; 1931 Primary School Report, 103, 179; Secondary School Regulations, 3, 18, 28; Suggested Secondary English syllabus, 29; *Suggestions for the Teaching of English in Secondary Schools*, 86, 99; *Supplementary Memoranda on Examinations*, 118; *The Teaching of English in England* (1921 Report), 3-4, 10, 19, 66-74, 77, 78, 90
Bolt, Sydney, 178
Bolton, Eric, 160
Bowen, H. Courthope, 7
Boyd, C. C., 90
Boyd, William, 15, 138
Bracken, Grace, 43, 59, 86
Bridge, G. F., 19
British Journal of Educational Psychology, 97, 118, 121, 143, 167
Britton, James, 168
Brown, C. J., 110, 121
Brown, Victoria, 144
Browne, E. G., 91
Burt, Cyril, 103
Burton, S. H., 173

Callan, Norman, 121, 128
Cambridge, 3
Campagnac, E. T., 44
Campbell, D., 58
Campbell, R., 171
Carpenter, G. R., 62
Cast, B. M. D., 118
Cattell, A., 155

Catty, Nancy, 121
Cawley, F., 143
Chalmers, J. S., 37
Chambers, R. W., 10
Child Art, 135
Child Vision, The, 53
Chubb, Percival, 42
Citizenship, 132–4
Cizek, F., 119, 135
Clarke, Fred, 124, 127
Class numbers, 14
Classical Studies, influence on English teaching, 6–9, 36–7, 66–7, 91, 97, 106
Clegg, Alec, 122, 159
Clements, S., 154, 170
Coleridge, 136, 137, 162
Coles, A. J., 79
Collins, J. Churton, 7
Colquhoun, B. S., 89
Composition, 10–17, 43–5, 47–9, 50–1, 64, 82, 101, 110; and grammar, 21–3; and pictures, 22; and imitation, 36; and imaginative expression, 53–4
Composition through Story Writing, 81
Comprehension, 79, 171
Comprehensive schools, 145
Cook, H. Caldwell, 45, 49–53, 68, 81, 119, 137
Cooper, Gertrude, 159
Cope, E., 175
Cornford, L. C., 7
'Correct' English, 168
'Correlation', 18
Covernton, E., 11, 14
Coxhead, G. E. S., 44
Creative Education and the Future, 132
Creative Experiment, 166
Creativity, 23, 105, 119, 135–6, 137, 139, 163–6; reaction to, 86–9, 105–8; Romantic aspects of, 85, 161–3
Creber, J. Patrick, 146, 156
Croker, W. G., 142
Crump, G. H., 89
Cruse, Amy, 80
CSE, 157, 174, 182–3
Culture and Environment, 129

Daily Mail Curriculum Contest, 91–2
Dalton Plan, 97–8
Daniels, John, 155
Dartmouth Seminar, 185
Davidson, E. F., 79, 87, 88
Davies, A. F., 110
Davies, L. A., 110
Davies, T. V., 110
Dawson, Ethel, 34
De la Mare, 100
Dent, H. C., 26
De Sola Pinto, V., 142
Dewey, Evelyn, 97
Dewey, John, 124, 133, 153
Dick, A. J., 155
Dictation, 12
Diltz, B. C., 110
'Direct Method', 35, 36, 80
Dixon, J., 154, 170, 185
Doughty, P., 168
Dover Wilson, John, 66, 85
'Dramatic Method', 41–2
Dramatic Method of Teaching, The, 41
Dyer, Ernest, 130

Eades, John, 16
Earnshaw, Judith, 159
Edmunds, E. W., 59, 90
Education Act of 1918, 93
Education and Social Change, 124
Education for Citizenship in Secondary Schools, 130, 132
Education: its Data and First Principles, 82
Education of the Poetic Spirit, The, 136
Education of the Whole Man, The, 94, 151
Education Through the Imagination, 23
Edwards, C. R., 170
Egford, R., 171
Elementary schools; English texts, 43, 57, 64; readers, 32–3
Eliot, T. S., 126
Emmens, P., 170
Empson, W., 126
English and the New Prospect, 109

English Association publications, 10, 22, 43, 97, 142–3
English for Maturity, 148
English for the English, 75, 76ff., 148, 184
English in the Modern School, 146, 147
Englishness of English Teaching, The, 147, 179
Examinations, 61, 62, 68–9, 99, 112–17, 145–6, 156, 157, 180–3; opposition to, 62; questions, 58; texts, 57–8, 99–100, 112–14
Excitement of Writing, The, 122, 159
Expression in Speech and Writing, 75, 84
Eye of Innocence, The, 159, 161

Fallacies: 'classical', 6; 'content', 19, 62; 'foreign language', 39, 70,90; 'imitation',10, 36; 'moral', 17–8, 132; 'Old English', 9
Finch, Robert, 47–8, 68, 98, 119
Finlay-Johnson, Harriet, 41–2
Finlayson, D., 118
First Fruits, 122
Ford, Boris, 159, 163
Fowler, J. H., 12, 25
Fowler, R. S., 155
Freedom and Authority in Education, 152
Fry, Isabel, 90

Gard, Roger, 178
Gardiner, H., 155
Garnett, Emmeline, 180
Glassey, S. C., 110, 142
Gradon, Pamela, 142
Grammar, 8, 19ff., 34, 37, 38, 50, 64, 69–70, 78, 89, 96–7, 101, 104, 108, 123, 142–4, 165, 167
Grammar schools, 92
Granville, C., 90
Green, G. H., 22
Green, J. A., 38, 130
Greenwood, R., 171
Griffiths, A., 171
Griffiths, D., 171
Griffiths, Ruth, 120, 137
Growth Through English, 185

Grugeon, D., 179
Gurrey, P., 126, 167
Gwillam, W. J., 21

Haddow, Alexander, 98
Hadow Report, 94
Hall, Stanley, 42
Halliday, M. A. K., 168
Handbooks of Suggestions, *see* Board of Education; influence of, 35
Hartog, Philip, 24, 62, 68, 116, 117, 129, 145
Hasan, R., 168
Hastings, Edith, 22
Hayward, F. H., 60–1
Henderson, B. L. K., 91
Henley, W. E., 17, 55
Higgins, D. S., 170
Hildick, E. W., 129
Hoggart, R., 129, 150
Holbrook, D., 148–52, 153, 163, 166, 169, 171, 176
Holmes, Edmond, 13–14, 39–40, 82, 140
Holroyd, G., 142
Hothersall, H., 110
Hourd, Marjorie, 54, 136–40, 151, 159, 161
How to Teach English Composition, 47
Huggler, S., 163
Hughes, A. G., 152
Hughes, Ted, 176
Humphreys, G. S., 142
Hunnisett, E. M., 170
Hunter, Jim, 171
Huntley, A., 110
Hyde, Mary, 20

IAAM, 117; 1923 *Memorandum*, 86, 90–1; 1952 *Memorandum*, 155
Infant schools, 40
Inglis, Fred, 146, 179, 180
Intellectual Growth in Young Children, 105
Isaacs, Susan, 40, 105, 140, 136

Jacks, L. P., 94, 151
Jackson, Brian, 149, 169

Jagger, J. H., 86
Jenkinson, A. J., 109, 130–2
Jepson, R. W., 110, 111
Jespersen, 70
Joint Committee on Grammatical Terminology, 38–9
Journal of Education, 4, 19, 20, 34, 43, 44, 79, 87, 95, 99, 115, 121, 126, 159
Journal of Experimental Pedagogy, 19, 38, 130
Junior school poetry texts, 179–80

Kemp, M., 164
Kenny, E. J., 12, 110
Kenwrick, Joyce, 94
Kerr, W., 110
Kimmins, C. W., 119
Kitchener, E. E., 13
Klein, Melanie, 151
Knights, L. C., 117, 126, 181
Koffka, 136
Kohler, 136

Lamborn, E. A. Greening, 45, 75, 82, 84, 85, 88
Lane, S. M., 164
Langbridge, F., 17
Langdon, Margaret, 121, 160, 163
Language and Mental Development of Children, The, 140
Language development, 140–2
Laurence, Margaret, 133, 144
Lawrence, D. H., 120
Lawrence, Gordon, 155
Leathes, Stanley, 10
Leavis, F. R., 111, 125, 126, 127, 128, 129, 150, 152, 156, 172
Leeds University, 3
Leopold, Kathleen, 121
Lesson in Appreciation, The, 60
Let the Children Write, 121, 163
Lewis, R. T., 81
Life through Young Eyes, 159
Literature: anthologies, 59; primers, 58–9; the teaching of, 33–4, 60, 109, 179
Literature as Exploration, 176
Little, W. B., 133
Liverpool University, 3
'Local' examinations, 4, 58, 61

London University, 3, 167–8
Lowe, Evelyn, 122
Lowndes, G. A. N., 25, 102
Lushington, S., 168
Lynch, A. J., 97
Lyon, P. H. B., 126

Macaulay, W. J., 97, 143
McKay, G. H., 142
Mackie, W. S., 171
Macmillan, Margaret, 23, 54
Manchester University, 3
Manners, Penelope, 175
Mansfield, R., 179
Marland, M., 129, 170, 187
Marriott, J. W., 90
Marsh, Lewis, 22, 35
Marshall, Sybil, 162, 163
Martin, Nancy, 170, 171
Mason, W. H., 155
Mass Civilization and Minority Culture, 127
Mass media, 149
Mattam, D., 179
Matter, Form and Style, 44
Maurice, F. D., 3
Maxwell, C. H., 22
Maybury, Barry, 164
Measuring Devices in Composition, Spelling and Arithmetic, 15
Meldrum, Roy, 126
Meredith, M., 171
Ministry of Education: Pamphlet No. 26 *Language*, 126, 157
Mock, Ruth, 120
'Model' essays, 15–16
Modern secondary schools, 144ff., 158
Montessori, Maria, 40–1, 82
Moody, H., 171
Moon, A. R., 110, 142
Morgan, R. B., 37, 90
Morley, Henry, 3
Morris, Norman, 122
Morrison, R. L., 118
Muller, Herbert, 185
Mushet, J., 20

NATE, 157, 181
Newbolt, Henry, 66, 73
'New critics', 85, 125–9

New Teaching, The, 60, 64, 74
Nesfield, J. C., 61
Newsom Report, 75, 158, 159, 179
Norman, J. S., 37
Nottingham University, 3
Nunn, Percy, 82–3, 103

Ogilvie, G., 61
O'Grady, H., 44
Old English (*see also* Fallacies), 69, 71, 106, 108
Oliphant, L., 90
O'Malley, R., 171
Owen, Dorothy Tudor, 53–5
Owens, G., 187
Oxford, 3, 9–10

Paintings, children's, 135–6
Palmer, D. J., 3, 25
Palmer, H. E., 107–8
Parkhurst, Helen, 97
Parsing, 20
Peel, Marie, 136, 162, 164
Perse Playbooks, 45, 49, 50, 51, 122
Pertwee, Ernest, 18
Phillips, Margaret, 120
Piaget, 136
Pickering, George, 185
Pickles, F., 36, 80
Pink, M. A., 110
Play Way, 53, 82
Plowden Report, 158–9, 186
Pocock, Guy, 81, 86
Poems: anthologies of pupils', 122, 159–61; popular in schools, 55–7; pupils writing of, 45–7, 48, 120–1, 160–1; pupils' own, 46–7, 49–50
Poems by Children 1950–61, 159, 162
Poetry anthologies, 56–7
Poetry study, 60–1
Polkinghorne, R. K., 110
Poole, R. H., 170
'Popular' culture, 124, 128
Potter, F. F., 108, 110
Potter, Stephen, 25
Powell, Brian, 160
Practical Criticism, 125, 169
Pritchard, F. H., 80, 98, 109
Pym, Dora, 163

Quiller-Couch, A., 10, 66

Rahtz, F. J., 21
Raleigh, Walter, 10
Ratcliff, A. J. J., 99
Read, Herbert, 135, 159
Reading and Discrimination, 126
Recapitulation theory, 42–3
Reeves, James, 160
Reflections, 154
'Relevance' in literature, 173–4, 176–8
Repetition, 31
Reproduction, 13
Revised Code, 5, 12, 26, 27, 39, 72, 76, 88, 93
Reynolds, E. E., 115
Rhetoric, 9
Rhodes, E. C., 117
Rich, R. W., 25
Richards, I. A., 125, 128, 129, 156, 169, 172
Roberts, A. E., 7, 20, 23, 41, 43, 62, 130
Roberts, J. C., 142
Robertson, A. S., 142
Robertson, J. Logie, 58
Robinson, Nora, 166
Robinson, Stewart, 20
Romantic aspects of 'creativity', 85, 161–3
Rooney, C., 36
Rose, J. D., 61
Rosenblatt, Louise, 176–8
Rousseau, 83, 135
Rowe, Albert, 149, 170, 171
Rudiments of Criticism, The, 45
Ruskin, 136
Russell, John, 142

Salmon, D., 11, 22
Sampson, George, 66, 67, 75, 76–9, 82, 148, 179, 184
Scholarship papers, 95–6, 111
Scotland, 2
Scott, A. F., 171
Scrutiny, 117, 125
Secondary literature study, 171ff.
Secondary School Examinations Council, 62–3, 157, 182–3

Secondary schools, 3; texts, 57–8, 59, 99, 106–7, 112–14, 131, 146, 155, 176, 179–80
'Self-expression', 85–6
Shelley, 137
'Silent social revolution', 93, 133, 146
Smith, A. E., 146–7, 150
Smith, Arnold, 18, 42, 45, 62, 130
Smith, J. C., 55
Smith, N. B., 79
Social studies, 154
Society for Teachers of English, 128
Spearman, 136
Speech work, 71, 74–6
Spens Report, 116, 128, 132
Spooner, Elizabeth, 56
Spooner, F., 59
Stanford, D., 174–5
Stanley, Oliver, 132
Steel, J. H., 118
Stephenson, N., 175
Stevens, Frances, 182
Stratta, R., 154, 170
Strong, L. A. G., 144
Stuart, Simon, 156
Summerfield, Geoffrey, 170, 179

Tant, Ethel, 43
Tappan, E. M., 58
Tawney, 94
Teacher's Certificate, 3, 30–1
Teacher's World, 95, 121
Teaching Fiction in Schools, 178
Teaching of English in England, The, see Board of Education
Teaching of English in Primary Schools, The, 87
Teaching of English Literature in Secondary Schools, The, 36, 59
Teaching of English Literature in Secondary Schools for Girls, The, 43, 59, 86
Teaching the Mother Tongue, 96
Themes, 170
Thomas, H. R., 171
Thompson, Denys, 126, 129, 156, 171
Thomson, L., 56
Thorpe, E. G., 171

Tillyard, E. M. W., 25
Times Educational Supplement, The, 47, 54, 55, 73, 79, 82, 89, 93, 106, 115, 126, 144, 184
Tipping, L., 110
Tomkinson, W. S., 75, 82, 84, 85, 94
Transference theory, 19–20
Treble, H. A., 13, 87, 88
Twentyman, G. A., 90

Use of English, The, 129, 137, 143, 148, 151, 156, 169, 180
Usill, H. V., 108
Urwin, G. C., 175

Vernon, P. E., 118
Viola, W., 135–6

Walsh, J. H., 146, 156, 160
Walsh, William, 162, 163
Watts, A. F., 140, 168
Weeks-Pearson, A., 171
Welton, James, 13, 18, 23
West, Alfred, 37, 38
Weston, W. J., 90
What Do Boys and Girls Read? 130
What Is and What Might Be, 13, 39, 40
Wheeler, Olive, 132
Whitehead, Frank, 146, 156, 163, 166, 169
Widdows, J., 144
Williams, G. P., 118
Williams, Raymond, 127
Williamson, W., 12, 20
Wilson, Richard, 79
Wiseman, S., 118
Wollman, M., 179
Wood, T. R., 170
Wordsworth, 136, 162
Writing of English, The, 24

Year Book of Education: 1932, 41; 1933, 108; 1936, 25, 128, 132; 1939, 132
Young, W. T., 58
Young Writers, Young Readers, 159, 163

Zimmern, Alice, 4